CASES AND MATERIALS ON
EMPLOYMENT DISCRIMINATION

1996 Supplement

CASES AND MATERIALS ON EMPLOYMENT DISCRIMINATION

Third Edition

1996 Supplement

MICHAEL J. ZIMMER
Professor of Law
Seton Hall University

CHARLES A. SULLIVAN
Professor of Law
Seton Hall University

RICHARD F. RICHARDS
Professor of Law
University of Arkansas, Fayetteville

DEBORAH A. CALLOWAY
Professor of Law
University of Connecticut

Little, Brown and Company
Boston   New York   Toronto   London

Library of Congress Catalog Card No. 93-80781

ISBN 0-316-98803-0

CCP

Published simultaneously in Canada
by Little, Brown & Company (Canada) Limited

Printed in the United States of America

CONTENTS

Special Note

PART I

Chapter 2

PART II

THE CONCEPT OF DISCRIMINATION UNDER TITLE VII, THE AGE DISCRIMINATION IN EMPLOYMENT ACT, AND SECTION 1981

Chapter 6

The Interrelation of the Disparate Treatment and Disparate Impact Theories of Discrimination   95

Chapter 7

Special Problems in Applying Title VII, Section 1981, and the ADEA   105

PART III

PART IV

PROCEDURES AND REMEDIES	187

Chapter 10

Procedures for Enforcing Antidiscrimination Laws	189

Chapter 11

Judicial Relief	195

TABLE OF CASES

Table of Cases

TABLE OF SELECTED SECONDARY AUTHORITIES

(References are to casebook page numbers.)

Articles

Abrams, Douglas E., Arbitrability in Recent Federal Civil Rights Legislation: The Need for Amendment, 26 Conn. L. Rev. 521 (1994), 982

Abrams, Kathryn, Gender Discrimination and the Transformation of Workplace Norms, 42 Vand. L. Rev. 1183, 1203 (1989), 578

Abrams, Kathryn, Title VII and the Complex Female Subject, 92 Mich. L. Rev. 2479, 2524 (1994), 358

Adler, Robert & Ellen Pierce, The Legal, Ethical, and Social Implications of the "Reasonable Woman" Standard in Sexual Harassment Cases, 61 Fordham L. Rev. 772 (1993), 578

Blumoff, Theodore Y. & Harold S. Lewis, Jr., The Reagan Court and Title VII: A Common-Law Outlook on a Statutory Task, 69 N.C.L. Rev. 1, 47 (1990), 192

Brookins, Robert, *Hicks*, Lies, and Ideology: The Wages of Sin Is Now Exculpation, 28 Creighton L. Rev. 939, 994 (1995), 156

Browne, Kingsley, Sex and Temperament in Modern Society: A Darwinian View of the Glass Ceiling and the Gender Gap, 27 Ariz. L. Rev. 971 (1995), 512

Calloway, Deborah A., Accommodating Pregnancy in the Workplace, 25 Stetson L. Rev. 1 (1995), 541, 552

Notes and Comments

PREFACE

The authors would like to thank a number of research assistants for their work on this supplement: Thomas Crino, Jessica Stein, and Matthew Sciappa, Seton Hall Class of 1996; Rachel Diehl, Linda Garibaldi, Megan Gula, and William Nossen, Seton Hall Class of 1997; and Denise Polivy and Deborah McKenna of the University of Connecticut School of Law.

We gratefully acknowledge the permissions granted to reproduce the following materials:

Linda Hamilton Krieger, The Content of Our Categories: A Cognitive Bias Approach to Discrimination and Equal Employment Opportunity, 47 Stan. L. Rev. 1161 (1995). Copyright © 1995 by the Board of Trustees of the Leland Stanford Junior University. Reprinted by permission of Stanford Law Review and Fred B. Rothman and Company.

Ramona L. Paetzold and Steven L. Willborn, Deconstructing Disparate Impact: A View of the Model Through New Lenses, 74 N.C.L. Rev. 325 (1995).

Michael J. Zimmer
Charles A. Sullivan
Richard F. Richards
Deborah A. Calloway

May 1996

CASES AND MATERIALS ON EMPLOYMENT DISCRIMINATION

1996 Supplement

Special Note

The Retroactivity of the
Civil Rights Act of 1991

Please read this Special Note in conjunction with the entire casebook.

The Civil Rights Act of 1991 was enacted on November 21, 1991, Pub. L. No. 102-166, 105 Stat. 1071 §105(b), to legislatively overrule a series of Supreme Court decisions that Congress believed to have radically reduced the protection offered by Title VII and other antidiscrimination statutes. The new Act makes one general reference to its effective date: §402(a) provides that "except as otherwise specifically provided, this Act and the amendments shall take effect upon enactment." While this clearly means that the Act is immediately effective, the significance of this provision for pending cases remained unresolved until 1994.[1] Indeed, the issue became one of major practical and theoretic importance as literally scores of district courts rendered opinions on the retroactivity of the Act.

---

1. Cases may be "pending" at various stages. Arguably, the effect of the new statute on a matter that has been fully tried but is on appeal may be different, at least as to such matters as jury trial, than a case that is pending trial as of November 21, 1991. See Mozee v. American Commercial Marine Serv. Co., 963 F.2d 929, 936-937 (7th Cir. 1992).

Although §402(a) begins with "except as otherwise specifically provided," the statute addressed its application more explicitly only in regard to two sections. Thus, §109(c) provides that the extension of Title VII and the Americans with Disabilities Act to employees in foreign countries "shall not apply with respect to conduct occurring before the date of the enactment of this Act." Section 402(b) states that "[n]otwithstanding any other provision of this Act, nothing in this Act shall apply to any disparate impact case for which a complaint was filed before March 1, 1975, and for which an initial decision was rendered after October 30, 1983." The Act, therefore, spoke unambiguously only with respect to the effect of two of its changes on pending cases, and as to them mandated prospective application.

In all other areas, the question remained unresolved until the Supreme Court addressed the question in two opinions in 1994. In Landgraf v. USI Film Products, 114 S. Ct. 1483 (1994), and Rivers v. Roadway Express, Inc., 114 S. Ct. 1510 (1994), the Supreme Court decided that most applications of the new statute were not retroactive.

In *Landgraf* the violation and the trial had both occurred before the effective date of the Act. The plaintiff nevertheless argued on appeal that since her case was still "pending" at the time the 1991 statute became effective, it should be remanded for a new trial at which she would be entitled to seek the compensatory and punitive damages that the new statute authorized. She also argued that at that new trial she should be accorded a jury, as provided by the new Act. A majority of the Court rejected that argument.

The Court approached the question as solely one of statutory interpretation and, because of the narrow approach it took, did not have to address the constitutional questions that a broader reading of the statute might have raised.[2] The Court found little express guidance in the language of the statute. It first focused on §402(a): "except as otherwise specifically provided, this Act and the amendments shall take effect upon enactment." The portion of this sentence requiring application on its enactment was not read as addressing the question of possible application to events prior to the passage of the law. The Court, however, had more trouble with the phrase "except as otherwise specifically provided." It stated that this probably referred to provisions of the new law explicitly restricting certain parts to prospective application,[3] and further recognized "some force" to plaintiff's argument that these exceptions created a negative implication that the rest of the Act was

2. Serious due process questions would arise if the statute were read to retroactively make actionable conduct that was legal at the time it took place. See Fray v. Omaha World Herald Co., 960 F.2d 1370, 1378 n.12 (8th Cir. 1992).

3. Sections 109(c) and 402(b). See also §110, establishing a Technical Assistance Training Institute, which states "this section shall take effect on the date of enactment of this Act." Similarly, §116 states "[n]othing in the amendments made by this title shall be construed to affect court-ordered remedies, affirmative action, or conciliation agreements, that are in accordance with the law."

to be applied retroactively. However, the Court said, "we find it most unlikely that Congress intended the introductory clause to carry the critically important meaning petitioner assigns it." 114 S. Ct. at 1494. Had Congress so intended, it could have chosen language better suited to reaching this result. Further,

> [i]t is entirely possible that Congress inserted the "otherwise specifically provided" language not because it understood the "takes effect" clause to establish a rule of retroactivity to which only two "other specific provisions" would be exceptions, but instead to assure that any specific timing provisions in the Act would prevail over the general "take effect on enactment" command.

Id. In short, the Court seemed to believe that §§109(c) and 402(b) were simply added out of an abundance of caution, to ensure that cases falling under these sections remain immune to the Act.

In light of the legislative history, particularly the fact that the vetoed 1990 version of the statute contained explicit provisions mandating retroactive application, the Court concluded that Congress had recognized the retroactivity problem but been unable to come to any agreement:

> It is entirely possible—indeed, highly probable—that, because it was unable to resolve the retroactivity issue. . . , Congress viewed the matter as an open issue to be resolved by the courts. Our precedents on retroactivity left doubts about what default rule would apply in the absence of congressional guidance, and suggested that some provisions might apply to cases arising before enactment while others might not. The only matters Congress did not leave to the courts were set out with specificity in §§109(c) and 402(b).

Id. at 1494-1495 (citations and footnote omitted). The Court found the legislative history indicated that Congress simply could not agree on retroactivity questions.

As this passage suggests, the Court's precedents on the general retroactivity question were unclear. These precedents took apparently divergent views of the presumption to be employed in the absence of a sufficiently clear indication of congressional intent. And, having found no strong indication of legislative intent on the retroactivity issue in the 1991 Act itself, the Court necessarily turned to the ultimate question of how to treat a statute's effective date where Congress has not resolved the issue. In the process, the Court had to reanalyze its earlier decisions.

Ultimately, the majority found a presumption against retroactivity to be fundamental to American jurisprudence, one expressed, inter alia, in several clauses of the Constitution, including the ex post facto clause. While such constitutional provisions would not necessarily have barred the retroactive application of the Civil Rights Act of 1991, "a requirement that Congress first make its intention clear helps ensure that Congress itself has determined that the benefits of retroactivity outweigh the potential for disruption or unfairness." Id. at 1498.

Given this presumption, the question for the Court was when to view a statute as operating retroactively. Formulating the proper approach, the *Landgraf* opinion states:

> the court must ask whether the new provision attaches new legal consequences to events completed before its enactment. The conclusion that a particular rule operates "retroactively" comes at the end of a process of judgment concerning the nature and extent of the change in the law and the degree of connection between the operation of the new rule and a relevant past event.[4]

Thus, many cases employing the presumption against retroactivity "involved new provisions affecting contractual or property rights, matters in which predictability and stability are of prime importance," id. at 1500, although the presumption was broader than that. In contrast, however, "[e]ven absent specific legislative authorization, application of new statutes passed after the events in suit is unquestionably proper in many situations." Id. at 1501. These included jurisdictional rules and, more generally, procedural rules, which often do not implicate retroactivity concerns: "Because rules of procedure regulate secondary rather than primary conduct, the fact that a new procedural rule was instituted after the conduct giving rise to the suit does not make application of the rule at trial retroactive." Id. at 1502.

Applying these principles to the case before it, the *Landgraf* Court read the statute's instruction that its provisions were to "'take effect upon enactment' to mean that courts should evaluate each provision of the Act in light of ordinary judicial principles concerning the application of new rules to pending cases and pre-enactment conduct." Id. at 1505. Under this approach, the Court stated that, while the right to jury trial established by §102(c)(1) would ordinarily govern trials conducted after the statute's effective date, it could not do so where the jury trial right was dependent on the right to compensatory or punitive damages accorded by §102. In turn, those provisions expanding liability for conduct that occurred prior to the passage of the statute could not be applied retroactively. This was clearly true as to punitive damages, which implicated ex post facto concerns, but also applied to compen-

---

4. Id. at 1499. At another point the Court wrote:

> [When the statute contains no express command by Congress], the court must determine whether the new statute would have retroactive effect, i.e., whether it would impair rights a party possessed when he acted, increase a party's liability for past conduct, or impose new duties with respect to transactions already completed. If the statute would operate retroactively, our traditional presumption teaches that it does not govern absent clear congressional intent favoring such a result.

Id. at 1505.

satory damages because of their effect in enhancing liability for prior conduct. Accordingly, the plaintiff had no right to either a jury trial or compensatory or punitive damages where the underlying conduct occurred prior to the Civil Rights Act of 1991.

Landgraf decided only two specific questions of retroactivity under the new Civil Rights Act, although it clearly established a paradigm that would limit application of the statute's provisions where some of the events in question occurred prior to the passage of the Act. The Supreme Court addressed some of the remaining issues in *Landgraf's* companion case, Rivers v. Roadway Express, Inc., 114 S. Ct. 1510 (1994). At issue there was whether the new law's amendment of §1981 to reach all aspects of contractual relationships could apply to cases that arose prior to its passage. The Court refused to so apply §101 of the Civil Rights Act of 1991, despite the argument that this provision merely restored the law to the state it had been prior to the Supreme Court's decision in Patterson v. McLean Credit Union, 491 U.S. 164 (1989) (and therefore merely reflected the law that was governing at the time of the conduct being challenged by the plaintiff).

Together, *Landgraf* and *Rivers* resolve three of the most important retroactivity questions under the new law, and set out a very stringent test for other questions. As might be expected, the circuits have been very reluctant to apply other provisions of the new law retroactively.[5] Ironically, one of the few instances in which a party has been prejudiced by application of the new Act was to the detriment of a plaintiff. The 1991 Civil Rights Act statute amended the Age Discrimination in Employment Act by eliminating the former statute of limitations and substituting a requirement for filing suit within 90 days of receipt of a right to sue notice from the EEOC. While this may sometimes increase the time limits for filing suit, in Million v. Frank, 47 F.3d 385 (10th Cir. 1995), the court found a suit untimely when filed more than 90 days after receipt of the EEOC's notice, although it would have been timely under the prior statute of limitation.

---

5. Rutland v. Moore, 54 F.3d 226 (5th Cir. 1995) (extension of Civil Rights Act of 1991 to appointee or elected official could not be applied retrospectively to special assistant Attorney General's discharge, which occurred prior to the new statute's enactment); Maitland v. University of Minnesota, 43 F.3d 357 (8th Cir. 1994) (§108 of the new act, specifying the effects of consent decrees, could not be applied to a decree entered prior to the effective date of the new law); Chenault v. United States Postal Serv., 37 F.3d 535 (9th Cir. 1994) (§107, providing that an employer has committed an unlawful employment practice whenever an improper consideration is a "motivating factor" in an employment decision, may not be applied retroactively; §114(1), extending the filing period for federal employees from 30 days to 90 days may not be applied retroactively to revive a claim barred under the old statute); Shipes v. Trinity Indust., 31 F.3d 347 (5th Cir. 1994) (§113(b), providing for payment of expert witness fees as part of costs, does not apply "retroactively" where both the relevant conduct and the trial court's denial of fees occurred before the effective date of the 1991 Act); Preston v. Virginia, 31 F.3d 203 (4th Cir. 1994) (§107, providing that an employer has committed an unlawful employment practice whenever an improper consideration is a "motivating factor" in an employment decision, may not be applied retroactively); Hook v. Ernst & Young, 28 F.3d 366 (3d Cir. 1994)(same).

PART I

THE EMPLOYMENT RELATION AND THE PROBLEM OF DISCRIMINAITON

Chapter 2

The Policy Bases for
Antidiscrimination Law

C. WHY PROHIBIT DISCRIMINATION?

*Page 66.   Add the following new Note 11 at the end of the
page:*

11. Richard H. McAdams, Cooperation and Conflict: The Economics of
Group Status Production and Race Discrimination, 108 Harv. L. Rev. 1003
(1995), argues that one explanation of discrimination is the desire to maintain
the status of one's "group," including racial groups:

> This Article offers an economic theory to explain why individuals make ma-
> terial sacrifices for group welfare. My thesis is that a material view of human
> motivation underestimates both the level of cooperation that groups elicit from
> their members and the level of conflict that groups elicit from each other. A sin-
> gle group dynamic connects these added increments of cooperation and con-
> flict: groups achieve solidarity and elicit loyalty beyond what economic
> analysis conventionally predicts, but solidarity and loyalty within groups lead
> predictably, if not inevitably, to competition and conflict between groups. The

connection is the desire for esteem or status. Groups use intra-group status rewards as a non-material means of gaining material sacrifice from members, but the attendant desire for inter-group status causes inter-group conflict. . . .

This two-fold importance of status is essential to a genuine understanding of race discrimination, which has eluded economics. Discrimination is a means by which social groups produce status for their members, but pivotal to understanding this form of inter-group conflict is the role that status plays in generating the intra-group cooperation necessary to make discrimination effective. Absent the desire for intra-group status, selfish individuals would not make the material sacrifices that discrimination requires.

Id. at 1007-1008. After sketching the economic challenges to discrimination, Professor McAdams goes on:

Many have questioned and criticized this economic analysis of discrimination. Yet legal criticism has generally taken one of two forms, neither of which offers an alternative economic theory of discrimination. The first accepts arguendo the starting point of the theory—that discrimination is "non-association"—and then challenges the economic implications Becker and others draw from this model. A second group of critics, including critical race theorists, feminists, and others skeptical of economic analysis, rejects not only the non-association description of discrimination, but also the entire method of economics. Thus, critics of Becker's model have generally not been interested in using economics to develop a comprehensive alternative theory.

This lack of interest is unfortunate. The economic theory of discrimination as non-association fails not because it employs the economic method, but because it is not sufficiently faithful to that method. Perhaps what seems so barren about the application of the economic method in this context is that it seems to require overlooking what many regard as the central realities of race discrimination: discrimination produces for its practitioners a gain beyond the mere avoidance of association, and discrimination victims suffer not just material harm, but also degradation.

Id. at 1034-1035. Perhaps needless to say, Professor Epstein responded. Richard A. Epstein, The Status-Production Sideshow: Why the Antidiscrimination Laws Are Still a Mistake, 108 Harv. L. Rev. 1085 (1995).

PART II

THE CONCEPT
OF DISCRIMINATION
UNDER TITLE VII,
THE AGE DISCRIMINATION
IN EMPLOYMENT ACT,
AND SECTION 1981

Chapter 3

Individual Disparate Treatment Discrimination

B. THE MEANING OF DISCRIMINATORY INTENT

Page 97. *Replace the citation to Smith v. Texas Department of Water Resources in Note 2 with the following:*

818 F.2d 363 (5th Cir. 1987), *cert. denied*, 484 U.S. 1059 (1988),

Page 98. *Add the following to the end of Note 4(b):*

See also Stacks v. Southwestern Bell Yellow Pages, Inc., 27 F.3d 1316, 1318 (8th Cir. 1994) ("women in sales were the worst thing that ever happened to this company"); EEOC v. Farmer Bros. Co., 31 F.3d 891, 896 (9th Cir. 1994) (company president announced he "would spend every last dime" to keep women employees from coming back); and Suggs v. ServiceMaster Education Food Management, 72 F.3d 1228, 1231 (6th Cir. 1996) (manager told plaintiff's male replacement that it was "time to show a man could run the operation better").

Page 98.   Add the following to the end of Note 4(d):

See also Mangold v. California Pub. Utils. Commn., 67 F.3d 1470, 1474 (9th Cir. 1995) (plaintiff's director told him "you know we want fresh young blood in this group").

Page 101.   Add new Note 8a:

8a. Linda Hamilton Krieger, in The Content of Our Categories: A Cognitive Bias Approach to Discrimination and Equal Employment Opportunity, 47 Stan. L. Rev. 1161 (1995), used the insights provided by cognitive psychology to explain that stereotyping by race and gender is an "unintended consequence" of the necessity for humans to categorize their sensory perceptions in order to make any sense of the world:

> [The] central premise of social cognition theory [is] that cognitive structures and processes involved in categorization and information processing can in and of themselves result in stereotyping and other forms of biased intergroup judgment previously attributed to motivational processes. The social cognition approach to discrimination comprises three claims relevant to our present inquiry. The first is that stereotyping . . . is nothing special. It is simply a form of categorization [of our sensory perceptions], similar in structure and function to the categorization of natural objects. According to this view, stereotypes, like other categorical structures, are cognitive mechanisms that *all* people, not just "prejudiced" ones, use to simplify the task of perceiving, processing, and retaining information about people in memory. They are central, and indeed essential to normal cognitive functioning.
>
> The second claim posited in social cognition theory is that, once in place, stereotypes bias intergroup judgment and decisionmaking. . . . [T]hey function as implicit theories, biasing in predictable ways the perception, interpretation, encoding, retention, and recall of information about other people. These biases are *cognitive* rather than *motivational*. They operate absent intent to favor or disfavor members of a particular social group. And, perhaps most significant for present purposes, they bias a decisionmaker's judgment long before the "moment of decision" [when the employment decision in question is made], as a decisionmaker attends to relevant data and interprets, encodes, stores, and retrieves it from memory. These biases "sneak up on" the decisionmaker, distorting bit by bit the data upon which his decision is eventually based.

> The third claim follows from the second. Stereotypes, when they function as implicit prototypes or schemas [by which we evaluate each other], operate beyond the reach of decisionmaker self-awareness. Empirical evidence indicates that people's access to their own cognitive processes is in fact poor. Accordingly, cognitive bias may well be both unintentional and unconscious.

Id. at 1187-1188. If acting on stereotypes is unintentional and unconscious, should that fall within the proscriptions of individual disparate treatment discrimination? It is treating people differently based on their race or gender, but is that what antidiscrimination law proscribes? Professor Krieger proposes a new theory of disparate treatment discrimination:

> To establish liability for disparate treatment discrimination, a Title VII plaintiff would simply be required to prove that his group status *played a role* in causing the employer's action or decision. Causation would no longer be equated with intentionality. The critical inquiry would be whether the applicant or employee's group status "made a difference" in the employer's action, not whether the decisionmaker intended that it make a difference.

Id. at 1242.

Page 106.   *Replace the citation to Binder v. Long Island Lighting Co. in Note 6 with the following:*

57 F.3d 193 (2d Cir. 1995)

Page 108.   *Add new Note 10a:*

10a. Suppose that a 38-year-old woman is discharged, and she thinks it was because of her gender and her age. Because the ADEA's protection from age discrimination applies only after age 40, she does not have a federal claim of age discrimination. If she sues only on the basis of sex discrimination, the employer can rebut that claim by admitting it acted because of her age. While such an admission is neither legitimate nor nondiscriminatory, would the *Biggins* Court find the employer's rebuttal sufficient?

Biggins pressures plaintiff to sue on every possible basis to avoid the employer "admitting" it acted on some ground plaintiff failed to assert and thereby defeating the ground plaintiff chose to sue on. On the other hand, if plaintiff adds a count of age discrimination based on a state law that prohibits all age discrimination to avoid the trap set by the first part of *Biggins*, she faces the risk of dilution established by the second part of *Biggins*, that is, that the power of an inference drawn from circumstantial evidence to support any one claim of discrimination diminishes as the range of claims expands.

Page 109.   Add new Note 12a:

12a. Is an employer who discharges workers because of its customers' objections to older workers in violation of the ADEA? Brownlee v. Lear Siegler Management Services Corp., 15 F.3d 976 (10th Cir.), *cert. denied*, 114 S. Ct. 2743 (1994), refused to attribute the alleged discriminatory motivation of the Saudi Arabian Air Force to defendant employer who discharged plaintiffs at the Air Force's instructions.

Page 109.   Add the following to the end of Note 13:

See also Sack v. Bentsen, 51 F.3d 264 (1st Cir.), *cert. denied*, 116 S. Ct. 384 (1995) (policy preferring recent law school graduation to more remote graduation did not discriminate on the basis of age). See generally Robert J. Gregory, There Is Life in That Old (I Mean, More "Senior") Dog Yet: The Age-Proxy Theory After *Hazen Paper Co. v. Biggins*, 11 Hofstra Lab. L.J. 391 (1994) (proxy theory can still be used as a tool for inferring intent to discriminate).

In Johnson v. New York, 49 F.3d 75 (2d Cir. 1995), the defendant required, as a condition of employment, the plaintiff to be a member of the New York Air National Guard, which had a mandatory retirement age of 60. When plaintiff was forced to retire from the Guard, he was discharged by the defendant. The court held that, while the National Guard's unquestionable age discrimination age was beyond the reach of the ADEA, the defendant's use of National Guard membership imposed an age-based criterion because it "inextricably linked" the plaintiff's age and his termination. Id. at 80. Is this the proxy theory or something different?

Page 110.   Add the following to the end of Note 16:

In Odima v. Westin Tucson Hotel, 53 F.3d 1484 (9th Cir. 1995), the court found the defendant's reason for not promoting the Nigerian-born plaintiff beyond the laundry room was a pretext for discrimination based on race and national origin. The defendant explained it had denied the plaintiff's requests for transfer because the plaintiff's accent would interfere with his communications with the public. Is this proxy or pretext?

C. INFERENTIAL EVIDENCE OF DISCRIMINATORY INTENT

1. The Plaintiff's Prima Facie Case

Page 117.   Add the following before the "Notes" section:

O'CONNOR v. CONSOLIDATED COIN CATERERS CORP.
116 S. Ct. 1307 (1996)

Justice SCALIA delivered the opinion of the Court.

This case presents the question whether a plaintiff alleging that he was discharged in violation of the Age Discrimination in Employment Act of 1967 (ADEA), must show that he was replaced by someone outside the age group protected by the ADEA to make out a prima facie case under the framework established by McDonnell Douglas Corp. v. Green.

Petitioner James O'Connor was employed by respondent Consolidated Coin Caterers Corporation from 1978 until August 10, 1990, when, at age 56, he was fired. Claiming that he had been dismissed because of his age in violation of the ADEA, petitioner brought suit. . . . [In] upholding summary judgment for defendant, the Court of Appeals for the Fourth Circuit stated that petitioner could establish a prima facie case under *McDonnell Douglas* only if he could prove that (1) he was in the age group protected by the ADEA; (2) he was discharged or demoted; (3) at the time of his discharge or demotion, he was performing his job at a level that met his employer's legitimate expectations; and (4) following his discharge or demotion, he was replaced by someone of comparable qualifications outside the protected class. Since petitioner's replacement was 40 years old, the Court of Appeals concluded that the last element of the prima facie case had not been made out. Finding that petitioner's claim could not survive a motion for summary judgment without benefit of the *McDonnell Douglas* presumption (i.e., "under the ordinary standards of proof used in civil cases") the Court of Appeals affirmed the judgment of dismissal. We granted O'Connor's petition for certiorari.

In *McDonnell Douglas*, we "established an allocation of the burden of production and an order for the presentation of proof in Title VII discriminatory-treatment cases." St. Mary's Honor Center v. Hicks. We held that a plaintiff alleging racial discrimination in violation of Title VII of the Civil Rights Act of 1964 could establish a prima facie case by showing "(i) that he belongs to a racial minority; (ii) that he applied and was qualified for a job for which the employer was seeking applicants; (iii) that, despite his qualifications, he was rejected; and (iv) that, after his rejection, the position remained open and the employer continued to seek applicants from persons of [the] complainant's qualifications." Once the plaintiff has met this initial burden, the burden of production shifts to the employer "to articulate some legitimate, nondiscriminatory reason for the employee's rejection." If the trier of fact finds that the elements of the prima facie case are supported by a preponderance of the evidence and the employer remains silent, the court must enter judgment for the plaintiff. *St. Mary's Honor Center*; Texas Dept. of Community Affairs v. Burdine.

In assessing claims of age discrimination brought under the ADEA, the Fourth Circuit, like others, has applied some variant of the basic evidentiary framework set forth in *McDonnell Douglas*. We have never had occasion to decide whether that application of the Title VII rule to the ADEA context is correct, but since the parties do not contest that point, we shall assume it. Cf. *St. Mary's Honor Center* (assuming that "the McDonnell Douglas Framework is fully applicable to racial-discrimination-in-employment claims under 42 U.S.C. §1983"). On that assumption, the question presented for our determination is what elements must be shown in an ADEA case to establish the prima facie case that triggers the employer's burden of production.

As the very name "prima facie case" suggests, there must be a least a logical connection between each element of the prima facie case and the illegal discrimination for which it establishes a "legally mandatory, rebuttable presumption," *Burdine*. The element of replacement by someone under 40 fails this requirement. The discrimination prohibited by the ADEA is discrimination "because of [an] individual's age," though the prohibition is "limited to individuals who are at least 40 years of age." This language does not ban discrimination against employees because they are aged 40 or older; it bans discrimination against employees because of their age, but limits the protected class to those who are 40 or older. The fact that one person in the protected class has lost out to another person in the protected class is thus irrelevant, so long as he has lost out because of his age. Or to put the point more concretely, there can be no greater inference of age discrimination (as opposed to "40 or over" discrimination) when a 40 year-old is replaced by a 39 year-old than when a 56 year-old is replaced by a 40 year-old. Because it lacks probative value, the fact that an ADEA plaintiff was replaced by someone outside the protected class is not a proper element of the *McDonnell Douglas* prima facie case.

Perhaps some courts have been induced to adopt the principle urged by respondent in order to avoid creating a prima facie case on the basis of very thin evidence—for example, the replacement of a 68 year-old by a 65 year-old. While the respondent's principle theoretically permits such thin evidence (consider the example above of a 40 year-old replaced by a 39 year-old), as a practical matter it will rarely do so, since the vast majority of age-discrimination claims come from older employees. In our view, however, the proper solution to the problem lies not in making an utterly irrelevant factor an element of the prima facie case, but rather in recognizing that the prima facie case requires "evidence adequate to create an inference that an employment decision was based on an [illegal] discriminatory criterion. . . ." Teamsters v. United States. In the age-discrimination context, such an inference can not be drawn from the replacement of one worker with another worker insignificantly younger. Because the ADEA prohibits discrimination on the basis of age and not class membership, the fact that a replacement is substantially younger than the plaintiff is a far more reliable indicator of age discrimination than is the fact that the plaintiff was replaced by someone outside the protected class.

Page 118. Add the following to the end of Note 3:

See, e.g., Suggs v. ServiceMaster Education Food Management, 72 F.3d 1228 (6th Cir. 1996).

Page 118. Add new Notes 4a and 4b:

4a. What would have been the effect of upholding the lower court in *O'Connor*? Would employers have a safe harbor from the application of *McDonnell Douglas* by replacing the older worker with one at least age 40? Why exactly is it irrelevant that O'Connor's replacement was at least age 40? At the same time O'Connor was fired, another manager, age 57, was demoted and replaced by a worker age 37. Is the inference of age discrimination equally powerful in both of these cases? How powerful must this inference be to make out a prima facie case? The Court emphasizes that "the fact that a replacement is substantially younger than plaintiff is a far more reliable indicator of age discrimination than is the fact that the plaintiff was replaced by someone outside the protected class." Thus, a case is made out when plaintiff is 56 and his replacement is 40. What about a 68-year-old replaced by a 65-year-old? What if a series of these decisions takes place so that the average age of the workers declines by three years? What about a 40-year-old replaced by a 38-year-old?

4b. The lower court in *O'Connor* also wrestled with the application of the *McDonnell Douglas* test in reduction-in-force situations as opposed to individual decisions not to hire or to fire. 56 F.3d 542 (4th Cir. 1995). The court found this inapplicable to plaintiff because he could point to the person who replaced him, but the opinion nevertheless analyzes the appropriate approach to such situations and concludes that plaintiff failed to establish a prima facie case under it.

In the typical reduction-in-force case, we apply a modified version of the *McDonnell Douglas* prima facie standard:

> (1) the employee was protected by the ADEA; (2) he was selected for discharge from a larger group of candidates; (3) he was performing at a level substantially equivalent to the lowest level of those of the group retained; and (4) the process of selection produced a residual work force of persons in the groups containing some unprotected persons who were performing at a level lower than that at which he was performing.

Id. at 546. Plaintiff failed to establish the third prong of this formula because "even prior to the reorganization that gave rise to the two new district manager positions, O'Connor was slow in dealing with problem accounts, his territorial responsibilities had already been greatly reduced [in a prior reorganization], and he experienced a problem with food delivery in an unrefrigerated truck." Id. at 547. Plaintiff's showing of satisfactory ratings and a large bonus was not sufficient to raise a genuine issue of material fact. Further, plaintiff failed to establish the fourth prong. Because his territory had been reduced prior to this termination due to his slow response to problem accounts, plaintiff could not compare himself to the two younger replacements.

Page 118.   Add the following to the end of the first paragraph of Note 5:

See also Hiatt v. Union Pac. R.R., 65 F.3d 838 (10th Cir. 1995) (employees could only show inconvenience in losing their priority for shift selection based on their seniority system).

Page 119.   Add the following before the last sentence of Note 6:

See also Panis v. Mission Hills Bank, 60 F.3d 1486 (10th Cir. 1996) (the plaintiff failed to establish that the defendant's reason for terminating her was a pretext for discrimination when it claimed that she was discharged for fear of the loss of its customers' confidence if the plaintiff were somehow linked to her husband's indictment for defrauding customers of another bank).

Page 124.   Add the following subsequent history to the citation to BoBo v. ITT, Continental Banking Co. in Note 2:

, cert. denied, 456 U.S. 933 (1982)

Page 124. Add the following to the end of Note 3:

See also Odima v. Westin Tucson Hotel, 53 F.3d 1484 (9th Cir. 1994) (plaintiff, born in Nigeria, brought suit for disparate treatment based on both race and national origin).

Page 127. Add the following subsequent history to the citation to Sinai v. New England Tel. & Tel. Co. in Note 6:

, cert. denied, 115 S. Ct. 597 (1994),

Page 128. Replace the citation to Garcia v. Gloor in Note 10 with the following:

618 F.2d 264, 269 (5th Cir. 1980), *cert. denied*, 449 U.S. 1113 (1981)

Page 136. Add the following subsequent history to the citation to Ezold v. Wolf, Block, Schorr & Solis-Cohen in Note 3:

, cert. denied, 114 S. Ct. 88 (1993)

Page 136. Add the following to the end of Note 3:

See also EEOC v. Ethan Allen, Inc., 44 F.3d 116 (2d Cir. 1994); Cronin v. Aetna Life Ins. Co., 46 F.3d 196 (2d Cir. 1995).

Page 137. Add new Note 5a:

5a. Deborah C. Malamud, The Last Minuet: Disparate Treatment After *Hicks*, 93 Mich. L. Rev. 2229 (1995), reviewed district courts' use of *McDonnell Douglas/Burdine* at the pretrial stage:

A review of district court summary judgment cases demonstrates that to accord legal significance to the plaintiff's satisfaction of the "requirements" of the prima facie "stage" and the pretext "stage" of *McDonnell Douglas-Burdine* is to engage in an act of misplaced concreteness. The world of practice under *McDonnell Douglas-Burdine* remains a disorderly one, in which the assignment of categories of facts to "stages" is unstable. Furthermore, to the extent that *McDonnell Douglas-Burdine does* constrain fact finding, it tends to discourage the kind of holistic fact finding that is most likely to reveal the truth about discrimination in the workplace.

Id. at 2237.

Page 137.   Add the following subsequent history to the citation to Hong v. Children's Memorial Hosp. in Note 10:

, *cert. denied*, 114 S. Ct. 1372 (1994)

Page 138.   Add the following subsequent history to the citation to Henn v. National Geographic Socy. in Note 12:

, *cert. denied*, 484 U.S. 964 (1987)

Page 138.   Change the citation to Paolillo v. Dresser Indus., Inc. in Note 12 as follows:

884 F.2d 707 (2d Cir. 1989)

2.   Defendant's Rebuttal and Plaintiff's Proof of Pretext

Page 141.   Add the following to the end of Note 4:

See also Grant v. News Group Boston, Inc., 55 F.3d 1 (1st Cir. 1994). In *Grant*, the plaintiff was able to establish a prima facie case of race discrimination by presenting evidence that, following a previous claim of racial discrimination (which the defendant had settled with the plaintiff), he was not called to work as a substitute paper handler while similarly situated white employees were being hired. However, the court held that the plaintiff failed to show pretext when the defendant presented evidence that the plaintiff had not shown up for work nine times in the past year and had the poorest overall record for the job. Id. at 7.

Page 142.   Add the following subsequent history to the citation to Walther v. LoneStar Gas Co. in Note 6:

, *reh'g denied*, 977 F.2d 161 (5th Cir. 1992),

Page 143.   Add new Note 9a:

See also Purkett v. Elem, 115 S. Ct. 1769 (1995), a case dealing with peremptory challenges to jurors where the prosecutor tried to explain its exclusion of several blacks because of their hair length and facial hair and not their race. The Supreme Court relied on Title VII's analysis to indicate that even nonsensical explanations—"implausible," "silly," "fantastic," or "superstitious"—satisfied defendant's burden of production.

Page 145.   Add the following subsequent history to the citation to CNA Fin. Corp. v. Donovan in Note 14:

, *cert. denied*, 485 U.S. 977 (1988),

Page 156.   Add the following to the end of Note 2:

Deborah A. Calloway, *St. Mary's Honor Center v. Hicks*: Questioning the Basic Assumption, 26 Conn. L. Rev. 997 (1995), argues that the Supreme Court's underlying assumption about the pervasiveness of the discrimination has changed and it is that change that is the significance of *Hicks*:

> *Hicks* is significant, not for its narrow legal holding, but for the attitude underlying that holding. The majority and dissent argue about parsing precedent and legal niceties such as the meaning of a rebuttable presumption and allocating burdens of proof. But this case is *not* about who bears the burden of proof. Instead, this case is about what evidence is sufficient to meet the plaintiff's burden of persuasion on discriminatory intent. What evidence makes it "more likely than not" that the defendant discriminated? The answer to this question depends on one's beliefs about the prevalence of discrimination. Whether a reasonable person (or judge) will be convinced that discrimination has been shown depends on whether he believes that discrimination is a logical inference in the absence of some other explanation for adverse conduct. The district court and the majority of the Supreme Court in *Hicks* reached their result, not because it

was required by any formal legal rules, but rather because they just plain do not believe in that basic assumption.

Id. at 1008-1009. In contrast, Deborah C. Malamud, The Last Minuet: Disparate Treatment After *Hicks*, 93 Mich. L. Rev. 2229 (1995), argues that *Hicks* is correctly decided, given that the Court's earlier decisions avoided dealing with the hard issues:

> [I analyze] the Court's prior disparate treatment decisions and conclude that the Supreme Court never succeeded in setting the prima facie case threshold high enough to permit the proven prima facie case to support a sufficiently strong inference of discrimination to mandate judgment for the plaintiff when combined only with disbelief of the employer's stated justification. . . . I conclude that the major thrust of the Court's disparate treatment jurisprudence is the attempt to insulate disparate treatment cases from the radical innovations of the disparate impact standard. There is a marked conservative overtone to the *McDonnell Douglas-Burdine* line of cases—and against its background, the nostalgic critique of *Hicks* is unacceptable.

Id. at 2236-2237. Articles critical of *Hicks* include Sherie L. Coons, Proving Disparate Treatment After *St. Mary's Honor Center v. Hicks*, 19 J. Corp L. 379 (1994); Robert Brookins, *Hicks*, Lies, and Ideology: The Wages of Sin Is Now Exculpation, 28 Creighton L. Rev. 939, 994 (1995) (criticizing *Hicks* because "Title VII's rules must help plaintiffs pierce corporate and governmental veils of secrecy and subjectivity, probe the nooks and crannies of decision-making arenas, and, ultimately, scrape away concreted discriminatory sediment"); Melissa A. Essary, The Dismantling of *McDonnell Douglas v. Green*: The High Court Muddies the Evidentiary Waters in Circumstantial Discrimination Cases, 21 Pepp. L. Rev. 385 (1994).

Page 157.   Add new Note 3a:

3a. In *Hicks*, the only evidence regarding personal animosity between the plaintiff and his supervisor was the testimony of the supervisor denying that it existed. Thus, the factfinder could not have found that the supervisor's personal animosity *was* the reason for the plaintiff's discharge. However, the factfinder need not determine that personal animosity was the reason for the employer's action. Instead, it must decide only whether unlawful discrimination was the actual reason for the challenged action. Because the plaintiff bears the burden of persuasion, he will lose if, based on the evidence in the record, the factfinder fails to conclude that it was the employer's intent to discriminate that motivated the adverse action plaintiff challenges.

*Page 158.   Add the following subsequent history to the
citation to Palmer v. District Bd. of Trustees
in Note 9:*

, *reh'g denied*, 752 F.2d 649 (11th Cir. 1985),

Page 159.   Add the following to the end of Note 10:

See Kralman v. Illinois Dept. of Veterans' Affairs, 23 F.3d 150 (7th Cir.), *cert. denied*, 115 S. Ct. 359 (1994) (defendant mistakenly believed it had to give priority in rehiring to a disabled veteran over the plaintiff).

D.   DIRECT EVIDENCE OF DISCRIMINATORY INTENT

Page 175.   Add the following to the end of Note 2(b):

In Starceski v. Westinghouse Elec. Corp., 54 F.3d 1089 (3d Cir. 1995), the plaintiff was discharged after working for the defendant for 36 years. The court held the testimony of a former supervisor that the defendant instructed him to transfer work from older to younger employees and to "doctor" the plaintiff's records to "reflect poor performance" was sufficient to satisfy the *Price Waterhouse* requirement of direct evidence. Id. at 1094.

In O'Connor v. Consolidated Coin Caterers Corp., 116 S. Ct. 1307 (1996), the Court addressed a *McDonnell Douglas* issue, see id. at 1309, but did not address a claim based on *Price Waterhouse*. The Fourth Circuit upheld the grant of summary judgment to the employer of plaintiff's *Price Waterhouse* claim, finding that three statements alleged to have been made by O'Connor's supervisor failed to raise material questions of fact. Several months before plaintiff's discharge, he and his supervisor were watching a golf match on television. In response to plaintiff saying he could not walk 18-hole rounds of golf on five consecutive days, his supervisor said that plaintiff was just "too old." Two weeks before plaintiff's discharge, his supervisor said, "O'Connor, you are too damn old for this kind of work." Two days before the discharge, the supervisor remarked to another employee while in plaintiff's presence that "it's about time we get some young blood in this company." These remarks, the court determined, did not raise material questions of fact as to intent to discriminate because they were not immediately connected with the employer's decision to terminate plaintiff, were in jest, or were "more accurately understood as a commentary on the fact that all people age." 56 F.3d 542, 549 (1995). Is the only statement that will qualify for *Price Waterhouse* analysis in the Fourth Circuit one made as the employee is being discharged that he is being discharged because of his age? What about the sterotypical thinking discussed in *Biggins*? Isn't the young blood comment an expression of stereotypical thinking that older workers are less competent than younger ones? Would all these statements be admissible in a *McDonnell Douglas* case?

Page 176.   Add the following subsequent history to the citation to *Griffiths v. CIGNA Corp.* in Note 3:

, *cert. denied*, 114 S. Ct. 186 (1993)

Page 178.   Add the following to the end of Note 8:

In Miller v. CIGNA Corp., 47 F.3d 586 (3d Cir. 1995) (en banc), the court overturned the sole cause rule announced in *Griffiths* (see Section E).

Page 180.   Add the following subsequent history to the citation to *Ezold v. Wolf, Block, Shorr & Solis-Cohen* in Note 12:

, *cert. denied*, 114 S. Ct. 88 (1993),

Page 184.   Add the following to the end of the Note on After-Acquired Evidence:

In McKennon v. Nashville Banner Pub. Co., 115 S. Ct. 879 (1995), the Supreme Court decided that after-acquired evidence does not cut off liability but instead limits the potential remedies of a plaintiff. The Court reviewed summary judgment granted against plaintiff on the assumption that plaintiff had been discharged because of age discrimination but that defendant had subsequently discovered evidence of plaintiff's prior misconduct that would justify her discharge.

The Court first found that an employee discharged because of discrimination is not barred from all relief when, after her discharge, her employer discovers wrongdoing that would have led to her termination on lawful and legitimate grounds had the employer known of it at the time of the discharge. Second, such after-acquired evidence is nevertheless relevant to the remedies plaintiff may recover in her underlying discrimination action if the employer seeking to rely on that evidence establishes that the wrongdoing was of such severity that the employee in fact would have been terminated on those grounds alone had the employer known of it at the time of the discharge. For an interesting article tieing *McKennon* with *Hicks* and critiquing both, see William R. Corbett, The Fall of *Summers*, the Rise of "Pretext Plus," and the Escalating Subordination of Federal Employment Discrimination Laws to Employment at Will: Lessons from *McKennon* and *Hicks*, 30 Ga. L. Rev. 305 (1996). Remedial questions are explored in more detail in Chapter 11 of this Supplement.

Page 186.   *Add the following subsequent history to the citation to Simpson v. Diversitech Gen., Inc. in the second full paragraph:*

, *cert. dismissed*, 502 U.S. 1083 (1992)

Page 191.   *Change the citation to Rivera v. Wichita Falls in the third full paragraph as follows:*

665 F.2d 531 (5th Cir. 1982)

Page 192.   *Add the following new Section at the end of the chapter:*

E. IS A NEW STRUCTURE OF INDIVIDUAL DISPARATE TREATMENT THEORY EMERGING?

There is considerable turmoil in the law of individual disparate treatment discrimination. First, new literature suggests that *McDonnell Douglas* and its progeny were never well founded and that the decisions in *Hicks* and *Biggins* have destroyed whatever coherence that had previously existed. Second, there is great confusion concerning the proper scope of application of and relationship between *McDonnell Douglas/Burdine* cases and *Price Waterhouse* cases. Third, the scope of applicable provisions of the 1991 Civil Rights Act is not yet clear within Title VII jurisprudence. Fourth, it is not clear what, if any, role the 1991 Act will have on the other antidiscrimination statutes that have been modeled on Title VII. It may be that out of this turmoil an entirely new structure will emerge to replace the existing theories. See Michael J. Zimmer, The Emerging Uniform Structure of Disparate Treatment Discrimination Litigation, 30 Ga. L. Rev. 563 (1996).

MILLER v. CIGNA CORP.
47 F.3d 586 (3d Cir. 1995) (en banc)

STAPLETON, Circuit Judge:

This appeal is before the court for rehearing in banc to clarify the proper standard for a jury charge in a pretext case alleging age discrimination.

Defendant Insurance Company of North America ("INA")[a CIGNA subsidiary] terminated plaintiff William J. Miller from his job after fifteen years of employment. Miller alleges that he was discriminated against on the basis of his age in violation of the Age Discrimination in Employment Act.

At trial, the district judge instructed the jury that it could return a verdict for Miller only if he proved that age was "the sole cause" of INA's decision. After the jury returned a verdict in INA's favor, Miller appealed, asserting that the district court improperly charged the jury regarding his burden of proof. We hold that in ADEA cases that do not qualify for a burden shifting charge under Price Waterhouse v. Hopkins, district courts should instruct the jury that the plaintiff's burden is to prove that age played a role in the employer's decisionmaking process and that it had a determinative effect on the outcome of that process. Because Miller should not have been required to prove that age was the sole cause of INA's decision, we conclude that he is entitled to a new trial.

I

Miller was hired in 1975 as an assistant to INA's Chief Financial Officer. In that position, he directed INA's reinsurance operations at the Newark Reinsurance Company, created a financial processing service center, and directed the production of summary financial documents. After serving as Vice President and Director of INA's Special Risk Facility, Miller was promoted to Senior Vice President, Field Operations. He created a new organization, managed a $200 million budget, and supervised over 8,000 employees. At this point in his career, Miller was compensated at pay grade sixty-one and his superior consistently evaluated his performance as exceeding expectations. After his promotion to Senior Vice President, Miller was asked to join a special team of executives called IMPACT. IMPACT's mission was to identify major strategic issues and market strategies for INA's Property and Casualty Division. Caleb Fowler, Chief Financial Officer of the Property and Casualty Division, and Richard Hoag, then Chief of Human Resources, indicated that they would find Miller a permanent position at the conclusion of the project. When IMPACT concluded in late 1984, Miller was assigned to a special project on reinsurance collection.

Upon completing the special project on reinsurance collection, Miller was appointed to the position of Senior Vice President, Finance and Administration in the Underwriting Division. In this position, Miller managed four departments, handled complaints from agents and regulatory agencies, prepared state filings and annual budgets, and managed a $70 million annual budget.

In late 1988, Miller's supervisor, Jack Morrison, advised Miller that he should search for another job because his position might be eliminated. In March of 1989, Miller's new superior, Nord Bjorke, informed Miller that his position was eliminated and sent him to Richard Hoag to receive a special assignment reducing real estate costs in the Property and Casualty Division.

One year later, Hoag informed Miller that, despite his success in reducing real estate costs, his position as "real estate czar" was being terminated. Hoag advised Miller that he could assist Robert O'Neil, head of the Corporate Real Estate Department, with special projects. In November of 1990, Miller was informed that this position was being eliminated and that he would be terminated at the end of December. At the time he was terminated, Miller was fifty-eight years old and had been downgraded to pay grade fifty-nine. At no time during 1990 did company officials apprise Miller of five vacancies at the company for which he might have applied.

The first vacancy was for the position of Vice President, Filing and Regulation. The company announced that Darrell DeMoss, age forty-two, had been selected. Miller had not known of the position and contends that he was qualified for it because, as Senior Vice President, Finance and Administration, he supervised the Filing and Regulation function. INA asserts that Miller was not considered because the position required legal analysis and Richard Franklin, the hiring manager for this position, decided to hire an attorney. Miller notes, however, that his name was not included on the list of nonlawyer candidates who were considered but disqualified, and that the previous Vice President, Filing and Regulation, was not a lawyer.

The second vacancy was in the position of General Manager of CIGNA Reinsurance Company, United Kingdom. Among the desired qualifications were "[w]ork experience with either United Kingdom accounting practices or reinsurance accounting practices and principles." Miller asserts that this position involved the same responsibilities he had when he supervised the Newark Reinsurance Company. James Godorecci, who was in charge of hiring for the position, acknowledged that he wrote the job qualifications with Michael Durkin, age thirty-five, in mind and that he never considered Miller for the position. INA contends that Miller lacked the desired academic credentials, work experience, and knowledge of United Kingdom accounting practices, although Miller testified that when he expressed interest in the position, Godorecci's superior told Miller he was "over qualified."

The third vacancy was for the position of Senior Vice President, Finance Systems and Administration, in the Claims Department. Qualifications desired for the position included: broad knowledge and experience in the property and casualty business; knowledge of financial measures and objectives; demonstrated credibility and the ability to work with other managers; skill in influencing managers and implementing strategy; and effective verbal and written skills. Miller contends he satisfied these requirements because of his management experience. James Engle, the hiring manager for this position, testified Miller was not qualified because he did not have a strong math and statistical background, was not familiar with loss control and statistical monitors, and lacked credibility among the actuaries. The company asserts that Victor DiFelice, age thirty-eight, was better qualified for the job.

The fourth vacancy, for the position of Head of Strategy Implementation, was filled by Ronald Peters, age forty-nine. The company conceded that Miller was qualified for the job, but maintained that Peters was better qualified. Although it was a temporary assignment, when his work in this position was completed Peters was retained by the company.

The fifth vacancy was for the position of Vice President, Property and Casualty Marketing. Hiring manager Thomas Cobb appointed Cynthia Cole-Dougherty, age thirty-eight. Job qualifications included an ability to conduct market studies, market research, competitive analyses, and segmentation studies. INA asserts that, although Cynthia Cole-Dougherty did not have insurance experience, one of the primary considerations in the hiring decision was a desire to hire from outside both the company and the industry.

The evidence at trial also focused on the nature of INA's hiring and promotion decisionmaking process. Human resource personnel testified about the company's formal placement process available for positions above pay grade fifty-four ("the 54 + placement process"). A department manager using the 54 + placement process would receive assistance from an assigned human resource contact who would act as the manager's agent within the company, helping to locate, sort through, and evaluate potential candidates for the position. Open positions above grade fifty-four were not publicly posted and a candidate could only access information about these openings through direct management contact. The 54 + placement process was not mandatory, however, and many of the managers who testified at trial explained that they had in fact filled their management vacancy through an informal process by assessing their own needs, reflecting on the qualifications of their staff members, and initiating contact with potential candidates directly. Richard Morrissey, director of human resources for CIGNA's property and casualty companies, also testified about the company's annual organizational review process through which department managers assess the qualifications, potential, and development needs of their staff with an eye toward identifying and developing future high level managers.

During trial, the district judge asked counsel if Miller's was a "pretext" or "mixed motives" case. This inquiry made reference to the distinction between employment discrimination cases in which the plaintiff seeks to carry his or her burden by showing that the employer's tendered reason for the challenged action is a pretext for discrimination and cases that qualify for a mixed motives, burden shifting instruction under Price Waterhouse v. Hopkins. Miller's counsel advised the district court that this was a "pretext" case. The district judge then "distribute[d] to counsel the questions [to be used] to submit the case to the jury." After reviewing those questions, Miller's counsel stated that she had an objection. Counsel asserted that plaintiff's burden of proof was to establish that age was "a determining factor," i.e., that it "made a difference" in the employer's decision.

Notwithstanding this objection, the district judge instructed the jury as follows:

> To recover under the pretext theory which the plaintiff asserts in this case, the plaintiff must establish by a preponderance of the evidence that his age was the sole cause of defendants' failure to hire him into vacancies that became available and to terminate his position as a real estate czar in the last of those listings that I've put on the page that you have; that he was qualified and rejected for the positions in question solely because of his age.

After two days of deliberations, the jury returned a verdict in favor of INA. . . .

III

Like Title VII which prohibits an employer from taking adverse employment actions against an employee "because of such individual's race, color, religion, sex, or national origin," the ADEA prohibits an employer from taking adverse employment actions against an employee "because of such individual's age." Not surprisingly, the ADEA jurisprudence concerning this prohibition has followed the Title VII jurisprudence interpreting the analogous prohibition. Trans World Airlines, Inc. v. Thurston. A district judge in a case under either statute must, of course, instruct the jury in a manner consistent with Congress' mandate that the adverse employment action must have been taken "because of" the prohibited consideration.

The nature of the causal connection mandated by the use of the phrase "because of" in Title VII was a focus of the Supreme Court's opinions in Price Waterhouse v. Hopkins. The members of the Court differed as to whether "because of" meant that the forbidden consideration must be a "but-for" cause (i.e., one without which the adverse employment action would not have been taken) or only that the impermissible consideration must have "played a motivating part" in the decision to take that action. See [the plurality opinion and Justice O'Connor, concurring in the judgment]. All members of the Court agreed, however, that "because of" did not mean "solely because of."

We find it clear from the opinions in *Price Waterhouse*, and from the legislative history they cite, that Congress, by using the phrase "because of," did not mean "solely because of." Even if we did not have this guidance, however, we would be reluctant to attribute to Congress an intention that an employer should be liable if a hiring or discharge decision is based solely on an employee's age and not liable if the decision is based primarily on the employee's age but also on the fact that the employee's supervisor did not like the employee's personality, hair color, or some other personal trait or conduct.

Having concluded that "because of" does not mean "solely because of," we now look to the governing precedents to determine the proper jury instruction in an employment discrimination case that does not qualify for a mixed motives, burden shifting charge under *Price Waterhouse*.

IV

The Justices concurring in the judgment in *Price Waterhouse* declined to apply to the situation before them the familiar rules for allocating the burdens of production and persuasion found in McDonnell Douglas Corp. v. Green and Texas Department of Community Affairs v. Burdine. They viewed those cases as "pretext" cases and the case before them as a "mixed motives" case. The Court held that, in cases where the plaintiff offers "direct evidence" of unlawful discrimination and the evidence as a whole permits a conclusion that both permissible and impermissible considerations played a role in the employer's decision, the plaintiff need only show that the unlawful motive was a substantial motivating factor in that decision. If the finder of fact concludes that the plaintiff has carried this burden, the burden of persuasion shifts to the defendant to prove that the unlawful motive was not a but-for cause, i.e., that the same action would have been taken, because of legitimate considerations, in the absence of the unlawful motive.

The members of the Court concurring in the judgment in *Price Waterhouse* reached this result by different routes. Justices Brennan, Marshall, Blackmun, and Stevens read the statute as imposing liability in any situation where the unlawful motive was a "motivating" factor, but recognized an "affirmative defense" where the employer shows that the same actions would have been taken in the absence of the unlawful motive. *Price Waterhouse.* Justice O'Connor agreed with the three dissenters that the statute required but-for cause as a predicate to liability, but favored a burden shifting rule for cases in which the plaintiff "show[s] by direct evidence that an illegitimate criterion was a substantial factor in the decision." In such cases, the burden shifts "to the employer to justify its decision," — "to show that the decision would have been the same absent discrimination." "[W]here a plaintiff has made this type of strong showing of illicit motivation, the factfinder is entitled to presume that the employer's discriminatory animus made a difference in the outcome, absent proof to the contrary from the employer." Justice White found it unnecessary "to get into semantic discussions on whether *Mt. Healthy . . .* creates an affirmative defense." *Price Waterhouse.* He agreed with Justice O'Connor, however, that the plaintiff in *Price Waterhouse* had made the requisite showing that sex was a substantial factor in the employer's decision and that the "burden of persuasion then should have shifted to *Price Waterhouse* to prove" the same decision would have been made absent the unlawful motive.

For present purposes, there are two important things to note about the several opinions in *Price Waterhouse.* First, a majority of the members of the Court did not endorse the plurality's view that Title VII imposed liability whenever a prohibited factor played a motivating role in the challenged decision. Justices O'Connor and White and the three dissenters rejected, in the words of Justice White, "a rule of causation that focused solely on whether [an impermissible motive] played a part, 'substantial' or otherwise, in a decision." Second, while the holding of the Court fashioned a special rule reducing the plaintiff's burden of persuasion in a defined category of Title VII individual discrimination cases, a majority of the Court endorsed views of Title VII that would leave plaintiffs in other individual discrimination cases with the burden of showing but-for cause.

All members of the Court now seem to agree that a showing of but-for causation by the plaintiff is required in ADEA cases that do not call for special treatment under *Price Waterhouse.* In Hazen Paper Co. v. Biggins, the plaintiff, like the plaintiff here, claimed that he had been discharged because of his age in violation of the ADEA. The Supreme Court was called upon to address the relationship between the standard of ordinary liability under the ADEA and the standard of liability for liquidated damages under the provision of that Act authorizing such damages for "willful" violations. With respect to the former, Justice O'Connor, writing for a unanimous Court, reviewed the case law applicable to disparate treatment (i.e., individual discrimination) cases and concluded as follows:

> Whatever the employer's decisionmaking process, a disparate treatment claim cannot succeed unless the employee's protected trait actually played a role in that process and had a determinative influence on the outcome.

With respect to the standard of liability for liquidated damages, the Court held:

> We therefore reaffirm that the *Thurston* definition of "willful"—that the employer either knew or showed reckless disregard for the matter of whether its conduct was prohibited by the statute—applies to all disparate treatment cases under the ADEA. Once a "willful" violation has been shown, the employee need not additionally . . . prove that age was the predominant rather than a determinative factor in the employment decision.

We find support in *Hazen Paper* for our earlier conclusion that "because of" does not mean "solely because of." If an ADEA plaintiff need not show that age was "the predominant factor" in order to establish liability for liquidated damages, surely such a plaintiff does not have to show that age was the sole cause of the challenged decision in order to establish a right to normal forms of relief. We also believe *Hazen Paper* provides an authoritative answer to our second inquiry. A plaintiff in an ADEA case who does not qualify for a burden shifting instruction under *Price Waterhouse* has the burden of persuading the trier of fact by a preponderance of the evidence that there is a "but-for" causal connection between the plaintiff's age and the employer's adverse action—i.e., that age "actually played a role in [the employer's decisionmaking] process and had a determinative influence on the outcome" of that process. *Hazen Paper.*

V

We find further support for our holding in the Supreme Court's decision in St. Mary's Honor Center v. Hicks. That decision makes clear that the trier of fact in a pretext case is not limited to a choice between finding that the alleged discriminatory motive or the employer's nondiscriminatory explanation was the sole cause of the employment action. At the time we decided Griffiths v. CIGNA Corp.,[8] it was possible to view all pretext cases as presenting only two possibilities: the fact finder could conclude either that the plaintiff had succeeded in proving that the employer's explanation was a pretext for discrimination, or that the plaintiff had failed to so prove. Under this view, if the plaintiff proved the employer's proffered reason was pretextual, the trier

8. INA insists that our decision in *Griffiths* mandated the "sole cause" instructions given by the district court in this case. INA's reading of *Griffiths* would be inconsistent with a long line of decisions of this court, including our in banc decision in Chipollini v. Spencer Gifts, Inc., 814 F.2d 893, 897 (3d Cir.) (holding that an ADEA plaintiff "need not prove that age was the employer's sole or exclusive consideration, but must prove that age made a difference in the decision"), *cert. dismissed*, 483 U.S. 1052 (1987); see also Bellissimo v. Westinghouse Elec. Corp., 764 F.2d 175, 179 n.1 (3d Cir. 1985) (finding the requirement of proving that the improper motive was "'the determinative factor' [to be] inconsistent with the 'but-for' causation test"), *cert. denied*, 475 U.S. 1035 (1986). To the extent language in *Griffiths* can be read to suggest that the charge in this case was appropriate, it is hereby overruled.

of fact presumed, as a matter of law, that the impermissible cause alleged by plaintiff was the sole cause of the employer's decision.

St. Mary's instructs that this bipolar view of pretext cases is inaccurate. A finding that the employer's nondiscriminatory explanation is a pretext permits, but does not require, the trier of fact to conclude that the employer discriminated against the plaintiff based on the ground alleged. St. Mary's Honor Ctr. v. Hicks. . . .

We think it clear from the Supreme Court's opinion in *St. Mary's* that the trier of fact in a pretext case, where the record will support it, may choose not to accept either party's litigating position as reflecting the whole truth. This may, as in *St. Mary's*, take the form of a conclusion that the adverse action was taken for a reason other than the reasons urged by the parties. It may also take the form of a conclusion that the alleged discrimination and the employer's nondiscriminatory explanation both played a role in the employer's decision. If the plaintiff, for example, argues that he or she was discharged because of age and the employer insists that it was because of the plaintiff's record of absenteeism, the trier of fact may conclude that the plaintiff's absenteeism record played a part, but that the plaintiff would not have been fired if he or she were twenty years younger. . . .

In most age discrimination cases that get to the jury, the record will support an inference that both a legitimate and an illegitimate reason played a role in the employer's decision and the charge must provide for the possibility that the jury will find the employer's decision to be the product of more than one consideration. In those cases, the court must charge, in accordance with *Hazen Paper*, that the plaintiff's burden is to show that the prohibited consideration played a role in the decisionmaking process and that it had a determinative influence on the outcome of that process.[9]

9. We are here, of course, describing cases in which the challenged action of the employer may be the product of two or more motives. It is important to understand, however, that these cases do not fall within the legal category of "mixed motives" cases reserved for special treatment under *Price Waterhouse*. As we explained more fully in *Griffiths*, and Hook v. Ernst & Young, 28 F.3d 366, 373-76 (3d Cir. 1994), "mixed motives" cases are cases not only where the record would support a conclusion that both legitimate and illegitimate factors played a role in the employer's decision, but where the plaintiff's evidence of discrimination is sufficiently "direct" to shift the burden of proof to the employer on the issue of whether the same decision would have been made in the absence of the discriminatory animus. The term of art "mixed motives" is thus misleading because it describes only a small subset of all employment discrimination cases in which the employer may have had more than one motive. Under *Price Waterhouse*, the correct wording of a causation instruction to a jury differs depending on whether the case before the court is a "mixed motives" or a "pretext" case *as those categories are defined in that case*. Only in a "mixed motives" ADEA case is the plaintiff entitled to an instruction that he or she need show only that the forbidden motive played a role, i.e., was "a motivating factor." Even then, the instruction must be followed by an explanation that the defendant may escape liability by showing that the challenged action would have been taken in the absence of the forbidden motive. In all other ADEA disparate treatment cases, the jury should be instructed that the plaintiff may meet his or her burden only by showing that age played a role in the employer's decisionmaking process and that it had a determinative effect on the outcome of that process.

VI

In this case, the district court's repeated reference to "sole cause" and "sole factor" was not harmless error. Miller alleged that because of his age, he was not selected for various open high level management positions for which he was qualified and that thereafter he was terminated. For each of the open positions his employer offered evidence to show that Miller was not qualified or that he was less qualified than the candidate ultimately selected. Based on the evidence presented at trial, a jury could well have concluded that both Miller's and the employer's explanations were accurate—that Miller was qualified for one or more of the open positions, that the employer's promotion and hiring decisionmaking process contained a bias in favor of younger employees, and that Miller's credentials did not sufficiently distinguish him from the competing candidates to overcome this bias.

For example, with respect to the vacancy for general manager with CIGNA Reinsurance Company, United Kingdom (the "CIGNA UK position"), the manager responsible for filling that position testified that he wrote the job description with Michael Durkin, the successful candidate, in mind; that Durkin had most of the qualities needed for that position; and that Durkin had more experience than Miller in reinsurance and accounting work. A jury who credited the employer's evidence could therefore conclude that Durkin's promotion was a legitimate hiring decision. However, Miller testified that he had extensive reinsurance experience as well as substantially more management experience and skills than Durkin—one of the qualifications for the position. Durkin had managed a staff of only twenty employees, while Miller had managed much larger groups. Miller also testified that when he expressed interest in the CIGNA UK position the president of that division told him he was "overqualified." Miller also offered evidence that Durkin had obtained his reinsurance experience in part through his manager's desire to cross-train and develop him for this type of managerial promotion. Miller additionally points out that many of the INA managers responsible for the hiring decisions at issue, including the manager who filled the CIGNA UK position, testified that they eschewed the company's formal inter-departmental placement process available for positions above grade fifty-four for an informal and personal decisionmaking process. This testimony lends credence to Miller's theory that the promotion and hiring decisions for upper level management positions were susceptible to age-animus. Accordingly, a jury crediting Miller's evidence could infer that the decision not to consider or select him for the CIGNA UK position was based on age.

Because INA's and Miller's explanations were not inherently contradictory, however, it would have been possible for the jury to find that the company considered both Miller's qualifications and his age, and that both factored into the relevant hiring decisions. Thus, the jury could have reasonably concluded that Miller was less than ideally qualified for a particular position and that this was a factor in INA's decisionmaking process. At the same time, it could reasonably have concluded that INA's decisionmakers were biased in favor of younger workers and a younger person with Miller's credentials would have been assigned to the post.

The ADEA's protection against age discrimination is not limited to perfectly qualified employees. As the court observed in Shager v. Upjohn Co., 913 F.2d 398, 403 (7th Cir. 1990): "The statute does not protect merely the older worker who is perfect from the standpoint of his employer; such a worker needs no protection except from irrational employers, and they are rare. It protects, as a practical matter, the imperfect older worker from being treated worse than the imperfect younger one." Cf. Mardell v. Harleysville Life Ins. Co., 31 F.3d 1221, 1233 (3d Cir. 1994) ("[N]either Title VII nor ADEA strips a wrongdoing employee of his or her entitlement to protection against unlawful discrimination."). Despite his imperfect credentials, Miller should have prevailed if he would not have been passed over but for his age. The district court's "sole cause" charge did not permit the jury to find in Miller's favor on this basis. It follows that Miller is entitled to a new trial.

VII

We hold that in an ADEA case which does not qualify for a burden shifting instruction under *Price Waterhouse*, a district court should instruct the jury that the plaintiff must prove by a preponderance of the evidence that age played a role in the employer's decisionmaking process and that it had a determinative effect on the outcome of that process.[10] Since the district court instructed that age must be shown to be the sole cause of the employer's decision and since the record would support a conclusion that, while other factors played a role, age was a determinative factor, we will reverse and remand for a new trial.

GREENBERG, Circuit Judge, concurring in part and concurring in the judgment.

To put it succinctly, the question before us is the effect of Hazen Paper Co. v. Biggins and St. Mary's Honor Center v. Hicks on our holding in Griffiths

---

10. In the course of this opinion, we have relied on Title VII cases because the development of the relevant case law under the two statutes prior to the Civil Rights Act of 1991 followed parallel courses. Section 107 of the 1991 Civil Rights Act, codified at 42 U.S.C. §2000e-2(m), provides that "an unlawful employment practice is established when the complaining party demonstrates that [a prohibited consideration] was a motivating factor for any employment practice, even though other factors also motivated the practice." The substantive provisions of the 1991 Act that amended Title VII did not amend the ADEA, and Miller does not contend that section 107 is applicable to ADEA cases.

v. CIGNA Corp., that there are two types of cases under the ADEA—mixed motives cases and pretext cases—and that in the latter, the plaintiff must show that age was the determinative factor in the adverse employment decision. The majority correctly concludes that "in ADEA cases that do not qualify for a burden shifting charge under *Price Waterhouse* . . . district courts should instruct the jury that the plaintiff's burden is to prove that age played a role in the employer's decisionmaking process and that it had a determinative effect on the outcome of that process." . . . [T]he area of employment discrimination law is cursed with elusive terms like "mixed motives" and "pretext," and with numerous presumptions, inferences and burden-shifting rules. Those terms and rules historically often have taken on lives of their own, independent of their connection to the underlying theories of liability that gave them birth. Thus, a "mixed motives" case is not about mixed motives, and a "pretext" case has little to do with pretext. I believe the time has come to clarify the current status of theories of ADEA liability, and to dispense with unhelpful monikers whenever possible. Thus, unlike the in banc majority, I would dispense altogether with the terms "pretext" and "mixed motives" and hold explicitly that the same standard applies to all disparate treatment cases. Finally, I believe that the entire debate over "but-for" causation makes something out of nothing, and that district courts should feel free to instruct juries in all ADEA cases that a plaintiff does not succeed unless but-for causation is shown.

I

In McDonnell Douglas Corp. v. Green, the Supreme Court first set forth the order of proof in disparate treatment cases, and the Court elaborated upon and explained the framework in Texas Dept. of Community Affairs v. Burdine. *Burdine* repeatedly speaks about the employer's "true" reason for the discharge, and therefore, the opinion was cast in either-or terms. Post-*Burdine* cases reaffirmed this proposition. See, e.g., NLRB v. Transportation Management Corp., 462 U.S. 393, 400, n. 5 (1983) (in *Burdine*, "[t]he Court discussed only the situation in which the issue is whether either illegal or legal motives, but not both, were the 'true' motives behind the decision"); United States Postal Service Bd. of Governors v. Aikens, 460 U.S. 711, 717, 718 (1983) ("a plaintiff prevail[s] when at the third stage of a Title VII trial he demonstrates that the legitimate, nondiscriminatory reason given by the employer is in fact not the true reason for the employment decision") (Blackmun, J., concurring). Thus, the pre-*Price Waterhouse* jurisprudence "assumed . . . that a single impulse moves the employer who discriminates," see Theodore Y. Blumoff & Harold S. Lewis, Jr., The Reagan Court and Title VII: A Common-Law Outlook on a Statutory Task, 69 N.C.L. Rev. 1, 47 (1990), and that all disparate treatment claims could be analyzed under *Burdine*'s either-or pretext framework. This did not mean that the Court foreclosed liability when more than one cause motivated the adverse employment decision, but only that the employment discrimination cases coming before the Court were argued under the *Burdine* pretext framework.

Price Waterhouse v. Hopkins changed the employment discrimination liability landscape, but not in the way the in banc majority suggests. In my view, the majority confuses *Price Waterhouse*'s general holding that plaintiffs may obtain relief despite their inability to fit their proofs into *Burdine*'s pretext framework, with the standard for causation in cases that do proceed under *Burdine*. The majority correctly points out that "[a]ll members of the [*Price Waterhouse*] Court agreed . . . that 'because of' did not mean 'solely because of.'" But the quotations from the *Price Waterhouse* opinions demonstrate only that in that case, all members of the Court agreed that plaintiffs were not without a remedy if their proofs did not fit into the classic *Burdine* mold. Rather, all members of the Court agreed that when there is no one true reason behind the discharge, the employer in certain circumstances still could be liable. The *Price Waterhouse* dissent suggested interpreting *Burdine* so that it could cover all claims of disparate treatment. But a majority of the Court chose to retain *Burdine*'s framework for pretext cases, and to provide a separate theory of liability, together with a separate order of proof, to apply in cases involving both legitimate and illegitimate reasons for the adverse employment action.

Thus, *Price Waterhouse* does not support the conclusion that in a pretext case, a plaintiff need not prove that age was the determinative factor in the employment decision. Quite the contrary, a majority of the justices explicitly reaffirmed *Burdine*'s assumption that in a pretext case, as opposed to a mixed motives case, the illicit reason must be the determinative cause. Crucial passages in the various opinions, that the in banc majority does not cite, demonstrate that a majority of the *Price Waterhouse* court viewed *Burdine*'s "one or the other" description of pretext liability as still viable in cases proceeding under a pretext theory. . . .

In fact, the *Price Waterhouse* plurality's theory of employment discrimination liability necessarily assumed that a plaintiff proceeding under a mixed motives theory could not succeed under a pretext theory. This is because of the following: In a pretext case, the defendant responds to the plaintiff's prima facie case by offering legitimate nondiscriminatory reasons for the discharge. The plaintiff then must prove that those reasons are pretextual. If a plaintiff cannot prove that the proffered reasons for the discharge were not in fact real reasons, then by definition the plaintiff has failed to demonstrate pretext, and has failed the third prong of the *Burdine* test. Assume, however, that the district court is convinced that even though the defendant's proof has gone unrebutted, the plaintiff nonetheless has proven that age played a role in the adverse employment decision. That is a scenario in which both legitimate and illegitimate factors played a role in the decision. Here, the *Price Waterhouse* scenario comes into play, and even though the claim fails under *Burdine*, the defendant would have the burden of disproving but-for causation.

Thus, *Price Waterhouse* is important not because it said anything about the standard for showing pretext liability but because it constituted the first time the Supreme Court explicitly decided that *Burdine* liability, while alive and well, did not provide the only framework for imposing liability. I believe, then, that the in banc majority is wrong to suggest that the *Price Waterhouse* majority used "mixed motives" as a "term of art" that describes "only a small subset of all employment discrimination cases in which the employer may have had more than one motive." To be sure, there is language in the various *Price Waterhouse* opinions addressing the evidence the plaintiff must adduce to prove that the illicit criterion played a role in the decision. But, at least in *Price Waterhouse*, the nature of the evidence that can be used "to satisfy the factfinder that it is more likely than not that a forbidden characteristic played a part in the employment decision," is a question separate and apart from how a plaintiff can proceed when he or she is unable to prove pretext. In fact, in the wake of *Price Waterhouse*, a number of courts have addressed the nature of the proofs required to shift the burden in an employment discrimination case, and have arrived at differing results. That is hardly surprising, since *Price Waterhouse* does not address that question. *Compare* White v. Federal Express Corp., 939 F.2d 157, 160 (4th Cir. 1991) ("To show discrimination in a mixed motive case . . . a plaintiff . . . may carry its burden under ordinary principles of proof by any sufficiently probative direct or indirect evidence") with Brown v. East Mississippi Elec. Power Assn., 989 F.2d 858, 861 (5th Cir. 1993) ("[w]hen a plaintiff presents credible *direct* evidence that discriminatory animus in part motivated or was a substantial factor in the contested employment action, the burden of proof shifts to the employer. . . .") (emphasis added). For our part, we have held that "[a]t a bare minimum, a plaintiff seeking to advance a mixed motive case will have to adduce circumstantial evidence 'of conduct or statements by persons involved in the decision-making process that may be viewed as directly reflecting the alleged discriminatory attitude.'" *Griffiths* (quoting Ostrowski v. Atlantic Mut. Ins. Cos., 968 F.2d 171, 182 (2d Cir. 1992)).

In short, then, a majority of the justices in *Price Waterhouse* held that Title VII provides two theories of liability: (1) pretext, or *Burdine* analysis, under which an employee only wins by showing that the employer's proffered reason for the adverse employment decision was pretextual and that, in fact, the decision was based solely on illegitimate factors; (2) mixed motives cases, in which the trier of fact concludes that both licit and illicit motives played a role in the employment decision, and where the burden shifts to the employer to prove that it would have made the same decision absent the illegitimate motive.

II . . .

In Hazen Paper Co. v. Biggins, the Court clarified the standards for proving disparate treatment under the ADEA. In no uncertain terms, the Court held that: whatever the employer's decisionmaking process, a disparate treatment claim cannot succeed unless the employee's protected trait actually played a role in that process and had a determinative influence on the outcome. One thing is clear from this language: In no disparate treatment case must a plaintiff prove that the illicit motive was the determinative factor. It necessarily follows that the Court's distinction in *Price Waterhouse* between pretext cases and mixed motives cases no longer proves a viable rationale for the *Price Waterhouse*'s burden-shifting approach. This is because in light of *Hazen*, a plaintiff need not prove that age was the determinative factor to prove liability in a pretext case—rather, under the language of *Hazen*, a plaintiff could succeed under *Burdine* without proving that the employer's reasons are *wholly* pretextual. And, if the reasons are not wholly pretextual, some of them must be true. Further still, if some of the employer's reasons are true, pretext cases sometimes involve mixed motives. Thus, after *Hazen*, the burden-shifting approach of *Price Waterhouse*—if it survives at all— must rest not on the distinction between cases involving mixed motives and cases involving pretexts for discrimination, but rather on the distinction between circumstantial evidence cases and direct evidence cases. Thus, in my view, this court should not continue to refer to the term "mixed motives" and then define it as meaning something other than mixed motives. Instead, we simply should abandon the term altogether.

Along with abandoning the notion of an independent category of "mixed motives" cases, *Hazen* is important for another reason as well—it signalled discomfort with the *Burdine* scheme of apportioning burdens and presumptions, and consequently, with the entire notion of "pretext" liability. In this regard, the Court foreshadowed its decision in *St. Mary's* by pointing out that "inferring age-motivation from the implausibility of the employer's explanation may be problematic in cases where other unsavory motives, such as pension interference, were present." Hence, the Court expressed wariness about the "one or the other" approach of the pretext cases. The Court supported this critique by pointing to language in pretext cases tending to show that liability could be imposed under the ADEA even when age was not a motivating factor. Thus, with the criticism of *Burdine* generally, and with the Court's holding that in all disparate treatment cases the plaintiff need only prove that the illicit factor had a determinative effect on the outcome, the Court strongly signalled the end of pretext liability as a distinct theory of disparate treatment liability.

St. Mary's made the point even more explicit, and abandoned the notion of pretext liability altogether. In that case, the Supreme Court rejected the view that when a plaintiff proves an employer's proffered reasons for the adverse employment action is pretextual, the plaintiff automatically wins. Rather, in a disparate treatment case, the plaintiff must prove intentional discrimination, and the concept of affirmative proof is analytically distinct from proving other explanations wrong. *St. Mary's* qualified this by saying that "[t]he factfinder's disbelief of the reasons put forward by the defendant (particularly if disbelief is accompanied by a suspicion of mendacity) may, together with the elements of the prima facie case, suffice to show intentional discrimination." And, as the in banc majority recognizes, "[a] finding that the employer's nondiscriminatory explanation is a pretext permits, but does not require, the trier of fact to conclude that the employer discriminated against the plaintiff based on the ground alleged." But by focusing on what *St. Mary's* says about "sole cause," the majority misses the real significance of *St. Mary's*, and may perpetuate misreadings of the case both in our own case law and in the commentary.

If we interpret *St. Mary's* purely within the pretext paradigm, as the in banc majority appears to do, the case can be read to say that in all disparate treatment cases proceeding within the *Burdine* framework, the plaintiff must, at a minimum, prove pretext. After all, that is how *Burdine* described the three-pronged test. And, we recently held in Armbruster v. Unisys Corp., 32 F.3d 768, 782 (3d Cir. 1994), that in a post-*St. Mary's* pretext case "a plaintiff who claims invidious discrimination but lacks overt evidence of discriminatory animus *must* point to evidence tending to show the defendant's explanation is pretextual." If that is true, however, we very nearly are back at sole cause again. This is because the plaintiff is being forced not only to make an affirmative showing but also affirmatively to disprove facts. See *Armbruster* ("After *St. Mary's*, it seems clear . . . that the trier of fact cannot find for the plaintiff merely because it disbelieves the defendant's proffered explanation; it must also be persuaded that the employment decision was the result of the bias that can be inferred from the falsity of the defendant's explanation."); ("an ultimate finding of illegal discrimination in a pretext case requires evidence showing a *prima facie* case and evidence showing pretext"); see also Michael A. Zubrensky, Despite the Smoke, There Is No Gun: Direct Evidence Requirements in Mixed-Motives Employment Law After *Price Waterhouse v. Hopkins*, 46 Stan. L. Rev. 959, 964 (1994) ("plaintiffs [must] disprove unstated reasons for the employment decision"). But, as *Hazen* makes clear, in no disparate treatment case must a plaintiff prove that the illicit factor was the sole or determinative cause of the adverse employment action. Therefore, to read *St. Mary's* as requiring a plaintiff to prove pretext is to misread the case.

The point of *St. Mary's* was not to place a dual burden on plaintiffs, but rather to treat disparate treatment discrimination cases—after the plaintiff has established a prima facie case and after the defendant has met its burden of production—just like any other case where the plaintiff bears the burden of proof. See also Gehring v. Case Corp., 43 F.3d 340, 343 (7th Cir. 1994) ("Once the judge finds that the plaintiff has made the minimum necessary demonstration (the 'prima facie case') and that the defendant has produced an age neutral explanation . . . the only remaining question . . . the jury need answer is whether the plaintiff is a victim of intentional discrimination."). After the plaintiff and the defendant have met their initial burdens, the entire *Burdine* procedure no longer is of any relevance (apart from the fact that the procedure provided a mechanism to get evidence before the court). To be sure, the plaintiff may attempt to prove intentional discrimination solely by focusing on the falsity of the defendant's explanations, but that only means that if a jury disbelieves the defendant's argument, it may believe the opposite. Nothing in that proposition is peculiar to age discrimination claims. In other words, the plaintiff certainly is not required to rebut the defendant's proffered reasons completely, if he or she nonetheless is able to establish that the illicit motive was a but-for cause of the adverse employment decision.

The problem probably arose with *St. Mary's* assumption that proving pretext is easier than affirmatively proving intentional discrimination. *St. Mary's* assumed that when the factfinder is focussed purely on whether the defendant's proffered reasons are true, the plaintiff is somehow getting off the hook. In some cases that may be true. But that assumption certainly is incorrect as a general proposition. Rather, it may be much more difficult to disprove an employer's explanation than to point to evidence tending to show that even if the employer's explanation is partly correct, the illicit motive also caused the action.

But putting that incorrect assumption aside, the real point of *St. Mary's* was to focus the factfinder in all disparate treatment cases away from the question of pretext and instead on the question of whether intentional discrimination took place. *St. Mary's* is important because it tells district courts to dispense with abstract pretext analysis altogether except insofar as it sheds light on whether intentional discrimination took place. As in all cases, there must be evidence in the record to support a finding in favor of the plaintiff on the ultimate question. As *Hazen* makes clear, when the plaintiff is not required to prove sole cause, it should not matter at all that a legitimate reason played a role in the process. Thus, once the defendant has met its proffer, the jury should be instructed that it should consider evidence of the prima facie case, evidence of legitimate explanations, evidence bearing on the credibility of those explanations, and all other relevant evidence in the case to determine whether the employer discriminated against the plaintiff.

By abandoning sole cause as the basis for pretext liability, *Hazen* makes clear that there is no separate category of mixed motives cases. By turning the focus in "pretext" cases away from evidence of pretext, *St. Mary's* makes clear that there is no separate category of pretext cases. What we are left with is one broad category of disparate treatment cases that, except for the limited category of *Price Waterhouse* cases, should be treated alike.[4]

III

This brings me to the question of causation. The majority goes to great lengths to show that plaintiffs must prove but-for causation in order to prevail, but the ultimate test it announces neglects all mention of but-for causation. Contrary to the majority's intimations, all the justices in *Price Waterhouse* itself agreed on this point. I believe that the majority is incorrect when it states that in *Price Waterhouse*, "Justices Brennan, Marshall, Blackmun, and Stevens read the statute as imposing liability in any situation where the unlawful motive was a 'motivating' factor." While the *Price Waterhouse* plurality pointed out that "Hopkins argues that once she made this showing [that the unlawful motive was a motivating factor] she was entitled to a finding that Price Waterhouse had discriminated against her on the basis of sex," it quickly rejected that argument. Justice Brennan really was concerned with burdens and presumptions; his point was that if the defendant could not prove its affirmative defense, the trier of fact could presume that but-for causation had been proven. ("[W]here an employer is unable to prove its claim that it would have made the same decision in the absence of discrimination, we are entitled to conclude that gender did make a difference to the outcome.") (plurality opinion); ("A court that finds for a plaintiff under this standard has effectively concluded that an illegitimate motive was a 'but-for' cause of the employment decision.") (plurality opinion); ("The theory of Title VII liability the plurality adopts . . . essentially incorporates the but-for standard.") (Kennedy, J., dissenting). In other words, all the justices always have agreed that a plaintiff cannot win in an age discrimination suit if but-for causation is not proved; the disagreement in *Price Waterhouse* involves the much different question of who bears the burden of proof and what can be inferred when those burdens are not met. ("The importance of today's decision is not the standard of causation it employs, but its shift to the defendant of the burden of proof.") (Kennedy, J., dissenting).

The in banc majority's belief that "but-for" causation is surrounded in controversy has induced it to shy away from the concept in articulating a jury charge — even though the majority opinion at one point explicitly recognizes that the *Hazen* test translates into but-for causation, see Opinion ("A plaintiff

4. In light of *Hazen* and *St. Mary's*, I agree with the majority's conclusion that *Price Waterhouse* cases are "cases not only where the record would support a conclusion that both legitimate and illegitimate factors played a role in the employer's decision, but where the plaintiff's evidence of discrimination is sufficiently 'direct' to shift the burden of proof to the employer on the issue of whether the same decision would have been made in the absence of the discriminatory animus."

in an ADEA case . . . has the burden of persuading the trier of fact . . . that there is a 'but-for' causal connection between the plaintiff's age and the employer's adverse action. . . ." I believe this unnecessarily complicates matters. Cf. *Gehring* ("'determining factor' is not a term in common usage, and it therefore does not illuminate the essential concepts. Putting unusual terms in jury instructions does little beyond confusing the jurors"). Thus, while it is true that in all non-*Price Waterhouse* cases, the test is whether the "plaintiff [has proven] by a preponderance of the evidence that age played a role in the employer's decisionmaking process and that it had a determinative effect on the outcome of that process," the jury also may be instructed that this technically worded test translates into but-for causation. *Gehring* ("one attractive formulation" is that the jury should be instructed to decide "whether the employer would have fired [demoted, laid off] the employee if the employee had been younger than 40 and everything else had remained the same"). In *Price Waterhouse* cases, the jury should be instructed that if the defendant fails to meet its burden of showing that it would have made the same decision in the absence of the illicit motive, it must conclude that the plaintiff *has proven* but-for causation.

NOTES

1. The court rejected a "sole cause" test for *McDonnell Douglas/Burdine* cases and instead ruled that "in an ADEA case which does not qualify for a burden shifting instruction under *Price Waterhouse*, a district court should instruct the jury that the plaintiff must prove by a preponderance of the evidence that age played a role in the employer's decision-making process and that it had a determinative effect on the outcome of that process." What is the difference between "sole cause" and this new test? Is it that plaintiff can still win if the employer's announced reason played some role in the decision as long as the factfinder finally decides that age had a determinative effect in that decision?

Do you agree with Judge Greenberg that this in essence is the same as "but-for" causation? Is the two-step analysis of plaintiff showing that age played a role in the decision with that role having a determinative effect on the outcome the same as showing "but-for" causation? Is there any meaning to this two-step approach if plaintiff has to prove both steps?

2. What test does the court say applies to what it calls *Price Waterhouse* cases? See footnote 9:

[W]here the plaintiff's evidence of discrimination is sufficiently "direct" . . . the plaintiff [is] entitled to an instruction that he or she need show only that the forbidden motive played a role, i.e., was "a motivating factor." Even then, the instruction must be followed by an explanation that the defendant may escape liability by showing that the challenged action would have been taken in the absence of the forbidden motive.

This maintains the distinction, ultimately based on Justice O'Connor's concurrence in *Price Waterhouse*, that two separate theories of individual disparate treatment liability exist, depending on whether plaintiff has direct or only circumstantial evidence. In another part of Griffiths v. CIGNA, the Third Circuit had defined "direct" evidence as really meaning good circumstantial evidence. See Note 3, page 176 of the casebook. Is that still good law after *Miller*?

The court appears not to require that plaintiff show the forbidden motive was "a substantial factor," another element of O'Connor's concurrence in *Price Waterhouse*.

3. What are the differences between the application of *Price Waterhouse* cases and cases that do not qualify for the *Price Waterhouse* approach? Is there much difference between plaintiff having to show that age "played a role" and that age was "a motivating factor"? Is there a greater difference between showing that age "played a role . . . and that it had a determinative effect on the outcome" and showing that age was "a motivating factor"?

Is the major difference simply the difference in the burden of persuasion? In *Price Waterhouse* cases, the burden of persuasion shifts to the defendant once the plaintiff proves the prohibited characteristic was "a motivating factor." To escape liability, the employer must then prove it would have made the same decision even if it had not considered the prohibited characteristic. In cases not qualifying for the *Price Waterhouse* approach, the plaintiff always carries the burden of persuasion that the prohibited characteristic played a role that had a determinative effect on the outcome.

4. The *Miller* court remanded for a new trial. What instructions should be given? Is there "direct" evidence so that *Price Waterhouse* should apply? Is the comment by a supervisor that Miller was "over qualified" direct evidence of stereotypical thinking? See Taggart v. Time, Inc., 924 F.2d 43 (2d Cir. 1991). In *Griffiths*, the Third Circuit adopted a "good circumstantial evidence" test for when *Price Waterhouse* applies. The Second Circuit in Ostrowski v. Atlantic Mut. Ins. Co., 968 F.2d 171, 182 (2d Cir. 1992), described that test. "[C]ircumstantial evidence must be tied directly to the alleged discriminatory animus. For example, purely statistical evidence would not warrant such a charge; nor would evidence merely of the plaintiff's qualification for and the availability of a given position; nor would 'stray' remarks in the workplace by persons who are not involved in the pertinent decision-making process." Would the explanations given Miller by various employer officials qualify under this test?

Could instructions be given under both theories or are they mutually exclusive? If both were available, how would they be given? In Abrams v.

Lightolier, Inc., 50 F.3d 1204 (3d Cir. 1995), a case tried during the era when sole cause was applied to age discrimination cases in the Third Circuit, the jury was given a sole cause charge on the ADEA count in the complaint but was given a but-for charge appropriate to an age discrimination claim under state law. Reviewing the same evidence, the jury found for the employer under the federal ADEA claim but found for the plaintiff under the state claim. If both theories apply under federal law, should the judge order the jury to review the whole case under each charge? Or should the *Price Waterhouse* charge be limited to the direct or good circumstantial evidence and the other test be applied to all of the evidence? How could a judge instruct a jury as to which evidence was relevant to which theory? If the plaintiff is entitled to both theories because both types of evidence are in the record, how can the plaintiff be put to the "either/or" decision?

5. Do you agree with Judge Greenberg's conclusion that the terms "mixed motive" and "pretext" should be abandoned?

> By abandoning sole cause as the basis for pretext liability, [Hazen Paper Co. v. Biggins] makes clear that there is no separate category of mixed motives cases. By turning the focus in "pretext" cases away from evidence of pretext, [*Hicks*] makes clear that there is no separate category of pretext cases. What we are left with is one broad category of disparate treatment cases that, except for the limited category of *Price Waterhouse* cases, should be treated alike.

Should the next step be to abandon both *McDonnell Douglas/Burdine* and *Price Waterhouse* paradigms of individual disparate treatment discrimination? If that were done, what should replace them?

6. *Hicks* has been criticized as abandoning a prophylactic rule necessary to counteract potential bias among judges and juries deciding discrimination cases:

> *Hicks'* restriction on the impact of the prima facie case and its questioning of the basic assumption, while consistent with the letter of the law, is clearly at odds with its purpose. A presumption is a judicially or legislatively created mechanism for predetermining the sufficiency of evidence to support a factual or legal conclusion. It saves time and legal resources, but it also can serve the purpose of forcing a correct decision that courts and juries are likely not to reach because of their personal prejudices and biases. Inferring discrimination is just such a situation and warrants exactly that treatment. Discrimination is rampant, but judges, academics and laypersons alike either underestimate its prevalence or believe that their group and not other groups are victimized. Under these circumstances, in a world in which most people are smart enough to avoid providing direct evidence of discriminatory intent, it is critical for the law to define a prima facie case which creates a presumption of discrimination absent evidence to the contrary.

Deborah A. Calloway, *St. Mary's Honor Center v. Hicks*: Questioning the Basic Assumption, 26 Conn. L. Rev. 997, 1037 (1994).

7. By contrast, Deborah C. Malamud, The Last Minuet: Disparate Treatment After *Hicks*, 93 Mich. L. Rev. 2229, 2237 (1995), concludes that *Hicks* is correctly decided. Based on her review of draft opinions and correspondence of the Justices available in the papers of Justice Thurgood Marshall, Professor Malamud argues that the Supreme Court had never decided in any of its individual disparate treatment cases that proving a simple prima facie case under *McDonnell Douglas* would by itself support an inference of discriminatory intent:

> If *Hicks* is correct, however, there remains what might well be thought of as a problem of judicial economy: *McDonnell Douglas-Burdine* is reduced to nothing but an empty ritual. If *McDonnell Douglas-Burdine* does nothing the normal rules of civil procedure cannot do, if it neither aids nor constrains judicial decisionmaking, one must ask whether it makes sense to continue to use the *McDonnell Douglas-Burdine* proof structure at all.

8. Still a third approach is found in Linda Hamilton Krieger's article, The Content of Our Categories: A Cognitive Bias Approach to Discrimination and Equal Employment Opportunity, 47 Stan. L. Rev. 1161 (1995), which criticizes the *McDonnell Douglas/Burdine* approach as it now exists because its emphasis on motivational, evil motive discrimination is inconsistent with the teachings of cognitive psychology that racial and gender stereotypes are the natural byproduct of the categorization of our sensory perceptions that are necessary for human beings to function:

> [N]ot only are many of the cognitive processes which cause discrimination automatic and beyond ordinary conscious self-awareness, they are adaptive, indeed, essential to effective cognitive functioning. People will divide the natural and social environment into categories; they will use stereotypes, scripts, and schemas to interpret, encode, and retrieve information relevant to social judgment. . . . And, because race, ethnicity, and gender have been made salient by our history and by observable patterns of economic, demographic, and political distribution, people will continue to categorize along those lines. . . . And so long as people categorize along lines of race, gender, or ethnicity, we can expect the resulting categorization-related distortions in social perception and judgment to bias intergroup decisionmaking.

Id. at 1239-1240. She fears that failing to take this into account in the law will result in vast underenforcement of the antidiscrimination laws:

> In the vast majority of cases now adjudicated under the pretext model of proof, the nondiscriminatory reason(s) articulated by the employer probably

did play an actuating role in the employer's decision. But it does not follow from this that no discrimination occurred. The same employer might have interpreted the same event differently and made a different decision had the target employee been a member of a different social group. To require a disparate treatment plaintiff to disprove the motivating significance of every nondiscriminatory reason articulated (or, after *Hicks* not articulated) by his employer imposes on plaintiffs an almost impossible burden, and will lead to the gross and utterly unjustifiable underidentification of biased employment decisions.

Id. at 1241.

9. Professor Malamud would replace *McDonnell Douglas/Burdine* with the general tests for civil litigation:

> If *McDonnell Douglas-Burdine* cannot be improved by tinkering at the margins and if we cannot eliminate either individual discrimination claims or the intent requirement, the best remaining alternative is to retain a cause of action for intentional discrimination but abandon the *McDonnell Douglas-Burdine* proof structure once and for all, at all stages of the case. Then it would be clear that the only relevant question at trial would be whether the plaintiff has proven intentional discrimination by a preponderance of the evidence. Since the function of the summary judgment court is to examine the sufficiency of the evidence for trial *in light of the questions the jury will be asked of the evidence at trial*, the only question on summary judgment would be the sufficiency of all the evidence to support a finding of intentional discrimination by a preponderance of the evidence.

93 Mich. L. Rev. at 2317-2318 (emphasis in original).

10. In coming to the rescue of antidiscrimination law with the 1991 Civil Rights Act, Congress modified *Price Waterhouse*. The *Miller* court did not consider the implications of the new Act. It may be that the Act can be the basis for a new unitary individual disparate treatment litigation structure. It may also be that the Supreme Court's decision in *Biggins* anticipates and lays the groundwork for just such an approach.

The 1991 Act modified *Price Waterhouse* in a number of important ways. First, new §703(m) rejects the "substantial factor" threshold test of the employer's state of mind that the concurrences of Justices White and O'Connor found so important. Instead, "an unlawful employment practice is established when the complaining party demonstrates that race, color, religion, sex, or national origin was a *motivating factor* for any employment practice, even though other factors also motivated the practice" (emphasis added). Second, Congress changed the effect of an employer carrying its same-decision defense. Instead of a defense to liability, it is now only a defense to full remedies if the employer is able to demonstrate that it would have made the same decision even if the protected characteristic had not been considered. Third, the terms of new §703(m) make it applicable to every Title VII case in which plaintiff proves that a characteristic protected by Title VII was "a motivating factor" for the employer. While not specifically rejecting Justice O'Connor's "direct" evidence threshold to the application of *Price Waterhouse*, there is no basis in the statute for limiting its application to only one type of disparate treatment case.

The Supreme Court in *Biggins*, a *McDonnell Douglas/Burdine* case, may have anticipated that the 1991 Act will be applicable to all cases involving claims of intentional discrimination. Justice O'Connor begins by laying out a general approach to all cases of intentional discrimination.

> In a disparate treatment case, liability depends on whether the protected trait . . . actually motivated the employer's decision. . . . The employer may have relied upon a formal, facially discriminatory policy requiring adverse treatment of employees with that trait[,] . . . [o]r the employer may have been motivated by the protected trait on an ad hoc, informal basis.

113 S. Ct. at 1706. The Court then described one test of liability for both systemic and individual disparate treatment discrimination. "Whatever the employer's decisionmaking process, a disparate treatment claim cannot succeed unless the employee's protected trait actually played a role in that process and had a determinative influence on that outcome." Id.

In addition to not mentioning "substantial factor" nor "direct" evidence, the new test appears to anticipate the burden-shifting approach of the 1991 Act. Under §703(m), a plaintiff bears the burden of proving that a protected trait was "a motivating factor." There is little difference between that and the "played a role in" language in *Biggins*. Once a plaintiff shows that a protected trait was "a motivating factor," liability is established but the burden shifts to the employer to try to limit full remedies by proving that it "would have taken the same action in the absence of the impermissible motivating factor." If the employer fails to carry its burden, then the protected trait, in the language of *Biggins*, "had a determinative influence on the outcome" because the employer would not have taken the same action in the absence of the protected trait. The two-step analysis of *Biggins* seems to be anticipating the two-step analysis of the 1991 Act with its shifting of the burden of persuasion between those steps. See Michael J. Zimmer, The Emerging Uniform Structure of Disparate Treatment Discrimination Litigation, 30 Ga. L. Rev. 563 (1996), for an extended analysis of this approach, including an attack on the idea that there is such a thing as "direct" evidence of discrimination. This article concludes:

> In sum, new sections 703(m) and 706(g)(2)(B) apply to all individual disparate treatment cases brought under Title VII. Because all evidence of dis-

crimination is circumstantial, courts should not attempt to categorize such evidence as direct or circumstantial. All relevant evidence, that is, evidence that is material and probative, should be equally weighed by the factfinder in determining whether the employer discriminated.

11. While the facts in *Miller* arose before the effective date of the Civil Rights Act of 1991 so that the new Act would not apply, a more difficult problem is whether the new Act should apply to an age discrimination case brought under the ADEA since new §§703(m) and 706(g)(2)(B) amended Title VII, not the ADEA, the Americans with Disabilities Act, or 42 U.S.C. §1981. See Howard Eglit, The Age Discrimination in Employment Act, Title VII, and the Civil Rights Act of 1991: Three Acts and a Dog That Didn't Bark, 39 Wayne L. Rev. 1093, 1114 (1993)(concluding that Congress did not intend to amend ADEA through amendment to Title VII); John L. Flynn, Note, Mixed-Motive Causation Under the ADA: Linked Statutes, Fuzzy Thinking, and Clear Statement, 83 Geo. L.J. 2009, 2026 (1995) (concluding the 1991 Act does not amend ADA absent clear statement by Congress). But see John C. Nagle, Waiving Sovereign Immunity in an Age of Clear Statement Rules, 1995 Wis. L. Rev. 771 (areas where Supreme Court has required clear statements by Congress limited to avoid constitutional concerns). Given the strong authority supporting a uniform structure of disparate treatment law across a number of antidiscrimination statutes, see Trans World Airlines v. Thurston, 469 U.S. 111, 121 (1985) ("interpretation of Title VII . . . applies with equal force in the context of age discrimination"); Patterson v. McLean Credit Union, 491 U.S. 164, 186 (1989) (individual disparate treatment discrimination structure of Title VII "should apply to claims of racial discrimination under section 1981"), Congress could not have meant to foreclose the courts in their development of the federal common law of discrimination from looking to and relying on the latest amendments to Title VII.

Chapter 4

Systemic Disparate Treatment Discrimination

C. PATTERNS AND PRACTICES OF DISCRIMINATION

Page 234. Add new Note 11a:

11a. The courts have been reluctant to find discrimination against older workers in a variety of situations involving benefits. See DiBiase v. Smith-Kline Beecham Co., 48 F.3d 719 (3d Cir.), *cert. denied,* 116 S. Ct. 306 (1995) (concluding there is no discrimination when an employer offers equal benefits to all those waiving rights, even though older workers are waiving ADEA rights that younger workers do not have); Lyon v. Ohio Education Assn., 53 F.3d 135 (6th Cir. 1995) (plan that imputed years of service to those seeking "early" retirement for the purpose of computing benefits did not discriminate on the basis of age even though the younger a worker at retirement the more years were imputed and the greater the resulting pension benefit); Goldman v. First Natl. Bank of Boston, 985 F.2d 1113 (1st Cir.), *amended,* 61 FEP Cases 439 (1st Cir. 1993) (restructuring of pension plan to provide earlier benefits to younger workers not evidence of age discrimination in absence of showing of harm to older workers).

Page 235.   Add the following to the end of Note 12:

In Winbush v. State of Iowa by Glenwood State Hosp., 66 F.3d 1471 (8th Cir. 1995), the court upheld a systemic disparate treatment claim as to promotions. The evidence established that the defendant used various preselection devices to avoid using a merit system of the civil service system in order to "fill open positions with friends and other favored individuals," which process "99% of the time" did not include African Americans. Id. at 1480 n.14. In response to the argument that African-American employees did not apply for promotions, the court upheld the lower court's finding that "application was futile due to the defendants' discriminatory practices." Id. at 1481.

Page 241.   Add new Note 4:

4. In Smith v. Virginia Commonwealth Univ., 62 F.3d 659 (4th Cir. 1995), plaintiffs were five male professors who challenged pay raises that VCU gave to its female faculty in response to a salary equity study showing that women faculty members had been underpaid. The pay equity study was a multiple regression that controlled for such differences as doctoral degree, academic rank, tenure status, number of years of VCU experience, and number of years of prior academic experience. Any difference in salary after controlling for these factors was attributed to sex. The difference attributed to sex was $1,354 to $1,982. Plaintiffs contended that salary was based on merit, with merit determined by an annual review of teaching load, teaching quality, quantity and quality of publications, and service to the community. Plaintiffs introduced expert testimony that the inclusion of the performance factors was possible and necessary to ensure accurate statistical data. Plaintiffs' expert, however, did not conduct his own pay study.

Applying the standards applicable to attacks on affirmative action plans, see pages 310 et seq. of the casebook, the court reversed the summary judgment for VCU. "Given the number of important variables omitted from the multiple regression analysis, and the evidence presented by the [plaintiffs] that these variables are crucial, a dispute of material fact remains as to the validity of the study." Id. at 663. Judge Michael dissented. "Plaintiffs argue that VCU's study should have included more variables, but they fail to demonstrate that the inclusion of those variables would have eliminated the statistically significant effect of gender on salaries. Thus, plaintiffs' response does not satisfy either Supreme Court precedent (*Bazemore*) or settled summary judgment principles." Id.

D. DEFENSES TO DISPARATE TREATMENT CASES

2. *Bona Fide Occupational Qualifications*

Page 307. Add new Note 7a:

7a. In Healey v. Southwood Psychiatric Hosp., 78 F.3d 128 (3d Cir. 1996), plaintiff challenged a gender-specific rule that male and female child care specialists had to be assigned to every shift at a hospital for emotionally disturbed children and adolescents, some of whom had been sexually abused. The court upheld summary judgment for the employer based on the BFOQ defense:

> The "essence" of Southwood's business is to treat emotionally disturbed and sexually abused adolescents and children. Southwood has presented expert testimony that staffing both males and females on all shifts is necessary to provide therapeutic care. "Role modeling," including parental role modeling, is an important element of the staff's job, and a male is better able to serve as a male role model than a female and vice versa. A balanced staff is also necessary because children who have been sexually abused will disclose their problems more easily to a member of a certain sex, depending on their sex and the sex of the abuser. If members of both sexes are not on a shift, Southwood's inability to provide basic therapeutic care would hinder the "normal operation" of its "particular business." Therefore, it is reasonably necessary to the normal operation of Southwood to have at least one member of each sex available to the patients at all times.

Id. at 132-133. Plaintiff had introduced an affidavit that showed that another hospital, Merck Multiple Disabilities Program at Western Psychiatric Institute, did not use gender in staffing because it did not play a role in the staff's ability to provide necessary care to the patients at that hospital. The court rejected the claim that this raised a genuine issue of material fact because the "essence" of the two institutions was different. "Merck treats mentally retarded patients ranging from three to twenty-four years old whose developmental age is lower than their chronological age. Southwood's mission, in contrast, is to treat emotionally disturbed and sexually abused children and adolescents. Southwood's therapeutic mission depends on subtle interactions such as 'role modeling' rather than the more concrete behavior modification techniques practiced at Merck." Id. at 134.

3.   Voluntary Affirmative Action

Page 334.   Add the following to Note 12:

In Smith v. Virginia Commonwealth Univ., 62 F.3d 659 (4th Cir. 1995), plaintiffs were five male professors who challenged pay raises that VCU gave to its female faculty in response to a salary equity study showing that women faculty members had been underpaid. The pay equity study was a multiple regression that controlled for such differences as doctoral degree, academic rank, tenure status, number of years of VCU experience, and number of years of prior academic experience. Any difference in salary after controlling for these factors was attributed to sex. The difference attributed to sex was $1,354 to $1,982. Plaintiffs contended that salary was based on merit, with merit determined by an annual review of teaching load, teaching quality, quantity and quality of publications, and service to the community. Plaintiffs introduced expert testimony that the inclusion of the performance factors was possible and was necessary to ensure accurate statistical data. Plaintiffs' expert, however, did not conduct his own pay study.

Applying *Johnson*, the court reversed the summary judgment for VCU. "Given the number of important variables omitted from the multiple regression analysis, and the evidence presented by the [plaintiffs] that these variables are crucial, a dispute of material fact remains as to the validity of the study." Id. at 663. Judge Michael dissented. "Plaintiffs argue that VCU's study should have included more variables, but they fail to demonstrate that the inclusion of those variables would have eliminated the statistically significant effect of gender on salaries. Thus, plaintiffs' response does not satisfy either Supreme Court precedent (*Bazemore*) or settled summary judgment principles." Id.

Page 341.   Add the following before Problem 4.3:

ADARAND CONSTRUCTORS v. PENA
115 S. Ct. 2097 (1995)

Justice O'CONNOR, J., announced the judgment of the Court and delivered an opinion, which was for the Court except insofar as it might be inconsistent with the views expressed in the concurrence of SCALIA's concurrence.

Petitioner Adarand Constructors, Inc., claims that the Federal Government's practice of giving general contractors on government projects a financial incentive to hire subcontractors controlled by "socially and economically

58

disadvantaged individuals," and in particular, the Government's use of race-based presumptions in identifying such individuals, violates the equal protection component of the Fifth Amendment's Due Process Clause. The Court of Appeals rejected Adarand's claim. We conclude, however, that courts should analyze cases of this kind under a different standard of review than the one the Court of Appeals applied. We therefore vacate the Court of Appeals' judgment and remand the case for further proceedings.

I

In 1989, the Central Federal Lands Highway Division (CFLHD), which is part of the United States Department of Transportation (DOT), awarded the prime contract for a highway construction project in Colorado to Mountain Gravel & Construction Company. Mountain Gravel then solicited bids from subcontractors for the guardrail portion of the contract. Adarand, a Colorado-based highway construction company specializing in guardrail work, submitted the low bid. Gonzales Construction Company also submitted a bid.

The prime contract's terms provide that Mountain Gravel would receive additional compensation if it hired subcontractors certified as small businesses controlled by "socially and economically disadvantaged individuals." Gonzales is certified as such a business; Adarand is not. Mountain Gravel awarded the subcontract to Gonzales, despite Adarand's low bid, and Mountain Gravel's Chief Estimator has submitted an affidavit stating that Mountain Gravel would have accepted Adarand's bid, had it not been for the additional payment it received by hiring Gonzales instead. Federal law requires that a subcontracting clause similar to the one used here must appear in most federal agency contracts, and it also requires the clause to state that "the contractor shall presume that socially and economically disadvantaged individuals include Black Americans, Hispanic Americans, Native Americans, Asian Pacific Americans, and other minorities, or any other individual found to be disadvantaged by the [Small Business] Administration pursuant to §8(a) of the Small Business Act." Adarand claims that the presumption set forth in that statute discriminates on the basis of race in violation of the Federal Government's Fifth Amendment obligation not to deny anyone equal protection of the laws.

These fairly straightforward facts implicate a complex scheme of federal statutes and regulations, to which we now turn. The Small Business Act declares it to be "the policy of the United States that small business concerns, [and] small business concerns owned and controlled by socially and economically disadvantaged individuals, . . . shall have the maximum practicable opportunity to participate in the performance of contracts let by any Federal agency." The Act defines "socially disadvantaged individuals" as "those who have been subjected to racial or ethnic prejudice or cultural bias because of their identity as a member of a group without regard to their individual qualities," and it defines "economically disadvantaged individuals" as "those socially disadvantaged individuals whose ability to compete in the free enterprise system has been impaired due to diminished capital and credit opportunities as compared to others in the same business area who are not socially disadvantaged."

In furtherance of the policy stated in §8(d)(1), the Act establishes "the Government-wide goal for participation by small business concerns owned and controlled by socially and economically disadvantaged individuals" at "not less than 5 percent of the total value of all prime contract and subcontract awards for each fiscal year." It also requires the head of each Federal agency to set agency-specific goals for participation by businesses controlled by socially and economically disadvantaged individuals.

The Small Business Administration (SBA) has implemented these statutory directives in a variety of ways, two of which are relevant here. One is the "8(a) program," which is available to small businesses controlled by socially and economically disadvantaged individuals as the SBA has defined those terms. The 8(a) program confers a wide range of benefits on participating businesses, one of which is automatic eligibility for subcontractor compensation provisions of the kind at issue in this case. To participate in the 8(a) program, a business must be "small," as defined in 13 C.F.R. §124.102 (1994); and it must be 51% owned by individuals who qualify as "socially and economically disadvantaged." The SBA presumes that Black, Hispanic, Asian Pacific, Subcontinent Asian, and Native Americans, as well as "members of other groups designated from time to time by SBA," are "socially disadvantaged." It also allows any individual not a member of a listed group to prove social disadvantage "on the basis of clear and convincing evidence," as described in §124.105(c). Social disadvantage is not enough to establish eligibility, however; SBA also requires each 8(a) program participant to prove "economic disadvantage" according to the criteria set forth in §124.106(a).

The other SBA program relevant to this case is the "8(d) subcontracting program," which unlike the 8(a) program is limited to eligibility for subcontracting provisions like the one at issue here. In determining eligibility, the SBA presumes social disadvantage based on membership in certain minority groups, just as in the 8(a) program, and again appears to require an individualized, although "less restrictive," showing of economic disadvantage, §124.106(b). A different set of regulations, however, says that members of minority groups wishing to participate in the 8(d) subcontracting program are entitled to a race-based presumption of social and economic disadvantage. We are left with some uncertainty as to whether participation in the 8(d) subcontracting program requires an individualized showing of economic disadvantage. In any event, in both the 8(a) and the 8(d) programs, the presumptions of disadvantage are rebuttable if a third party comes forward with evidence suggesting that the participant is not, in fact, either economically or socially disadvantaged.

The contract giving rise to the dispute in this case came about as a result of the Surface Transportation and Uniform Relocation Assistance Act of 1987

(STURAA), a DOT appropriations measure. Section 106(c)(1) of STURAA provides that "not less than 10 percent" of the appropriated funds "shall be expended with small business concerns owned and controlled by socially and economically disadvantaged individuals." STURAA adopts the Small Business Act's definition of "socially and economically disadvantaged individual," including the applicable race-based presumptions, and adds that "women shall be presumed to be socially and economically disadvantaged individuals for purposes of this subsection." STURAA also requires the Secretary of Transportation to establish "minimum uniform criteria for State governments to use in certifying whether a concern qualifies for purposes of this subsection." The Secretary has done so in 49 C.F.R. pt. 23, subpt. D (1994). Those regulations say that the certifying authority should presume both social and economic disadvantage (i.e., eligibility to participate) if the applicant belongs to certain racial groups, or is a woman. As with the SBA programs, third parties may come forward with evidence in an effort to rebut the presumption of disadvantage for a particular business.

The operative clause in the contract in this case reads as follows:

> *Subcontracting.* This subsection is supplemented to include a Disadvantaged Business Enterprise (DBE) Development and Subcontracting Provision as follows: Monetary compensation is offered for awarding subcontracts to small business concerns owned and controlled by socially and economically disadvantaged individuals. . . . A small business concern will be considered a DBE after it has been certified as such by the U.S. Small Business Administration or any State Highway Agency. Certification by other Government agencies, counties, or cities may be acceptable on an individual basis provided the Contracting Officer has determined the certifying agency has an acceptable and viable DBE certification program. If the Contractor requests payment under this provision, the Contractor shall furnish the engineer with acceptable evidence of the subcontractor(s) DBE certification and shall furnish one certified copy of the executed subcontract(s).

"The Contractor will be paid an amount computed as follows:"

> 1. If a subcontract is awarded to one DBE, 10 percent of the final amount of the approved DBE subcontract, not to exceed 1.5 percent of the original contract amount.
> 2. If subcontracts are awarded to two or more DBEs, 10 percent of the final amount of the approved DBE subcontracts, not to exceed 2 percent of the original contract amount.

To benefit from this clause, Mountain Gravel had to hire a subcontractor who had been certified as a small disadvantaged business by the SBA, a state highway agency, or some other certifying authority acceptable to the Contracting Officer. Any of the three routes to such certification described above—SBA's

8(a) or 8(d) program, or certification by a State under the DOT regulations—would meet that requirement. The record does not reveal how Gonzales obtained its certification as a small disadvantaged business.

After losing the guardrail subcontract to Gonzales, Adarand filed suit against various federal officials in the United States District Court for the District of Colorado, claiming that the race-based presumptions involved in the use of subcontracting compensation clauses violate Adarand's right to equal protection. The District Court granted the Government's motion for summary judgment. The Court of Appeals for the Tenth Circuit affirmed. It understood our decision in Fullilove v. Klutznick to have adopted "a lenient standard, resembling intermediate scrutiny, in assessing" the constitutionality of federal race-based action. Applying that "lenient standard," as further developed in Metro Broadcasting, Inc. v. FCC, the Court of Appeals upheld the use of subcontractor compensation clauses. We granted certiorari.

III

The Government urges that "the Subcontracting Compensation Clause program is . . . a program based on disadvantage, not on race," and thus that it is subject only to "the most relaxed judicial scrutiny." To the extent that the statutes and regulations involved in this case are race neutral, we agree. The Government concedes, however, that "the race-based rebuttable presumption used in some certification determinations under the Subcontracting Compensation Clause" is subject to some heightened level of scrutiny. The parties disagree as to what that level should be. (We note, incidentally, that this case concerns only classifications based explicitly on race, and presents none of the additional difficulties posed by laws that, although facially race neutral, result in racially disproportionate impact and are motivated by a racially discriminatory purpose.)

Adarand's claim arises under the Fifth Amendment to the Constitution, which provides that "No person shall . . . be deprived of life, liberty, or property, without due process of law." Although this Court has always understood that Clause to provide some measure of protection against *arbitrary* treatment by the Federal Government, it is not as explicit a guarantee of equal treatment as the Fourteenth Amendment, which provides that "No State shall . . . deny to any person within its jurisdiction the *equal* protection of the laws" (emphasis added). Our cases have accorded varying degrees of significance to the difference in the language of those two Clauses. We think it necessary to revisit the issue here.

A

Through the 1940s, this Court had routinely taken the view in non-race-related cases that, "unlike the Fourteenth Amendment, the Fifth contains no equal protection clause and it provides no guaranty against discriminatory legislation by Congress." Detroit Bank v. United States, 317 U.S. 329, 337 (1943). . . . When the Court first faced a Fifth Amendment equal protection challenge to a federal racial classification, it adopted a similar approach, with most unfortunate results. In Hirabayashi v. United States, 320 U.S. 81 (1943), the Court considered a curfew applicable only to persons of Japanese ancestry. The Court observed—correctly—that "[d]istinctions between citizens solely because of their ancestry are by their very nature odious to a free people whose institutions are founded upon the doctrine of equality," and that "racial discriminations are in most circumstances irrelevant and therefore prohibited." But it also cited *Detroit Bank* for the proposition that the Fifth Amendment "restrains only such discriminatory legislation by Congress as amounts to a denial of due process," and upheld the curfew because "circumstances within the knowledge of those charged with the responsibility for maintaining the national defense afforded a rational basis for the decision which they made."

Eighteen months later, the Court again approved wartime measures directed at persons of Japanese ancestry. Korematsu v. United States, 323 U.S. 214 (1944), concerned an order that completely excluded such persons from particular areas. The Court did not address the view, expressed in cases like *Hirabayashi* and *Detroit Bank*, that the Federal Government's obligation to provide equal protection differs significantly from that of the States. Instead, it began by noting that "all legal restrictions which curtail the civil rights of a single racial group are immediately suspect . . . [and] courts must subject them to the most rigid scrutiny." That promising dictum might be read to undermine the view that the Federal Government is under a lesser obligation to avoid injurious racial classifications than are the States. But in spite of the "most rigid scrutiny" standard it had just set forth, the Court then inexplicably relied on "the principles we announced in the *Hirabayashi* case," to conclude that, although "exclusion from the area in which one's home is located is a far greater deprivation than constant confinement to the home from 8 P.M. to 6 A.M.," the racially discriminatory order was nonetheless within the Federal Government's power.

In Bolling v. Sharpe, 347 U.S. 497 (1954), the Court for the first time explicitly questioned the existence of any difference between the obligations of the Federal Government and the States to avoid racial classifications. *Bolling* did note that "the 'equal protection of the laws' is a more explicit safeguard of prohibited unfairness than 'due process of law.'" But *Bolling* then concluded that, "in view of [the] decision that the Constitution prohibits the states from maintaining racially segregated public schools, it would be unthinkable that the same Constitution would impose a lesser duty on the Federal Government."

Bolling's facts concerned school desegregation, but its reasoning was not so limited. The Court's observations that "distinctions between citizens solely because of their ancestry are by their very nature odious," *Hirabayashi*, 320 U.S. at 100, and that "all legal restrictions which curtail the civil rights of a single racial group are immediately suspect," *Korematsu*, [323 U.S. at 216,] carry no less force in the context of federal action than in the context of action by the States—indeed, they first appeared in cases concerning action by the Federal Government. *Bolling* relied on those observations and reiterated "'that the [C]onstitution of the United States, in its present form, forbids, so far as civil and political rights are concerned, discrimination by the [G]eneral [G]overnment, or by the [S]tates, against any citizen because of his race.'" [347 U.S. at 499.] The Court's application of that general principle to the case before it, and the resulting imposition on the Federal Government of an obligation equivalent to that of the States, followed as a matter of course.

Later cases in contexts other than school desegregation did not distinguish between the duties of the States and the Federal Government to avoid racial classifications. Consider, for example, the following passage from McLaughlin v. Florida, [379 U.S. 184, 191-192,] a 1964 case that struck down a race-based state law:

> [W]e deal here with a classification based upon the race of the participants, which must be viewed in light of the historical fact that the central purpose of the Fourteenth Amendment was to eliminate racial discrimination emanating from official sources in the States. This strong policy renders racial classifications "constitutionally suspect," Bolling v. Sharpe, and subject to the "most rigid scrutiny," Korematsu v. United States, and "in most circumstances irrelevant" to any constitutionally acceptable legislative purpose, Hirabayashi v. United States.

McLaughlin's reliance on cases involving federal action for the standards applicable to a case involving state legislation suggests that the Court understood the standards for federal and state racial classifications to be the same.

Cases decided after *McLaughlin* continued to treat the equal protection obligations imposed by the Fifth and the Fourteenth Amendments as indistinguishable. Loving v. Virginia, 388 U.S. 1 (1967), which struck down a race-based state law, cited *Korematsu* for the proposition that "the Equal Protection Clause demands that racial classifications . . . be subjected to the 'most rigid scrutiny.'" The various opinions in Frontiero v. Richardson, 411 U.S. 677 (1973), which concerned sex discrimination by the Federal Government, took their equal protection standard of review from Reed v. Reed, 404 U.S. 71 (1971), a case that invalidated sex discrimination by a State, without mentioning any possibility of a difference between the standards applicable to state and federal action. Thus, in 1975, the Court stated explicitly that "this Court's approach to Fifth Amendment equal protection claims has always been precisely the same as to equal protection claims under the Fourteenth Amendment." Weinberger v. Wiesenfeld, 420 U.S. 636, 638 (1975); see also

Buckley v. Valeo, 424 U.S. 1 (headnote) (1976) ("Equal protection analysis in the Fifth Amendment area is the same as that under the Fourteenth Amendment."); United States v. Paradise, 480 U.S. 149, 166 (1987) (plurality opinion of Brennan, J.) ("The reach of the equal protection guarantee of the Fifth Amendment is coextensive with that of the Fourteenth"). We do not understand a few contrary suggestions appearing in cases in which we found special deference to the political branches of the Federal Government to be appropriate, e.g., Hampton v. Mow Sun Wong, 426 U.S. 88 (1976) (federal power over immigration), to detract from this general rule.

B

Most of the cases discussed above involved classifications burdening groups that have suffered discrimination in our society. In 1978, the Court confronted the question whether race-based governmental action designed to benefit such groups should also be subject to "the most rigid scrutiny." Regents of Univ. of California v. Bakke involved an equal protection challenge to a state-run medical school's practice of reserving a number of spaces in its entering class for minority students. The petitioners argued that "strict scrutiny" should apply only to "classifications that disadvantage 'discrete and insular minorities.'" Regents of Univ. of California v. Bakke, 438 U.S. 265 (1978). *Bakke* did not produce an opinion for the Court, but Justice Powell's opinion announcing the Court's judgment rejected the argument. In a passage joined by Justice White, Justice Powell wrote that "the guarantee of equal protection cannot mean one thing when applied to one individual and something else when applied to a person of another color." He concluded that "racial and ethnic distinctions of any sort are inherently suspect and thus call for the most exacting judicial examination." On the other hand, four Justices in *Bakke* would have applied a less stringent standard of review to racial classifications "designed to further remedial purposes." And four Justices thought the case should be decided on statutory grounds.

Two years after *Bakke*, the Court faced another challenge to remedial race-based action, this time involving action undertaken by the Federal Government. In Fullilove v. Klutznick the Court upheld Congress' inclusion of a 10% set-aside for minority-owned businesses in the Public Works Employment Act of 1977. As in *Bakke*, there was no opinion for the Court. Chief Justice Burger, in an opinion joined by Justices White and Powell, observed that "any preference based on racial or ethnic criteria must necessarily receive a most searching examination to make sure that it does not conflict with constitutional guarantees." That opinion, however, "did not adopt, either expressly or implicitly, the formulas of analysis articulated in such cases as [*Bakke*]." It employed instead a two-part test which asked, first, "whether the objectives of the legislation are within the power of Congress," and second, "whether the limited use of racial and ethnic criteria, in the context presented, is a constitutionally permissible means for achieving the congressional objectives." It then upheld the program under that test, adding at the end of the opinion that the program also "would survive judicial review under either 'test' articulated in the several *Bakke* opinions." Justice Powell wrote separately to express his view that the plurality opinion had essentially applied "strict scrutiny" as described in his *Bakke* opinion—i.e., it had determined that the set-aside was "a necessary means of advancing a compelling governmental interest"—and had done so correctly. Justice Stewart dissented, arguing that the Constitution required the Federal Government to meet the same strict standard as the States when enacting racial classifications and that the program before the Court failed that standard. Justice Stevens also dissented, arguing that "racial classifications are simply too pernicious to permit any but the most exact connection between justification and classification," id., at 537, and that the program before the Court could not be characterized "as a 'narrowly tailored' remedial measure." Justice Marshall (joined by Justices Brennan and Blackmun) concurred in the judgment, reiterating the view of four Justices in *Bakke* that any race-based governmental action designed to "remedy the present effects of past racial discrimination" should be upheld if it was "substantially related" to the achievement of an "important governmental objective"—i.e., such action should be subjected only to what we now call "intermediate scrutiny."

In Wygant v. Jackson Board of Education, the Court considered a Fourteenth Amendment challenge to another form of remedial racial classification. The issue in *Wygant* was whether a school board could adopt race-based preferences in determining which teachers to lay off. Justice Powell's plurality opinion observed that "the level of scrutiny does not change merely because the challenged classification operates against a group that historically has not been subject to governmental discrimination," and stated the two-part inquiry as "whether the layoff provision is supported by a compelling state purpose and whether the means chosen to accomplish that purpose are narrowly tailored." In other words, "racial classifications of any sort must be subjected to 'strict scrutiny.' " The plurality then concluded that the school board's interest in "providing minority role models for its minority students, as an attempt to alleviate the effects of societal discrimination," was not a compelling interest that could justify the use of a racial classification. It added that "societal discrimination, without more, is too amorphous a basis for imposing a racially classified remedy," and insisted instead that "a public employer . . . must ensure that, before it embarks on an affirmative-action program, it has convincing evidence that remedial action is warranted. That is, it must have sufficient evidence to justify the conclusion that there has been prior discrimination," id., at 277. Justice White concurred only in the judgment, although he agreed that the school board's asserted interests could not, "singly or together, justify this racially discriminatory layoff policy." Four Justices dissented, three of whom again argued for intermediate scrutiny of remedial race-based government action.

The Court's failure to produce a majority opinion in *Bakke*, *Fullilove*, and *Wygant* left unresolved the proper analysis for remedial race-based governmental action. See United States v. Paradise (plurality opinion of Brennan, J.) ("Although this Court has consistently held that some elevated level of scrutiny is required when a racial or ethnic distinction is made for remedial purposes, it has yet to reach consensus on the appropriate constitutional analysis."). Lower courts found this lack of guidance unsettling. See, e.g., Kromnick v. School Dist. of Philadelphia, 739 F.2d 984 (3rd Cir. 1984) ("The absence of an opinion of the Court in either *Bakke* or *Fullilove* and the concomitant failure of the Court to articulate an analytic framework supporting the judgments makes the position of the lower federal courts considering the constitutionality of affirmative action programs somewhat vulnerable.").

The Court resolved the issue, at least in part, in 1989. Richmond v. J. A. Croson Co. concerned a city's determination that 30% of its contracting work should go to minority-owned businesses. A majority of the Court in *Croson* held that "the standard of review under the Equal Protection Clause is not dependent on the race of those burdened or benefited by a particular classification," and that the single standard of review for racial classifications should be "strict scrutiny." As to the classification before the Court, the plurality agreed that "a state or local subdivision . . . has the authority to eradicate the effects of private discrimination within its own legislative jurisdiction," but the Court thought that the city had not acted with "a 'strong basis in evidence for its conclusion that remedial action was necessary.'" The Court also thought it "obvious that [the] program is not narrowly tailored to remedy the effects of prior discrimination."

With *Croson*, the Court finally agreed that the Fourteenth Amendment requires strict scrutiny of all race-based action by state and local governments. But *Croson* of course had no occasion to declare what standard of review the Fifth Amendment requires for such action taken by the Federal Government. *Croson* observed simply that the Court's "treatment of an exercise of congressional power in *Fullilove* cannot be dispositive here," because *Croson*'s facts did not implicate Congress' broad power under §5 of the Fourteenth Amendment. On the other hand, the Court subsequently indicated that *Croson* had at least some bearing on federal race-based action when it vacated a decision upholding such action and remanded for further consideration in light of *Croson*. H.K. Porter Co. v. Metropolitan Dade County, 489 U.S. 1062 (1989). Thus, some uncertainty persisted with respect to the standard of review for federal racial classifications.

Despite lingering uncertainty in the details, however, the Court's cases through *Croson* had established three general propositions with respect to governmental racial classifications. First, skepticism: "'any preference based on racial or ethnic criteria must necessarily receive a most searching examination,'" *Wygant*; *Fullilove*; see also *McLaughlin* ("Racial classifications [are] 'constitutionally suspect.'"); *Hirabayashi* ("Distinctions between citizens solely because of their ancestry are by their very nature odious to a free people"). Second, consistency: "the standard of review under the Equal Protection Clause is not dependent on the race of those burdened or benefited by a particular classification," *Croson*; see also *Bakke* (opinion of Powell, J.), i.e., all racial classifications reviewable under the Equal Protection Clause must be strictly scrutinized. And third, congruence: "equal protection analysis in the Fifth Amendment area is the same as that under the Fourteenth Amendment," Buckley v. Valeo; see also Weinberger v. Wiesenfeld; Bolling v. Sharpe. Taken together, these three propositions lead to the conclusion that any person, of whatever race, has the right to demand that any governmental actor subject to the Constitution justify any racial classification subjecting that person to unequal treatment under the strictest judicial scrutiny. Justice Powell's defense of this conclusion bears repeating here:

> If it is the individual who is entitled to judicial protection against classifications based upon his racial or ethnic background because such distinctions impinge upon personal rights, rather than the individual only because of his membership in a particular group, then constitutional standards may be applied consistently. Political judgments regarding the necessity for the particular classification may be weighed in the constitutional balance, [*Korematsu*], but the standard of justification will remain constant. This is as it should be, since those political judgments are the product of rough compromise struck by contending groups within the democratic process. When they touch upon an individual's race or ethnic background, he is entitled to a judicial determination that the burden he is asked to bear on that basis is precisely tailored to serve a compelling governmental interest. The Constitution guarantees that right to every person regardless of his background. *Bakke*.

A year later, however, the Court took a surprising turn. *Metro Broadcasting* involved a Fifth Amendment challenge to two race-based policies of the Federal Communications Commission. In *Metro Broadcasting*, the Court repudiated the long-held notion that "it would be unthinkable that the same Constitution would impose a lesser duty on the Federal Government" than it does on a State to afford equal protection of the laws. It did so by holding that "benign" federal racial classifications need only satisfy intermediate scrutiny, even though *Croson* had recently concluded that such classifications enacted by a State must satisfy strict scrutiny. "Benign" federal racial classifications, the Court said, "—even if those measures are not 'remedial' in the sense of being designed to compensate victims of past governmental or societal discrimination—are constitutionally permissible to the extent that they serve *important* governmental objectives within the power of Congress and are *substantially related* to achievement of those objectives." *Metro Broadcasting* (emphasis added). The Court did not explain how to tell whether a racial classification should be deemed "benign," other than to express "confidence that an 'examination of the legislative scheme and its history' will separate benign measures from other types of racial classifications."

Applying this test, the Court first noted that the FCC policies at issue did not serve as a remedy for past discrimination. Proceeding on the assumption that the policies were nonetheless "benign," it concluded that they served the "important governmental objective" of "enhancing broadcast diversity," and that they were "substantially related" to that objective. It therefore upheld the policies.

By adopting intermediate scrutiny as the standard of review for congressionally mandated "benign" racial classifications, *Metro Broadcasting* departed from prior cases in two significant respects. First, it turned its back on *Croson*'s explanation of why strict scrutiny of all governmental racial classifications is essential: "Absent searching judicial inquiry into the justification for such race-based measures, there is simply no way of determining what classifications are 'benign' or 'remedial' and what classifications are in fact motivated by illegitimate notions of racial inferiority or simple racial politics. Indeed, the purpose of strict scrutiny is to 'smoke out' illegitimate uses of race by assuring that the legislative body is pursuing a goal important enough to warrant use of a highly suspect tool. The test also ensures that the means chosen 'fit' this compelling goal so closely that there is little or no possibility that the motive for the classification was illegitimate racial prejudice or stereotype." We adhere to that view today, despite the surface appeal of holding "benign" racial classifications to a lower standard, because "it may not always be clear that a so-called preference is in fact benign." *Bakke.*

Second, *Metro Broadcasting* squarely rejected one of the three propositions established by the Court's earlier equal protection cases, namely, congruence between the standards applicable to federal and state racial classifications, and in so doing also undermine the other two—skepticism of all racial classifications, and consistency of treatment irrespective of the race of the burdened or benefitted group. Under *Metro Broadcasting*, certain racial classifications ("benign" ones enacted by the Federal Government) should be treated less skeptically than others; and the race of the benefited group is critical to the determination of which standard of review to apply. *Metro Broadcasting* was thus a significant departure from much of what had come before it.

The three propositions undermined by *Metro Broadcasting* all derive from the basic principle that the Fifth and Fourteenth Amendments to the Constitution protect persons, not groups. It follows from that principle that all governmental action based on race—a group classification long recognized as "in most circumstances irrelevant and therefore prohibited," *Hirabayashi*—

should be subjected to detailed judicial inquiry to ensure that the personal right to equal protection of the laws has not been infringed. These ideas have long been central to this Court's understanding of equal protection, and holding "benign" state and federal racial classifications to different standards does not square with them. "[A] free people whose institutions are founded upon the doctrine of equality," ibid., should tolerate no retreat from the principle that government may treat people differently because of their race only for the most compelling reasons. Accordingly, we hold today that all racial classifications, imposed by whatever federal, state, or local governmental actor, must be analyzed by a reviewing court under strict scrutiny. In other words, such classifications are constitutional only if they are narrowly tailored measures that further compelling governmental interests. To the extent that *Metro Broadcasting* is inconsistent with that holding, it is overruled.

In dissent, Justice Stevens criticizes us for "delivering a disconcerting lecture about the evils of governmental racial classifications." With respect, we believe his criticisms reflect a serious misunderstanding of our opinion.

Justice Stevens concurs in our view that courts should take a skeptical view of all governmental racial classifications. He also allows that "nothing is inherently wrong with applying a single standard to fundamentally different situations, as long as that standard takes relevant differences into account." What he fails to recognize is that strict scrutiny does take "relevant differences" into account—indeed, that is its fundamental purpose. The point of carefully examining the interest asserted by the government in support of a racial classification, and the evidence offered to show that the classification is needed, is precisely to distinguish legitimate from illegitimate uses of race in governmental decisionmaking. And Justice Stevens concedes that "some cases may be difficult to classify," all the more reason, in our view, to examine all racial classifications carefully. Strict scrutiny does not "treat dissimilar race-based decisions as though they were equally objectionable"; to the contrary, it evaluates carefully all governmental race-based decisions in order to decide which are constitutionally objectionable and which are not. By requiring strict scrutiny of racial classifications, we require courts to make sure that a governmental classification based on race, which "so seldom provides a relevant basis for disparate treatment," *Fullilove* (Stevens, J., dissenting), is legitimate, before permitting unequal treatment based on race to proceed.

Justice Stevens chides us for our "supposed inability to differentiate between 'invidious' and 'benign' discrimination," because it is in his view sufficient that "people understand the difference between good intentions and bad." But, as we have just explained, the point of strict scrutiny is to "differentiate between" permissible and impermissible governmental use of race. And Justice Stevens himself has already explained in his dissent in *Fullilove* why "good intentions" alone are not enough to sustain a supposedly "benign" racial classification: "Even though it is not the actual predicate for this legislation, a statute of this kind inevitably is perceived by many as resting on an assumption that those who are granted this special preference are less qualified in some respect that is identified purely by their race. Because that perception—especially when fostered by the Congress of the United States—can only exacerbate rather than reduce racial prejudice, it will delay the time when race will become a truly irrelevant, or at least insignificant, factor. Unless Congress clearly articulates the need and basis for a racial classification, and also tailors the classification to its justification, the Court should not uphold this kind of statute." *Fullilove* (dissenting opinion); *Croson* ("Although [the legislation at issue] stigmatizes the disadvantaged class with the unproven charge of past racial discrimination, it actually imposes a greater stigma on its supposed beneficiaries."). These passages make a persuasive case for requiring strict scrutiny of congressional racial classifications.

Perhaps it is not the standard of strict scrutiny itself, but our use of the concepts of "consistency" and "congruence" in conjunction with it, that leads Justice Stevens to dissent. According to Justice Stevens, our view of consistency "equates remedial preferences with invidious discrimination," and ignores the difference between "an engine of oppression" and an effort "to foster equality in society," or, more colorfully, "between a 'No Trespassing' sign and a welcome mat." It does nothing of the kind. The principle of consistency simply means that whenever the government treats any person unequally because of his or her race, that person has suffered an injury that falls squarely within the language and spirit of the Constitution's guarantee of equal protection. It says nothing about the ultimate validity of any particular law; that determination is the job of the court applying strict scrutiny. The principle of consistency explains the circumstances in which the injury requiring strict scrutiny occurs. The application of strict scrutiny, in turn, determines whether a compelling governmental interest justifies the infliction of that injury.

Consistency does recognize that any individual suffers an injury when he or she is disadvantaged by the government because of his or her race, whatever that race may be. This Court clearly stated that principle in *Croson*; see also Shaw v. Reno, 509 U.S. 630 (1993); Powers v. Ohio, 499 U.S. 400 (1991). Justice Stevens does not explain how his views square with *Croson*, or with the long line of cases understanding equal protection as a personal right.

Justice Stevens also claims that we have ignored any difference between federal and state legislatures. But requiring that Congress, like the States, enact racial classifications only when doing so is necessary to further a "compelling interest" does not contravene any principle of appropriate respect for a co-equal Branch of the Government. It is true that various Members of this Court have taken different views of the authority §5 of the Fourteenth Amendment confers upon Congress to deal with the problem of racial discrimination, and the extent to which courts should defer to Congress' exercise of that authority. We need not, and do not, address these differences today. For now, it is enough to observe that Justice Stevens' suggestion that any Member of this Court has repudiated in this case his or her previously expressed views on the subject is incorrect. . . .

D

Our action today makes explicit what Justice Powell thought implicit in the *Fullilove* lead opinion: federal racial classifications, like those of a State, must serve a compelling governmental interest, and must be narrowly tailored to further that interest. See *Fullilove*. Of course, it follows that to the extent (if any) that *Fullilove* held federal racial classifications to be subject to a less rigorous standard, it is no longer controlling. But we need not decide today whether the program upheld in *Fullilove* would survive strict scrutiny as our more recent cases have defined it.

Some have questioned the importance of debating the proper standard of review of race-based legislation. But we agree with Justice Stevens that, "because racial characteristics so seldom provide a relevant basis for disparate treatment, and because classifications based on race are potentially so harmful to the entire body politic, it is especially important that the reasons for any such classification be clearly identified and unquestionably legitimate," and that "racial classifications are simply too pernicious to permit any but the most exact connection between justification and classification." *Fullilove*. We think that requiring strict scrutiny is the best way to ensure that courts will consistently give racial classifications that kind of detailed examination, both as to ends and as to means. *Korematsu* demonstrates vividly that even "the most rigid scrutiny" can sometimes fail to detect an illegitimate racial classification. Any retreat from the most searching judicial inquiry can only increase the risk of another such error occurring in the future.

Finally, we wish to dispel the notion that strict scrutiny is "strict in theory, but fatal in fact." *Fullilove*. The unhappy persistence of both the practice and the lingering effects of racial discrimination against minority groups in this country is an unfortunate reality, and government is not disqualified from acting in response to it. As recently as 1987, for example, every Justice of this Court agreed that the Alabama Department of Public Safety's "pervasive, systematic, and obstinate discriminatory conduct" justified a narrowly tailored race-based remedy. See United States v. Paradise. When race-based action is necessary to further a compelling interest, such action is within constitutional constraints if it satisfies the "narrow tailoring" test this Court has set out in previous cases.

IV

Because our decision today alters the playing field in some important respects, we think it best to remand the case to the lower courts for further consideration in light of the principles we have announced. The Court of Appeals, following *Metro Broadcasting* and *Fullilove*, analyzed the case in terms of intermediate scrutiny. It upheld the challenged statutes and regulations because it found them to be "narrowly tailored to achieve [their] significant governmental purpose of providing subcontracting opportunities for small disadvantaged business enterprises." The Court of Appeals did not decide the question whether the interests served by the use of subcontractor compensation clauses are properly described as "compelling." It also did not address the question of narrow tailoring in terms of our strict scrutiny cases, by asking, for example, whether there was "any consideration of the use of race-neutral means to increase minority business participation" in government contracting, *Croson*, or whether the program was appropriately limited such that it "will not last longer than the discriminatory effects it is designed to eliminate," *Fullilove*.

Moreover, unresolved questions remain concerning the details of the complex regulatory regimes implicated by the use of subcontractor compensation clauses. For example, the SBA's 8(a) program requires an individualized inquiry into the economic disadvantage of every participant, whereas the DOT's regulations implementing STURAA §106(c) do not require certifying authorities to make such individualized inquiries. And the regulations seem unclear as to whether 8(d) subcontractors must make individualized showings, or instead whether the race-based presumption applies both to social and economic disadvantage, compare 13 C.F.R. §124.106(b) (apparently requiring 8(d) participants to make an individualized showing), with 48 C.F.R. §19.703(a)(2) (1994) (apparently allowing 8(d) subcontractors to invoke the race-based presumption for social and economic disadvantage). We also note an apparent discrepancy between the definitions of which socially disadvantaged individuals qualify as economically disadvantaged for the 8(a) and 8(d) programs; the former requires a showing that such individuals' ability to compete has been impaired "as compared to others in the same or similar line of business *who are not socially disadvantaged*," 13 C.F.R. §124.106(a)(1)(i) (1994) (emphasis added), while the latter requires that showing only "as compared to others in the same or similar line of business," §124.106(b)(1). The question whether any of the ways in which the Government uses subcontractor compensation clauses can survive strict scrutiny, and any relevance distinctions such as these may have to that question, should be addressed in the first instance by the lower courts.

Accordingly, the judgment of the Court of Appeals is vacated, and the case is remanded for further proceedings consistent with this opinion.

It is so ordered.

Justice SCALIA, concurring in part and concurring in the judgment.

I join the opinion of the Court, except Part III-C, and except insofar as it may be inconsistent with the following: In my view, government can never have a "compelling interest" in discriminating on the basis of race in order to "make up" for past racial discrimination in the opposite direction. See Richmond v. J. A. Croson Co. Individuals who have been wronged by unlawful racial discrimination should be made whole; but under our Constitution there can be no such thing as either a creditor or a debtor race. That concept is alien to the Constitution's focus upon the individual and its rejection of dispositions based on race or based on blood. To pursue the concept of racial entitlement—even for the most admirable and benign of purposes—is to reinforce and preserve for future mischief the way of thinking that produced race slavery, race privilege and race hatred. In the eyes of government, we are just one race here. It is American.

It is unlikely, if not impossible, that the challenged program would survive under this understanding of strict scrutiny, but I am content to leave that to be decided on remand.

Justice THOMAS, concurring in part and concurring in the judgment.

I agree with the majority's conclusion that strict scrutiny applies to all government classifications based on race. I write separately, however, to express my disagreement with the premise underlying Justice Stevens' and Justice Ginsburg's dissents: that there is a racial paternalism exception to the principle of equal protection. I believe that there is a "moral [and] constitutional equivalence" between laws designed to subjugate a race and those that distribute benefits on the basis of race in order to foster some current notion of equality. Government cannot make us equal; it can only recognize, respect, and protect us as equal before the law.

That these programs may have been motivated, in part, by good intentions cannot provide refuge from the principle that under our Constitution, the government may not make distinctions on the basis of race. As far as the Constitution is concerned, it is irrelevant whether a government's racial classifications are drawn by those who wish to oppress a race or by those who have a sincere desire to help those thought to be disadvantaged. There can be no doubt that the paternalism that appears to lie at the heart of this program is at war with the principle of inherent equality that underlies and infuses our Constitution.

These programs not only raise grave constitutional questions, they also undermine the moral basis of the equal protection principle. Purchased at the price of immeasurable human suffering, the equal protection principle reflects our Nation's understanding that such classifications ultimately have a destructive impact on the individual and our society. Unquestionably, "invidious [racial] discrimination is an engine of oppression." It is also true that "remedial" racial preferences may reflect "a desire to foster equality in society." But there can be no doubt that racial paternalism and its unintended consequences can be as poisonous and pernicious as any other form of discrimination. So-called "benign" discrimination teaches many that because of chronic and apparently immutable handicaps, minorities cannot compete with them without their patronizing indulgence. Inevitably, such programs engender attitudes of superiority or, alternatively, provoke resentment among those who believe that they have been wronged by the government's use of race. These programs stamp minorities with a badge of inferiority and may cause them to develop dependencies or to adopt an attitude that they are "entitled" to preferences. Indeed, Justice Stevens once recognized the real harms stemming from seemingly "benign" discrimination. See Fullilove v. Klutznick.

In my mind, government-sponsored racial discrimination based on benign prejudice is just as noxious as discrimination inspired by malicious prejudice. In each instance, it is racial discrimination, plain and simple.

Justice STEVENS, with whom Justice GINSBURG joins, dissenting.

Instead of deciding this case in accordance with controlling precedent, the Court today delivers a disconcerting lecture about the evils of governmental racial classifications. For its text the Court has selected three propositions, represented by the bywords "skepticism," "consistency," and "congruence." I shall comment on each of these propositions, then add a few words about stare decisis, and finally explain why I believe this Court has a duty to affirm the judgment of the Court of Appeals.

I

The Court's concept of skepticism is, at least in principle, a good statement of law and of common sense. Undoubtedly, a court should be wary of a governmental decision that relies upon a racial classification. "Because racial characteristics so seldom provide a relevant basis for disparate treatment, and because classifications based on race are potentially so harmful to the entire body politic," a reviewing court must satisfy itself that the reasons for any such classification are "clearly identified and unquestionably legitimate." Fullilove v. Klutznick. But, as the opinions in *Fullilove* demonstrate, substantial agreement on the standard to be applied in deciding difficult cases does not necessarily lead to agreement on how those cases actually should or will be resolved. In my judgment, because uniform standards are often anything but uniform, we should evaluate the Court's comments on "consistency," "congruence," and stare decisis with the same type of skepticism that the Court advocates for the underlying issue.

II

The Court's concept of "consistency" assumes that there is no significant difference between a decision by the majority to impose a special burden on the members of a minority race and a decision by the majority to provide a benefit to certain members of that minority notwithstanding its incidental burden on some members of the majority. In my opinion that assumption is untenable. There is no moral or constitutional equivalence between a policy that is designed to perpetuate a caste system and one that seeks to eradicate racial subordination. Invidious discrimination is an engine of oppression, subjugating a disfavored group to enhance or maintain the power of the majority. Remedial race-based preferences reflect the opposite impulse: a desire to foster equality in society. No sensible conception of the Government's constitutional obligation to "govern impartially" should ignore this distinction.

To illustrate the point, consider our cases addressing the Federal Government's discrimination against Japanese Americans during World War II. The discrimination at issue in those cases was invidious because the Government imposed special burdens—a curfew and exclusion from certain areas on the West Coast—on the members of a minority class defined by racial and ethnic characteristics. Members of the same racially defined class exhibited exceptional heroism in the service of our country during that War. Now suppose Congress decided to reward that service with a federal program that gave all Japanese-American veterans an extraordinary preference in Government employment. If Congress had done so, the same racial characteristics that motivated the discriminatory burdens in *Hirabayashi* and *Korematsu* would have defined the preferred class of veterans. Nevertheless, "consistency" surely would not require us to describe the incidental burden on everyone else in the country as "odious" or "invidious" as those terms were used in those cases. We should reject a concept of "consistency" that would view the special preferences that the National Government has provided to Native Americans since 1834 as comparable to the official discrimination against African Americans that was prevalent for much of our history.

The consistency that the Court espouses would disregard the difference between a "No Trespassing" sign and a welcome mat. It would treat a Dixiecrat Senator's decision to vote against Thurgood Marshall's confirmation in order to keep African Americans off the Supreme Court as on a par with President Johnson's evaluation of his nominee's race as a positive factor. It would equate a law that made black citizens ineligible for military service with a program aimed at recruiting black soldiers. An attempt by the majority to exclude members of a minority race from a regulated market is fundamentally different from a subsidy that enables a relatively small group of newcomers to enter that market. An interest in "consistency" does not justify treating differences as though they were similarities.

The Court's explanation for treating dissimilar race-based decisions as though they were equally objectionable is a supposed inability to differentiate between "invidious" and "benign" discrimination. But the term "affirmative action" is common and well understood. Its presence in everyday parlance shows that people understand the difference between good intentions and bad. As with any legal concept, some cases may be difficult to classify, but our equal protection jurisprudence has identified a critical difference between state action that imposes burdens on a disfavored few and state action that benefits the few "in spite of" its adverse effects on the many. *Feeney.*

Nothing is inherently wrong with applying a single standard to fundamentally different situations, as long as that standard takes relevant differences into account. For example, if the Court in all equal protection cases were to insist that differential treatment be justified by relevant characteristics of the members of the favored and disfavored classes that provide a legitimate basis for disparate treatment, such a standard would treat dissimilar cases differently while still recognizing that there is, after all, only one Equal Protection Clause. Under such a standard, subsidies for disadvantaged businesses may be constitutional though special taxes on such businesses would be invalid. But a single standard that purports to equate remedial preferences with invidious discrimination cannot be defended in the name of "equal protection."

Moreover, the Court may find that its new "consistency" approach to race-based classifications is difficult to square with its insistence upon rigidly separate categories for discrimination against different classes of individuals. For example, as the law currently stands, the Court will apply "intermediate scrutiny" to cases of invidious gender discrimination and "strict scrutiny" to cases of invidious race discrimination, while applying the same standard for benign classifications as for invidious ones. If this remains the law, then today's lecture about "consistency" will produce the anomalous result that the Government can more easily enact affirmative-action programs to remedy discrimination against women than it can enact affirmative-action programs to remedy discrimination against African Americans—even though the primary purpose of the Equal Protection Clause was to end discrimination against the former slaves. When a court becomes preoccupied with abstract standards, it risks sacrificing common sense at the altar of formal consistency.

As a matter of constitutional and democratic principle, a decision by representatives of the majority to discriminate against the members of a minority race is fundamentally different from those same representatives' decision to impose incidental costs on the majority of their constituents in order to provide a benefit to a disadvantaged minority. Indeed, as I have previously argued, the former is virtually always repugnant to the principles of a free and democratic society, whereas the latter is, in some circumstances, entirely consistent with the ideal of equality. By insisting on a doctrinaire notion of "consistency" in the standard applicable to all race-based governmental actions, the Court obscures this essential dichotomy.

III

The Court's concept of "congruence" assumes that there is no significant difference between a decision by the Congress of the United States to adopt an affirmative-action program and such a decision by a State or a municipality. In my opinion that assumption is untenable. It ignores important practical and legal differences between federal and state or local decisionmakers.

These differences have been identified repeatedly and consistently both in opinions of the Court and in separate opinions authored by members of today's majority.

In her plurality opinion in *Croson*, Justice O'Connor also emphasized the importance of this distinction when she responded to the City's argument that *Fullilove* was controlling. She wrote:

"What appellant ignores is that Congress, unlike any State or political subdivision, has a specific constitutional mandate to enforce the dictates of the Fourteenth Amendment. The power to 'enforce' may at times also include the power to define situations which Congress determines threaten principles of equality and to adopt prophylactic rules to deal with those situations. The Civil War Amendments themselves worked a dramatic change in the balance between congressional and state power over matters of race."

An additional reason for giving greater deference to the National Legislature than to a local law-making body is that federal affirmative-action programs represent the will of our entire Nation's elected representatives, whereas a state or local program may have an impact on nonresident entities who played no part in the decision to enact it. Thus, in the state or local context, individuals who were unable to vote for the local representatives who enacted a race-conscious program may nonetheless feel the effects of that program. This difference recalls the goals of the Commerce Clause, which permits Congress to legislate on certain matters of national importance while denying power to the States in this area for fear of undue impact upon out-of-state residents.

Ironically, after all of the time, effort, and paper this Court has expended in differentiating between federal and state affirmative action, the majority today virtually ignores the issue. It provides not a word of direct explanation for its sudden and enormous departure from the reasoning in past cases. Such silence, however, cannot erase the difference between Congress' institutional competence and constitutional authority to overcome historic racial subjugation and the States' lesser power to do so.

Presumably, the majority is now satisfied that its theory of "congruence" between the substantive rights provided by the Fifth and Fourteenth Amendments disposes of the objection based upon divided constitutional powers. But it is one thing to say (as no one seems to dispute) that the Fifth Amendment encompasses a general guarantee of equal protection as broad as that contained within the Fourteenth Amendment. It is another thing entirely to say that Congress' institutional competence and constitutional authority entitles it to no greater deference when it enacts a program designed to foster equality than the deference due a State legislature. The latter is an extraordinary proposition; and, as the foregoing discussion demonstrates, our precedents have rejected it explicitly and repeatedly.

Our opinion in *Metro Broadcasting* relied on several constitutional provisions to justify the greater deference we owe to Congress when it acts with respect to private individuals. In the programs challenged in this case, Congress has acted both with respect to private individuals and, as in *Fullilove*, with respect to the States themselves. When Congress does this, it draws its power directly from §5 of the Fourteenth Amendment. That section reads: "The Congress shall have power to enforce, by appropriate legislation, the provisions of this article." One of the "provisions of this article" that Congress is thus empowered to enforce reads: "No State shall make or enforce any law which shall abridge the privileges or immunities of citizens of the United States; nor shall any State deprive any person of life, liberty, or property, without due process of law; nor deny to any person within its jurisdiction the equal protection of the laws." U.S. Const., Amdt. 14, §1. The Fourteenth Amendment directly empowers Congress at the same time it expressly limits the States. This is no accident. It represents our Nation's consensus, achieved after hard experience throughout our sorry history of race relations, that the Federal Government must be the primary defender of racial minorities against the States, some of which may be inclined to oppress such minorities. A rule of "congruence" that ignores a purposeful "incongruity" so fundamental to our system of government is unacceptable.

In my judgment, the Court's novel doctrine of "congruence" is seriously misguided. Congressional deliberations about a matter as important as affirmative action should be accorded far greater deference than those of a State or municipality.

V

The Court's holding in *Fullilove* surely governs the result in this case. The Public Works Employment Act of 1977 (1977 Act), which this Court upheld in *Fullilove*, is different in several critical respects from the portions of the Small Business Act (SBA) and the Surface Transportation and Uniform Relocation Assistance Act challenged in this case. Each of those differences makes the current program designed to provide assistance to disadvantaged business enterprises (DBE's) significantly less objectionable than the 1977 categorical grant of $400 million in exchange for a 10% set-aside in public contracts to "a class of investors defined solely by racial characteristics." *Fullilove*. In no meaningful respect is the current scheme more objectionable than the 1977 Act. Thus, if the 1977 Act was constitutional, then so must be the SBA and STURAA. Indeed, even if my dissenting views in *Fullilove* had prevailed, this program would be valid.

Unlike the 1977 Act, the present statutory scheme does not make race the sole criterion of eligibility for participation in the program. Race does give rise to a rebuttable presumption of social disadvantage which, at least under STURAA, gives rise to a second rebuttable presumption of economic disadvantage. But a small business may qualify as a DBE, by showing that it is both socially and economically disadvantaged, even if it receives neither of these presumptions. Thus, the current preference is more inclusive than the 1977 Act because it does not make race a necessary qualification.

More importantly, race is not a sufficient qualification. Whereas a millionaire with a long history of financial successes, who was a member of numerous social clubs and trade associations, would have qualified for a preference under the 1977 Act merely because he was an Asian American or an African American, see *Fullilove*, neither the SBA nor STURAA creates any such anomaly. The DBE program excludes members of minority races who are not, in fact, socially or economically disadvantaged. The presumption of social disadvantage reflects the unfortunate fact that irrational racial prejudice — along with its lingering effects — still survives. The presumption of economic disadvantage embodies a recognition that success in the private sector of the economy is often attributable, in part, to social skills and relationships. Unlike the 1977 set-asides, the current preference is designed to overcome the social and economic disadvantages that are often associated with racial characteristics. If, in a particular case, these disadvantages are not present, the presumptions can be rebutted. The program is thus designed to allow race to play a part in the decisional process only when there is a meaningful basis for assuming its relevance. In this connection, I think it is particularly significant that the current program targets the negotiation of subcontracts between private firms. The 1977 Act applied entirely to the award of public contracts, an area of the economy in which social relationships should be irrelevant and in which proper supervision of government contracting officers should preclude any discrimination against particular bidders on account of their race. In this case, in contrast, the program seeks to overcome barriers of prejudice between private parties — specifically, between general contractors and subcontractors. The SBA and STURAA embody Congress' recognition that such barriers may actually handicap minority firms seeking business as subcontractors from established leaders in the industry that have a history of doing business with their golfing partners. Indeed, minority subcontractors may face more obstacles than direct, intentional racial prejudice: they may face particular barriers simply because they are more likely to be new in the business and less likely to know others in the business. Given such difficulties, Congress could reasonably find that a minority subcontractor is less likely to receive favors from the entrenched businesspersons who award subcontracts only to people with whom — or with whose friends — they have an existing relationship. This program, then, if in part a remedy for past discrimination, is most importantly a forward-looking response to practical problems faced by minority subcontractors.

The current program contains another forward-looking component that the 1977 set-asides did not share. §8(a) of the SBA provides for periodic review of the status of DBE's and DBE status can be challenged by a competitor at any time under any of the routes to certification. Such review prevents ineligible firms from taking part in the program solely because of their minority ownership, even when those firms were once disadvantaged but have since become successful. The emphasis on review also indicates the Administration's anticipation that after their presumed disadvantages have been overcome, firms will "graduate" into a status in which they will be able to compete for business, including prime contracts, on an equal basis. As with other phases of the statutory policy of encouraging the formation and growth of small business enterprises, this program is intended to facilitate entry and increase competition in the free market.

Significantly, the current program, unlike the 1977 set-aside, does not establish any requirement—numerical or otherwise—that a general contractor must hire DBE subcontractors. The program we upheld in *Fullilove* required that 10% of the federal grant for every federally funded project be expended on minority business enterprises. In contrast, the current program contains no quota. Although it provides monetary incentives to general contractors to hire DBE subcontractors, it does not require them to hire DBE's, and they do not lose their contracts if they fail to do so. The importance of this incentive to general contractors (who always seek to offer the lowest bid) should not be underestimated; but the preference here is far less rigid, and thus more narrowly tailored, than the 1977 Act.

Finally, the record shows a dramatic contrast between the sparse deliberations that preceded the 1977 Act and the extensive hearings conducted in several Congresses before the current program was developed. However we might evaluate the benefits and costs—both fiscal and social—of this or any other affirmative-action program, our obligation to give deference to Congress' policy choices is much more demanding in this case than it was in *Fullilove*. If the 1977 program of race-based set-asides satisfied the strict scrutiny dictated by Justice Powell's vision of the Constitution—a vision the Court expressly endorses today—it must follow as night follows the day that the Court of Appeals' judgment upholding this more carefully crafted program should be affirmed.

VI

My skeptical scrutiny of the Court's opinion leaves me in dissent. The majority's concept of "consistency" ignores a difference, fundamental to the idea of equal protection, between oppression and assistance. The majority's concept of "congruence" ignores a difference, fundamental to our constitutional system, between the Federal Government and the States. And the majority's concept of stare decisis ignores the force of binding precedent. I would affirm the judgment of the Court of Appeals.

Justice SOUTER, with whom Justice GINSBURG and Justice BREYER join, dissenting.

. . . I agree with Justice Stevens's conclusion that stare decisis compels the application of *Fullilove*. Although *Fullilove* did not reflect doctrinal consistency, its several opinions produced a result on shared grounds that petitioner does not attack: that discrimination in the construction industry had been subject to government acquiescence, with effects that remain and that may be addressed by some preferential treatment falling within the congressional power under §5 of the Fourteenth Amendment. Once *Fullilove* is applied, as Justice Stevens points out, it follows that the statutes in question here pass muster under Fifth Amendment due process and Fourteenth Amendment equal protection. . . .

In assessing the degree to which today's holding portends a departure from past practice, it is also worth noting that nothing in today's opinion implies any view of Congress's §5 power and the deference due its exercise that differs from the views expressed by the *Fullilove* plurality. . . .

Finally, I should say that I do not understand that today's decision will necessarily have any effect on the resolution of an issue that was just as pertinent under *Fullilove*'s unlabeled standard as it is under the standard of strict scrutiny now adopted by the Court. The Court has long accepted the view that constitutional authority to remedy past discrimination is not limited to the power to forbid its continuation, but extends to eliminating those effects that would otherwise persist and skew the operation of public systems even in the absence of current intent to practice any discrimination. This is so whether the remedial authority is exercised by a court or some other legislature. Indeed, a majority of the Court today reiterates that there are circumstances in which Government may, consistently with the Constitution, adopt programs aimed at remedying the effects of past invidious discrimination.

When the extirpation of lingering discriminatory effects is thought to require a catch-up mechanism, like the racially preferential inducement under the statutes considered here, the result may be that some members of the historically favored race are hurt by that remedial mechanism, however innocent they may be of any personal responsibility for any discriminatory conduct. When this price is considered reasonable, it is in part because it is a price to be paid only temporarily; if the justification for the preference is eliminating the effects of a past practice, the assumption is that the effects will themselves recede into the past, becoming attenuated and finally disappearing. Thus, Justice Powell wrote in his concurring opinion in *Fullilove* that the "temporary nature of this remedy ensures that a race-conscious program will not last longer than the discriminatory effects it is designed to eliminate."

Surely the transition from the *Fullilove* plurality view (in which Justice Powell joined) to today's strict scrutiny (which will presumably be applied as Justice Powell employed it) does not signal a change in the standard by which the burden of a remedial racial preference is to be judged as reasonable or not at any given time. If in the District Court Adarand had chosen to press a challenge to the reasonableness of the burden of these statutes, more than a decade after *Fullilove* had examined such a burden, I doubt that the claim would have fared any differently from the way it will now be treated on remand from this Court.

Justice GINSBURG, with whom Justice BREYER joins, dissenting.

For the reasons stated by Justice Souter, and in view of the attention the political branches are currently giving the matter of affirmative action, I see no compelling cause for the intervention the Court has made in this case. I further agree with Justice Stevens that, in this area, large deference is owed by the Judiciary to "Congress' institutional competence and constitutional authority to overcome historic racial subjugation." I write separately to underscore not the differences the several opinions in this case display, but the considerable field of agreement—the common understandings and concerns—revealed in opinions that together speak for a majority of the Court.

I

The statutes and regulations at issue, as the Court indicates, were adopted by the political branches in response to an "unfortunate reality": "the unhappy persistence of both the practice and the lingering effects of racial discrimination against minority groups in this country" (lead opinion). The United States suffers from those lingering effects because, for most of our Nation's history, the idea that "we are just one race" (Scalia, J., concurring in part and concurring in judgment), was not embraced. For generations, our lawmakers and judges were unprepared to say that there is in this land no superior race, no race inferior to any other. In Plessy v. Ferguson not only did this Court endorse the oppressive practice of race segregation, but even Justice Harlan, the advocate of a "color-blind" Constitution, stated: "The white race deems itself to be the dominant race in this country. And so it is, in prestige, in achievements, in education, in wealth and in power. So, I doubt not, it will continue to be for all time, if it remains true to its great heritage and holds fast to the principles of constitutional liberty." Not until Loving v. Virginia, which held unconstitutional Virginia's ban on interracial marriages, could one say with security that the Constitution and this Court would abide no measure "designed to maintain White Supremacy."

The divisions in this difficult case should not obscure the Court's recognition of the persistence of racial inequality and a majority's acknowledgement of Congress' authority to act affirmatively, not only to end discrimination, but also to counteract discrimination's lingering effects (lead opinion).

Those effects, reflective of a system of racial caste only recently ended, are evident in our workplaces, markets, and neighborhoods. Job applicants with identical resumes, qualifications, and interview styles still experience different receptions, depending on their race. White and African-American consumers still encounter different deals. People of color looking for housing still face discriminatory treatment by landlords, real estate agents, and mortgage lenders. Minority entrepreneurs sometimes fail to gain contracts though they are the low bidders, and they are sometimes refused work even after winning contracts. Bias both conscious and unconscious, reflecting traditional and unexamined habits of thought, keeps up barriers that must come down if equal opportunity and nondiscrimination are ever genuinely to become this country's law and practice.

Given this history and its practical consequences, Congress surely can conclude that a carefully designed affirmative action program may help to realize, finally, the "equal protection of the laws" the Fourteenth Amendment has promised since 1868.

II

The lead opinion uses one term, "strict scrutiny," to describe the standard of judicial review for all governmental classifications by race. But that opinion's elaboration strongly suggests that the strict standard announced is indeed "fatal" for classifications burdening groups that have suffered discrimination in our society. That seems to me, and, I believe, to the Court, the enduring lesson one should draw from Korematsu v. United States; for in that case, scrutiny the Court described as "most rigid" nonetheless yielded a pass for an odious, gravely injurious racial classification. A *Korematsu*-type classification, as I read the opinions in this case, will never again survive scrutiny: such a classification, history and precedent instruct, properly ranks as prohibited.

For a classification made to hasten the day when "we are just one race" (Scalia, J., concurring in part and concurring in judgment), however, the lead opinion has dispelled the notion that "strict scrutiny" is "'fatal in fact.'" Properly, a majority of the Court calls for review that is searching, in order to ferret out classifications in reality malign, but masquerading as benign (lead opinion). The Court's once lax review of sex-based classifications demonstrates the need for such suspicion. See, e.g., Hoyt v. Florida, 368 U.S. 57, 60, (1961) (upholding women's "privilege" of automatic exemption from jury service); Goesaert v. Cleary, 335 U.S. 464 (1948) (upholding Michigan law barring women from employment as bartenders). Today's decision thus usefully reiterates that the purpose of strict scrutiny "is precisely to distinguish legitimate from illegitimate uses of race in governmental decisionmaking" (lead opinion), "to 'differentiate between' permissible and impermissible governmental use of race," to distinguish " 'between a "No Trespassing" sign and a welcome mat.' "

Close review also is in order for this further reason. As Justice Souter points out, and as this very case shows, some members of the historically favored race can be hurt by catch-up mechanisms designed to cope with the lingering effects of entrenched racial subjugation. Court review can ensure that preferences are not so large as to trammel unduly upon the opportunities of others or interfere too harshly with legitimate expectations of persons in once-preferred groups. . . .

While I would not disturb the programs challenged in this case, and would leave their improvement to the political branches, I see today's decision as one that allows our precedent to evolve, still to be informed by and responsive to changing conditions.

NOTES

1. Is any part of *Metro Broadcasting* consistent with the Court's holding in *Adarand*?

2. Is any part of *Fullilove* consistent with the court's holding in *Adarand*?

3. Does an affirmative action program designed to promote diversity among the guards at a federal correctional facility serve a compelling state interest? See Memorandum to General Counsels, Post-*Adarand* Guidance on Affirmative Action in Federal Employment, U.S. Dept. of Justice, Feb. 29, 1996.

4. Reconsider Johnson v. Transportation Agency of Santa Clara County. We already considered whether the affirmative action decision in that case would violate the equal protection clause. Does *Adarand* change that analysis in any way?

5. Does Johnson "deserve" to get the dispatcher's position at issue in the *Santa Clara* case? Why? How is he wronged if he does not get it? What if he did not get the job because a "less qualified" person applied who was given the job pursuant to a veteran's preference requirement? Who "deserves" the job, the veteran or Johnson? Why?

6. Is there any remaining difference between the way the Court will treat an affirmative action program devised by a state legislative body and affirmative action programs designed by Congress? After *Adarand*, what is the meaning of §5 of the Fourteenth Amendment, delegating authority to the federal government to enforce the restriction of the Fourteenth Amendment?

The 1972 amendments to Title VII were enacted under §5 of the Fourteenth Amendment in order to reach state actors and avoid problems with the Tenth Amendment. Reliance on §5 as an enumerated power justifying other parts of the Civil Rights Act of 1964 was upheld in Katzenbach v. Morgan, 384 U.S. 641 (1966). In response to Justice Stevens' point in dissent that §5 distinguishes the power of Congress from the power of states, Justice O'Connor remarked that "[i]t is true that various Members of this Court have taken different views of the authority §5 of the Fourteenth Amendment confers upon Congress to deal with the problem of racial discrimination, and the extent to which courts should defer to Congress' exercise of that authority. We need not, and do not, address these differences today." If Congress did pass a statute requiring the use of race to redress societal discrimination and relied on its power under the Fourteenth Amendment, what result? Would it be found a legislative interference with constitutional rights as finally established by the Supreme Court or would it be upheld as an extension of rights consistent with the Fourteenth Amendment?

7. *Weber* and *Johnson* hold that, in passing Title VII, Congress did not intend to ban voluntary affirmative action. While employees of public employers will now surely use *Croson* and *Adarand* to attack affirmative action, what effect do these two holdings have on the voluntary use of affirmative action by private employers? *Croson* and *Adarand* do not appear to require Congress to ban affirmative action by statute, but do these cases suggest that the present Supreme Court will find that *Weber* and *Johnson* are wrong in their interpretation of what Congress intended in enacting Title VII? See Lara Hudgins, Comment, Rethinking Affirmative Action in the 1990s: Tailoring the Cure to Remedy the Disease, 47 Baylor L. Rev. 815 (1995), suggesting that Congress should enact legislation authorizing affirmative action.

8. What if a construction firm owned and run by females applies for the contract that Adarand wanted and gets it pursuant to the federal preference program at issue in *Adarand*? What standard of review applies? Why? Should an intermediate standard of review apply to evaluate preference programs that help women? Does the Court's decision mean that it is easier to satisfy equal protection when women are given preferences than when African Americans are given preferences? Is this a logical rule? If female set-aside programs should be evaluated under strict scrutiny, what about discrimination against female contractors?

9. Does the Court's analysis raise questions about the constitutional viability of class-based remedial preferences? How would you argue this case on remand if you represented the government? Does the articulated standard of review actually make any difference if strict scrutiny can be satisfied?

10. The debate within the majority as to whether strict scrutiny is "fatal in fact" to affirmative action was answered in the affirmative in the lower courts. In Hopwood v. Texas, 78 F.3d 932 (5th Cir. 1996), the court rejected

the idea that student body diversity could be a compelling state interest for using affirmative action by an educational institution. "[A]ny consideration of race or ethnicity by the law school for the purpose of achieving a diverse student body is not a compelling interest under the Fourteenth Amendment." Id at 944. In Podberesky v. Kirwan, 38 F.3d 147 (4th Cir. 1994), *cert. denied*, 115 S. Ct. 2001 (1995), the court rejected an attempt to justify an affirmative action of the University of Maryland as a remedy of the present effects of the past discrimination of a state actor that had engaged in de jure discrimination.

Chapter 5

Systemic Disparate Impact
Discrimination

A. THE GENERAL STRUCTURE OF
DISPARATE IMPACT DISCRIMINATION

Page 358.   Add the following at the end of carryover Note 5:

Ramona L. Paetzold and Steven L. Willborn, Deconstructing Disparate Impact: A View of the Model Through New Lenses, 74 N.C. L. Rev. 325, 353-354 (1995), argue that the cause of impact is irrelevant to disparate impact:

> The employment practice was one cause of the disparate impact in *Griggs*; if the employer had not required a high school diploma, the criterion obviously could not have caused a disparate impact on blacks. But the disparate impact was also "caused" by the social conditions that resulted in a lower proportion of blacks than whites with high school diplomas. The high school diploma requirement would not have caused a disparate impact if social conditions had produced the same proportion of high school graduates within the black and white subpopulations. Every disparate impact case depends on an interaction of at least two "causes" in this sense. In *Griggs*, each of the two relevant "causes"

(the employment criterion and the social conditions) was necessary to cause the disparate impact on blacks. If either had been absent, no disparate impact would have been present. . . .

Ordinary disparate impact cases, then, view causation with blinders. The law treats the employer's criterion as the cause of a disparity, even though it may be only one of a wide array of factors necessary to produce the disparity.[92] Ordinary disparate impact cases view causation with blinders, not because the cases arise in a single-cause context, but because they ignore causes external to the employer that contribute to the impact. The blinders necessarily mean that employers may be held legally responsible for impacts that are "caused" in substantial part by factors external to the employers.

See also Kathryn Abrams, Title VII and the Complex Female Subject, 92 Mich. L. Rev. 2479, 2524 (1994).

Page 361. *Add the following in Note 17 before "See Chapter 8":*

See generally Rebecca Hanner White, The EEOC, the Courts, and Employment Discrimination Policy: Recognizing the Agency's Leading Role in Statutory Interpretation, 1995 Utah L. Rev. 51.

Page 364. *Add the following after the carryover paragraph:*

Since the publication of the casebook, two appellate courts have squarely held that disparate impact is inapplicable to ADEA cases, Ellis v. United Airlines, Inc., 64 U.S.L.W. 2423 (10th Cir. 1996); EEOC v. Francis W. Parker School, 41 F.3d 1073 (7th Cir. 1994) (2-1), *cert. denied*, 115 S. Ct. 2577 (1995), and other decisions have questioned its relevance under this statute. E.g., Graffam v. Scott Paper Co., 60 F.3d 809 (1st Cir. 1995) (assuming arguendo that disparate impact applied under the ADEA but went on to hold that any disparate impact on older workers from a system for deciding who should be laid off in a downsizing was justified). See also DiBiase v. SmithKline Beecham Co., 48 F.3d 719, 732 (3d Cir. 1995) (assuming disparate impact applied when an employer offers equal severance benefits to all those waiving rights, "such a neutral policy—which does not rely on an invidious stereotype about older workers, which clearly is not motivated by a discrim-

---

92. Another way of saying this is that factors external to the employer are treated as givens and that an employer may be held responsible for them if, jointly with the employer's criterion, they produce a disparity.

inatory impulse, and which could be demonstrated to have a disparate impact only by an incredibly sophisticated statistical analysis simply cannot be the basis of ADEA liability"). See generally Michael C. Sloan, Comment, Disparate Impact in the Age Discrimination in Employment Act: Will the Supreme Court Permit It?, 1995 Wis. L. Rev. 507. See also Earl M. Maltz, The Legacy of *Griggs v. Duke Power Co.*: A Case Study in the Impact of a Modernist Statutory Precedent, 1994 Utah L. Rev. 1353.

Page 365.   Add the following at the end of the section:

See Faulkner v. Super Value Stores, Inc., 3 F.3d 1419, 1429 n.8 (10th Cir. 1993) (applicability of Civil Rights Act of 1991 to ADEA remains an open question). In Houghton v. SIPCO, Inc., 38 F.3d 953 (8th Cir. 1994), the court, purporting to apply the law in effect at the time because the case had been filed before the effective date of the 1991 Civil Rights Act, ordered a new trial because the jury was improperly instructed that, once the plaintiff proved a prima facie case, defendants can show by a preponderance of the evidence that their actions were justified by business necessity. Id. at 959. The court noted the proper charge should not place the burden of proof on the defendant and must use the standard set forth in *Wards Cove* of business justification. Id.

B. PLAINTIFF'S PRIMA FACIE CASE: PROVING THE IMPACT ELEMENT

1. *Actual Versus Theoretical Disparate Impact*

Page 372.   Add new Note 6a:

6a. Ramona L. Paetzold and Steven L. Willborn, Deconstructing Disparate Impact: A View of the Model Through New Lenses, 74 N.C.L. Rev. 325, 356 (1995), argue that the plaintiff in a disparate impact case need not prove actual causation:

> Causation is also blindered in ordinary disparate impact cases because it does not require that the plaintiff prove that the employer's criterion has actually produced a disparate impact in the workplace. In *Griggs*, for example, the same disparate impact on blacks may have occurred even if the employer had not utilized the high school diploma requirement. Employees applying for the jobs at issue in *Griggs* also had to attain a certain score on a general "intelligence" test that approximated the national median score for high school graduates. Blacks

as a class may have suffered from the same (or even a greater) disparate impact as a result of the test requirement. The disparate impact model as applied in *Griggs*, then, did not require any proof that the criterion at issue actually produced a disparate impact; it merely required proof that the criterion at issue would have screened out protected class members disproportionately if applied independently of any other factors at play in the selection process.[101]

Do you agree? Is *Beazer* consistent with this view?

Page 379.   Add the following to the end of Note 6:

In Muzquiz v. W.A. Foote Memorial Hosp., 70 F.3d 422 (6th Cir. 1995), a Mexican-Indian doctor failed to show the existence of disparate impact in his challenge to the hospital's rule requiring all doctors seeking work to present actual X-ray films and original records of patient care. Plaintiff claimed this rule had disparate impact on Mexicans because Mexican hospitals gave X-ray films to the patients and refused to ever release original patient records. The court found that, at most, this credential rule had disparate impact on doctors who trained in Mexico and not those of Mexican origin.

2.   Discrete Practices, Multicomponent Selection Processes, and the Bottom Line

Page 397.   Add at the end of the page:

See Ramona L. Paetzold and Steven L. Willborn, Deconstructing Disparate Impact: A View of the Model Through New Lenses, 74 N.C.L. Rev. 325, 380-386 (1995).

Page 399.   Add at the end of the carryover paragraph:

See Ramona L. Paetzold and Steven L. Willborn, Deconstructing Disparate Impact: A View of the Model Through New Lenses, 74 N.C.L. Rev. 325, 387-395 (1995).

---

101. The principal reason for this result is that courts, following the Supreme Court's lead in *Griggs*, do not inquire into whether other factors make the effects of the questioned factor redundant for individuals affected by the questioned factor. The "particular employment practice" requirement of Title VII also implies the result. [703(k)(1)(A)(i).] A different result would require inquiry beyond the "particular" criterion to other factors simultaneously in play in the selection process, to see how the interplay of factors would affect individuals. . . .

4. Identifying Criteria Appropriate for Impact Analysis

Page 409.   Add the following to the end of Note 7:

In West Virginia Univ. v. Deckerm, 447 S.E.2d 259 (W. Va. 1994), the court commented on the proper scope of application of disparate impact theory in a case in which a tenured faculty member used that theory to attack a university policy of paying incoming faculty members market salaries while having a separate system for incumbents that sometimes resulted in new faculty earning more than incumbents. In finding that the policy of meeting the demand of the market for new hires was justified by business necessity, the court indicated that disparate impact theory worked best to attack barriers to entry to employment and not the terms and conditions of employment of incumbent workers.

> The objective of anti-discrimination statutes was to break stereotypes and give people a chance who had previously been unjustifiably excluded from the work force. The strongest examples of disparate impact occur in entry level positions, and as a worker gains more seniority and moves up in rank, it becomes progressively harder to prove disparate impact using entry level positions as a reference point. This is because the longer a person is in a particular position, the less likely it is that his or her current position is equal in duties, benefits, and responsibilities, to an entry level position.
>
> In the area of salary adjustments, an employer should be able to take into account different credentials and different qualifications of employees. Imposing too many restrictions on employers at the firing, or salary compensation level has a counterproductive effect on the goals of civil rights statutes in general. Indeed, all discrimination litigation that arises after entry level provides perverse incentives for employers to avoid potential liability or governmental control over business decisions, by refusing to let members of protected classes get a foot in the door.

Page 428.   Replace the third sentence in the first full
paragraph with the following:

Other courts have held that the presence of good faith alone is insufficient to establish business necessity. Burwell v. Eastern Air Lines, Inc., 633 F.2d 361, 373 (4th Cir. 1980), *cert. denied*, 450 U.S. 965 (1981); Blake v. City of Los Angeles, 595 F.2d 1367, 1376 (9th Cir. 1979), *cert. denied*, 446 U.S. 928 (1980); see Griggs v. Duke Power Co., 401 U.S. 424, 432 (1971).

C.   DEFENDANT'S CASE: BUSINESS NECESSITY AND JOB RELATEDNESS

Page 432.   Add the following to the end of the carryover paragraph:

See Susan S. Grover, The Business Necessity Defense in Disparate Impact Discrimination Cases, 30 Ga. L. Rev. 387 (1996), justifying a stringent reading of the business necessity defense.

Chapter 6

The Interrelation of the Disparate Treatment and Disparate Impact Theories of Discrimination

B. THE RELATIONSHIP BETWEEN DISPARATE IMPACT AND TREATMENT WHERE THERE IS A STATISTICAL SHOWING OF EFFECTS

Page 502. *Insert before Note on the Relationship Between Individual and Systemic Disparate Treatment Cases:*

Are any of these points clarified by the following case?

FISHER v. TRANSCO
SERVICES-MILWAUKEE, INC.
979 F.2d 1239 (7th Cir. 1992)

DILLIN, District Judge.

Plaintiffs John W. Fisher and Richard R. Kirchhoff sued their former employer, Transco Services-Milwaukee, Inc., alleging unlawful discrimination in violation of the Age Discrimination in Employment Act. They appeal the District Court's grant of summary judgment in favor of Transco. For the following reasons, we reverse and remand for proceedings consistent with this opinion.

BACKGROUND

At all relevant times prior to March of 1984, The Great Atlantic & Pacific Tea Company, Inc. (A&P), through its subsidiary Kohl's Food Stores, Inc., owned and operated a retail grocery warehouse where plaintiffs-appellants Fisher and Kirchhoff had worked since 1970 as order selectors (selectors). As selectors, appellants were responsible for processing requests for goods, which included retrieving and loading the goods, and completing some required paperwork.

In March of 1984, A&P contracted with Transco Service Corporation, through its subsidiary, defendant-appellee Transco Services-Milwaukee, Inc. (Transco), to operate the warehouse. Approximately five months after the transfer of management, Transco instituted A&P's "Measured Day Work Program" in order to measure and evaluate the performance of its full-time selectors, including appellants.

At the heart of A&P's Program was a computer which analyzed each incoming order and assigned the number of "leveled minutes" needed for a selector to complete it. In calculating this time, the computer considered the goods requested, particularly their sizes, weights, and locations in the warehouse, and made adjustments for such variables as the distance between the starting area and the loading platform, and the degree of difficulty in loading a particular good.

Every leveled minute of work assigned to a selector earned the selector a proportional number of "rest allowance minutes" for personal needs. The leveled minutes and rest allowance minutes were summed to determine the "standard minutes" needed to complete an order. A selector's performance was calculated by taking the ratio of standard minutes to the actual time expended.

During an eight hour day, which is 480 minutes, a selector was expected under the Program to perform 407 minutes of leveled work and receive 73 minutes of rest allowance. At all times relevant, Transco expected a standard-to-actual ratio of one to one, i.e., 100 percent. Any selector who failed to maintain this ratio on a weekly basis might be subject to discipline.

Specifically, until all selectors achieved a 100 percent performance ratio, those selectors whose performance ratios fell into the lower 20 percent of those working that week were subject to progressive discipline. After the first week of low production, counseling and an oral warning were to be given. If a second week of low production occurred, additional counseling and a written warning were to be given. If a third, another written warning, as well as a one day suspension; for a fourth, a written warning and a three day suspension. Finally, if the employee's performance level fell in the bottom 20 percent for a fifth time, the employee became subject to discharge. The weeks of poor performance did not need to be consecutive, but if discipline was administered, a one week grace period was to be granted before discipline would again be given.

According to Transco, appellant Fisher failed to rank in the upper 80 percent of selectors for the weeks ending October 13, October 27, and December 15, 1984, and the weeks of January 12 and March 8, 1985. Fisher was terminated on March 8, 1985, at the age of 45. Appellant Kirchhoff failed to rank in the upper 80 percent the first week of the Program's implementation, that is, the week ending September 8, 1984. After an accident rendered him unable to work for nearly two months commencing in November of 1984, Kirchhoff failed to rank in the upper 80 percent for the weeks ending February 2, February 23, March 23 and April 12, 1985. Kirchhoff was terminated on April 12, 1985, at the age of 42. However, according to appellants, they were each erroneously disciplined three times and should not have been terminated. There is evidence to support these contentions.

Transco ended its Program on August 3, 1985, after 48 weeks. During this time 1,182 weekly measurements were taken, of which only 20 were at or above the 100 percent level. As a result of the Program, 11 out of the 52 selectors who worked for at least five weeks were fired, of whom 10 were age 40 or older.

To succeed in this action, Fisher and Kirchhoff must prove that they would not have been discharged "but for" their age. There exist two possible theories under which Fisher and Kirchhoff may assert their claims. First, they may argue that they have suffered disparate treatment because of their age. Second, they may assert that their employer's practice, while not necessarily intended, resulted in a significant disparate impact upon its older workers.

We will first consider the theory of disparate treatment. Under it, appellants may prove their claim in two ways. First they may meet their burden head on by presenting evidence, direct or circumstantial, that age was the determining factor in their discharge. Second, and the more common, they may utilize the indirect, burden-shifting method of proof used in Title VII cases. See McDonnell Douglas Corp. v. Green. Appellants have opted for the latter.

Under the indirect method of proving disparate treatment, appellants must set forth a prima facie case to create a presumption of discrimination. In discharge cases such as the present, plaintiffs must show that (1) they were in the protected class (persons over the age of 40), (2) they were doing their jobs well enough to meet their employer's legitimate expectations, (3) they were discharged or demoted, and (4) the employer sought a replacement for them.

If the plaintiff is successful, the burden of production shifts to his employer to articulate a legitimate, nondiscriminatory reason for the discharge. If such an articulation is forthcoming, the presumption dissolves, and the burden of production shifts back to the plaintiff to show that the employer's proffered reason is a pretext for discrimination.

It is clear that appellants were members of the class protected by the ADEA, and that they were discharged. In addition, we agree with appellants that until this appeal Transco had not challenged the contention that appellants were replaced and cannot do so now. Thus, remaining at issue is whether the appellants were performing their jobs well enough to meet Transco's legitimate expectations.

Transco's expectations as to the appellants' performances are wholly dependent upon the Program alleged by appellants to be a pretext for discrimination. We find that in this situation, the issue of legitimate performance is best merged with the issue of pretext. This approach is logical, for if the conditions placed upon the appellants by the Program are found to be illegitimate, it follows that Transco's expectations were likely pretextual, and vice-versa. Further, to hold otherwise would unnecessarily insulate Transco from the burden of articulating a nondiscriminatory reason for the discharge of the appellants. This would clearly not further the purpose of the ADEA.

For the above reasons, we believe that the appellants have effectively created a rebuttable presumption of discrimination. Thus, the burden of production is shifted to Transco to articulate a legitimate reason for appellants' discharge. This burden is not difficult to satisfy. Transco "need not persuade the court that it was actually motivated by the proffered reasons." Texas Department of Community Affairs v. Burdine. It is sufficient if its proffered reason raises a genuine issue of material fact as to whether it discriminated against the plaintiff. Id.

Transco relies upon appellants' poor performance under the Program as the basis for discharging the appellants. Since the Program was created after extensive studies, we find that Transco has met its burden of production. Therefore, the burden of production now shifts back to Fisher and Kirchhoff to show that the Program was really a pretext for discrimination. In support of a finding of pretext, appellants contend that Transco's Program was unreasonable in its demands and was not implemented in a neutral manner.

Despite the fact that Transco's standard under the Program, i.e., a 100 percent performance level, was seemingly unreasonable in that this level was achieved very rarely by any selector, and in most weeks was not achieved at all, we agree with the District Court that this does not, standing alone, show intentional discrimination. However, we believe that this standard, when coupled with the alleged manner of the Program's implementation, raises a genuine issue of material fact as to the Program being a pretext for age discrimination.

Appellants argue that erroneous disciplines occurred under the Program twenty-two times, of which 18 were applied against older workers and four against younger ones, and that the rate at which Transco disciplined workers decreased substantially after it had terminated several of its older workers. Because of this, appellants contend that eight younger workers who should have been fired were not, and that six older workers, including appellants, were fired when they should not have been.

To support its argument, appellants rely upon exhibit 6 to their expert's deposition. This exhibit sets forth the names and ages of Transco's warehouse workers, the performance level achieved for each week under the Program, whether the performance rendered an employee in the bottom 20% of those receiving scores, whether discipline had been given, and the form of the discipline.

An examination of exhibit 6 reveals that some errors were indeed committed. For example, for the week ending 10/13/84, 35 selectors were measured and none achieved a 100 percent level. Thus, seven of these constituted the lower 20 percent. However, appellant Fisher, who had received a performance level of 70.0% was disciplined despite his being one person above the 20 percent cut-off, while a younger selector, who had a level of 69.7%, was not.

Transco argues that this error and others "are nothing more than rounding problems in . . . [appellants' expert's] data base." However, this is merely an assertion and is not documented. In sum, we believe that whether the alleged errors present in Transco's implementation of the Program, coupled with the very high standards under the Program, render the Program a pretext for age discrimination presents a genuine issue of material fact.

Next to consider is the least developed aspect of this case, the appellants' claim of disparate impact. To establish unlawful disparate impact under the ADEA, as under Title VII, an employee must first show that an employer utilizes a particular employment practice that results in a disparate impact upon a protected class of workers. If the employee makes such a showing, the employer must then set forth how the challenged practice serves, in a significant way, its legitimate employment goals, i.e., the business necessity of the practice. However, no proof of discriminatory intent is necessary.

The appellants maintain that Transco's Program, while having facially neutral criteria, fell more harshly upon Transco's older employees. In granting Transco's motion for summary judgment, the District Court held, as the appellees now urge, that no conclusions could be gleaned from the statistical samples, as they were too small and too poorly presented. In the alternative, the District Court found that appellants had not rebutted Transco's claim that its Program was consistent with a business necessity.

Eleven terminations took place as a result of the Program, and 52 selectors were involved, of which 27 were age 40 or above. Of the 11 terminated, 10 were of a protected age. It is true that we, like other courts, are reluctant to render conclusions in a disparate impact claim based upon small statistical samples. However, this is not a hard and fast rule and generally some substantial evidence of the unreliability of the statistics is asserted before it is applied. In this case, where 10 of 27 older employees were terminated, as against 1 of 25 younger ones, it does not require expertise in differential equations to observe that an adverse ratio of approximately 10 to 1 is disproportionate. Thus, while the statistical analysis will have to be fully developed and presented at trial, we believe that the granting of summary judgment in favor of Transco on this issue by the District Court was premature.

The District Court found in the alternative that even if the appellants could show a disparate impact, the appellants had not rebutted Transco's claim that the Program was justified by business necessity. We disagree.

The standard required under the Program was so high that out of 1,182 attempts to meet it, the workers were successful only 20 times. Moreover, the Program was abandoned after 48 weeks, after several older employees had been eliminated, and was replete with errors in its administration. Under these circumstances, we believe that the District Court's grant of summary judgment was inappropriate. Simply put, whether the Program implemented at Transco was consistent with business necessity likewise presents a genuine issue of material fact.

NOTES

1. We saw in Chapter 5 that it is not clear that the disparate impact theory applies under the ADEA, but this case could arise as easily if the Measured Day Work Program resulted in adverse impact on women or minorities. In any event, *Transco* offers an opportunity to assess the interaction of disparate treatment and disparate impact theories.

2. Disparate treatment is relatively easy to analyze: Fisher, for example, seems to have been treated worse than the plan would, in theory, permit. In these circumstances, the discharge of an older worker might itself establish a prima facie case since one might expect an employer with an elaborate plan for rating job performance to ensure that the plan was implemented correctly. A failure to do so to the disadvantage of an older worker might be sufficient to create a prima facie case.

3. The plaintiffs had more than this: not only were there two older workers who sued, but they also offered evidence that instances of erroneous discipline occurred more frequently against older workers, and that "the rate at which Transco disciplined workers decreased substantially after it had terminated several of its older workers." In short, the plaintiffs presented evidence from which it could be found "that eight younger workers who should have been fired were not, and that six older workers, including appellants, were fired when they should not have been."

4. Whether all this proof was necessary merely to make out a prima facie case of disparate treatment discrimination is debatable, but the disproportionate effects on older workers clearly became relevant (indeed, critical) when the employer proffered a nondiscriminatory explanation. Obviously, a mere mistake by the employer in implementing its system, however unfortunate, would not justify relief under the ADEA. For the plaintiffs to prevail, then, they would have to establish that the supposed "mistakes" were really pretexts for Transco's efforts to discharge older workers. A pattern of "mistaken" dismissals that disproportionately fell on older workers would tend to rebut the mistake claim.

5. In this regard, the pattern of treating older workers less favorably than younger workers is offered not to prove mere disparate impact but rather to provide a basis for the trier of fact's inferring that an age-discriminatory motive underlay the supposedly neutral Measured Day Work Program. Assuming that the only evidence at trial is that which was proffered in the summary judgment motion, who is likely to prevail before a jury? Is your answer affected by the fact that, no matter the instructions, a jury is unlikely to be sympathetic to an employer that not only mistakenly fired two workers but also failed to offer them their jobs back when it realized its mistake?

6. Assuming that the jury draws the inference that the operation of the Measured Day Work Program was intentional age discrimination, could the employer assert the bfoq defense? Would any jury believe a claim of bfoq after the employer has in the first instance denied that it was using age in its decision-making?

7. Is there sufficient showing of impact to raise an inference of age discrimination, even if the evidence of the mistakes is factored out of the operation of the system? If the jury concludes that the employer's mistakes in administering were just that and that the mistakes did not support the inference that the Measured Day Work Program was adopted with an intent to discriminate on the basis of age, must the jury render a verdict in favor of the employer on the systemic disparate treatment theory? What significance should be given to the fact that the system was abandoned?

8. Is the level of showing of impact sufficient to make out a prima facie case of disparate impact discrimination? How do the "mistakes" fit in showing disparate impact of the Measured Day Work Program? Is there sufficient

showing of impact to make out a prima facie case of disparate impact if the evidence of the mistakes in administration is factored out of the challenge to the system as an employment practice of the employer? Should a lesser showing of impact than is necessary to raise an inference of systemic disparate treatment be sufficient to make out a disparate impact case?

9. Presumably, neither side will be able to put on different statistical evidence, although each may offer different expert analyses of the data. Does this decision require the factfinder to find disparity of impact? Does the opinion mean at a minimum that the factfinder is permitted to find such impact, even if expert testimony cannot establish any statistical significance to the age impact?

10. For disparate treatment, the age pattern of the supposed "mistakes" seems probative on the intent issue, even if there are not enough data for a statistical analysis. But is a statistical analysis necessary for the impact theory? After all, the conceptual underpinning of the theory is that the practice in question (the Measured Day Work Program) has an impact on older workers generally, not merely the particular persons who happened to be employed in this case. Could a jury be allowed to make that finding absent testimony that there is a statistically significant relationship between age and the system?

11. If there were such a relationship, wouldn't it suggest that older workers are less efficient? If so, wouldn't it be permissible to discharge less efficient workers? The problem is not with efficiency per se—selecting or firing workers on the basis of efficiency would undoubtedly be justified as a business necessity and obviously has a strong job relation—but rather with the Measured Day Work Program as a test for efficiency. The employer's mistakes in implementing it and its abandonment suggest that, as a measure for efficiency, it is flawed.

12. What about the defenses to disparate impact discrimination? The Measured Day Work Program seems to be job related because it is a means of analyzing the elements of the job and judging how well people were performing them. Do the mistakes in administration undermine the claim that the system is job related? Is necessary for business? How necessary is a system that, at best, is administered so sloppily?

13. Is the Measured Day Work Program a professionally developed test? Looking back at the methods for validating these tests, isn't this system an example of a content valid test? It is, after all, more than just a sample of the job; it is a measurement of the people actually doing the job. What significance should the mistakes in administration have to whether the test is valid?

14. Is the Measured Day Work Program an example of a bona fide merit system? Section 703(h) provides that "it shall not be an unlawful employment practice for an employer to apply . . . different terms, conditions, or privileges of employment pursuant to a bona fide . . . merit system, or a system which measures earnings by quantity or quality of production . . . provided that such

differences are not the result of an intention to discriminate because of race, color, religion, sex, or national origin. . . ." Given the mistakes in administration, the system may not have been a good measurement of merit or quantity of production but does that mean the defense is not available to the employer?

C. RECONCILING THE TENSION BETWEEN DISPARATE TREATMENT AND DISPARATE IMPACT

Page 511.   Add the following at the end of the carryover paragraph:

The debate over genetic racial differences in intelligence broke out anew with the publication in 1995 of The Bell Curve: Intelligence and Class Structure in American Life by Richard Herrnstein and Charles Murray. This book's central thesis is that social ills can largely be traced to the low intelligence of people who cause or suffer from them, and that intelligence is largely inherited. Because intelligence is largely hereditary, and blacks consistently score lower than whites on standard intelligence tests and other criteria, the book also argues that blacks as a race are significantly less intelligent than whites as a race. Needless to say, The Bell Curve prompted an enormous amount of criticism of its methods and conclusions. E.g., F. Allan Hanson, Testing, "The Bell Curve," and the Social Construction of Intelligence, 10 Tikkun 22 (1995).

Page 512.   Add the following at the end of the carryover paragraph:

More recently, Kingsley R. Browne published a lengthy article, Sex and Temperament in Modern Society: A Darwinian View of the Glass Ceiling and the Gender Gap, 27 Ariz. L. Rev. 971 (1995), which questions whether most differences in female achievement (the "glass ceiling" limiting women's access to the highest levels of employer hierarchies and the gender gap in wages) result from discrimination. Instead, he argues, a substantial part of these phenomena is

> the product of basic biological sex differences in personality and temperament. These differences have resulted from differential reproductive strategies that have been adopted by the two sexes during human history and are every bit as much a product of natural selection as our bidpedal locomotion and opposable

thumbs. Although these temperamental traits evolved in our hunting-and-gath-
ering ancestral environment, they remain with us today whether or not they remain adaptive.

Id. at 984. Professor Browne is not explicit about how acceptance of such a
view should affect the law of employment discrimination, but it is apparent
that such an approach would lead to a very different analysis than that offered
by those who argue that most sex differences are socially constructed.

Chapter 7

Special Problems in Applying Title VII, Section 1981, and the ADEA

B. COVERAGE OF TITLE VII, THE ADEA, AND SECTION 1981

Page 518. *Add the following at the end of carryover Note 3:*

Even if partnerships are beyond the reach of the antidiscrimination statutes, other legal protections may apply. See Mark S. Kende, Shattering the Glass Ceiling: A Legal Theory for Attacking Discrimination Against Women Partners, 46 Hastings L.J. 17 (1994) (arguing that the glass ceiling problem for women law partners and others not protected by Title VII can be addressed through the implied covenant of good faith and fair dealing, which can be read to prohibit partners from discriminating against each other on the basis of gender).

Page 519. *Add the following at the end of carryover Note 5:*

In Nationwide Mut. Ins. Co. v. Darden, 502 U.S. 318, 326 (1992), the Supreme Court held that common law agency principles govern the definition of "employee" under ERISA. In an opinion with implications for Title VII, the ADEA, and the ADA, the Court indicated that where a statute is not helpful in defining "employee," the courts should look to the common law definition as well as common law principles of agency. Id. at 321, citing Kelley v. Southern Pac. Co., 419 U.S. 318 (1974). The Court stated that "[c]ommon law agency principles comport moreover with our precedents and with the common understanding reflected in these precedents, of the difference between an employee and an independent contractor." Id. at 326. In short, *Darden* declared that, when the language of a statute is unclear, a court should not imply a broader meaning than the common law definition of employee. This suggests that either the economic realities or hybrid tests would be inapplicable to Title VII and the ADEA. Nevertheless, subsequent lower court cases have not rejected these approaches. E.g., Wilde v. County of Kandiyohi, 15 F.3d 103 (8th Cir. 1993); Frankel v. Balley, Inc., 987 F.2d 86 (2d Cir. 1993). In the latter decision, the court saw "no significant difference" between the hybrid test and the common law test articulated by the Supreme Court in *Darden*.

Page 520.   Add the following text at the end of Note 10:

A number of recent decisions have continued the split in authority. While some courts continue to hold that the language "agent of employer" means that an agent can be sued under Title VII and be personally liable for actions that violate Title VII, e.g., Ball v. Renner, 54 F.3d 664 (10th Cir. 1995), the majority view is that the language "agent of employer" merely means the employer is liable by virtue of respondeat superior for employee misconduct and that only statutory employers can be subject to Title VII liability. EEOC v. AIC Security Investigations, 55 F.3d 1276 (7th Cir. 1995) (ADA); Tomka v. Seiler Corp., 66 F.3d 1295 (2d Cir. 1995) (Title VII); Gary v. Long, 59 F.3d 1391 (D.C. Cir. 1995); Smith v. Lomax, 45 F.3d 402 (11th Cir. 1995) (Title VII and ADEA); Birbeck v. Marvel Lighting Co., 30 F.3d 507 (4th Cir. 1994); Grant v. Lone Star Co., 21 F.3d 649 (5th Cir.), *cert. denied*, 115 S. Ct. 574 (1994); Busby v. City of Orlando, 931 F.2d 764 (11th Cir. 1991). See generally Rebecca Hanner White, Vicarious and Personal Liability for Employment Discrimination, 30 Ga. L. Rev. 509 (1996); Steven K. Sanborn, Note, *Miller v. Maxwell's International, Inc.*: Individual Liability for Supervisory Employees Under Title VII and the ADEA, 17 W. New Eng. L. Rev. 143 (1995); Scott B. Goldberg, Comment, Discrimination by Managers and Supervisors: Recognizing Agent Liability Under Title VII, 143 U. Pa. L. Rev. 571 (1994); Christopher Greer, Note, "Who Me?": A Supervisor's Individual Liability for Discrimination in the Workplace, 62 Fordham L. Rev. 1835 (1994).

Page 522.   Add the following at the end of the first full
sentence in the carryover paragraph of Note 13:

Pursuant to the "Contract with America," the new Republican Congress enacted the Congressional Accountability Act of 1995, Pub. L. No. 104-1 (Jan. 23, 1995), under which employees of the House and of the Senate were protected similarly to other federal employees under §717.

Page 523.   Add the following in Note 16 after the EEOC
v. Fond du Lac citation:

See generally Vicki J. Limas, Application of Federal Labor and Employment Statutes to Native American Tribes: Respecting Sovereignty and Achieving Consistency, 26 Ariz. St. L.J. 681 (1994).

Page 524.   Add the following to Note 18 at the end of the
last full paragraph:

See Mahoney v. RFE/RL, Inc., 47 F.3d 447 (D.C. Cir.), *cert. denied*, 116 S. Ct. 181 (1995) (foreign law exemption applied when application of the ADEA would require violating a collective bargaining agreement in a country where departures from such agreements are illegal without approval by government-established "works councils").

C.   GENDER DISCRIMINATION

1.   Pregnancy

Page 539.   Add the following new text to Note 7:

In Thompson v. La Petite Academy, 838 F. Supp. 1478 (D. Kan. 1993), an employee alleged that her employer criticized a change in attitude coinciding with her pregnancy. After Thompson told her employer she was pregnant, she was fired for being "too ho-hum," walking around with her head down, not smiling, and not being perky or happy, reasons the court found clearly tied to her pregnancy.

Page 541.   Add the following new text to Note 15:

The EEOC's "Questions and Answers on the Pregnancy Discrimination Act" indicates that employers must process a pregnant employee's requests for benefits based on her pregnancy in the same way as any other employee's request. 29 C.F.R. pt. 1604 app. Questions 5, 6 (1994). In applying the PDA, courts have followed *Johnson Controls* and the EEOC guidelines and required employers to accommodate pregnant employees' needs *only* when failure to accommodate treats pregnant women differently than other employees who are similarly able or unable to work. See, e.g., EEOC v. Ackerman, Hoods & McQueen, 956 F.2d 944, 948 (10th Cir.), cert. denied, 113 S. Ct. 60 (1992) (pregnant worker was entitled to be excused from overtime work because employer had unwritten policy of granting work schedule requests for personal and medical reasons).

Commentators have noted that the PDA, as currently interpreted, is inadequate to deal with the needs of pregnant women for accommodation in the workplace. These commentators suggest a variety of responses ranging from reinterpreting the PDA to enacting new legislation. See Deborah A. Calloway, Accommodating Pregnancy in the Workplace, 25 Stetson L. Rev. 1 (1995); Samuel Issacharoff & Elyse Rosenblum, Women and the Workplace: Accommodating the Demands of Pregnancy, 94 Colum. L. Rev. 2154 (1994); Laura Schlichtmann, Accommodation of Pregnancy-Related Disabilities on the Job, 15 Berkeley J. Employment & Lab. L. 335 (1994).

Page 541.   Add the following new text to Note 16:

Two commentators have argued that the PDA can be construed to require not just accommodation but preferential treatment of pregnant employees. Under this interpretation, the first clause standing alone could require an employer to treat pregnant employees preferentially because this clause prevents employers from discharging employees who are disabled due to their pregnancies, even if similarly situated nonpregnant employees are discharged. Ann C. McGinley & Jeffrey W. Stempel, Condescending Contradiction: Richard Posner's Pragmatism and Pregnancy Discrimination, 46 Fla. L. Rev. 193, 242 (1994). To reach this result, the second clause must be read as not limiting or explaining the first clause. Id. at 245.

Preferential treatment may be necessary in some circumstances to put women in the workforce on an equal footing with men. The PDA could be interpreted to require equal opportunity, not just equal treatment. The majority opinion in *Guerra* uses this reasoning, but lower courts have been reluctant to read *Guerra* to mandate, rather than merely permit, preferential treatment. See Samuel Issacharoff & Elyse Rosenblum, Women and the Workplace: Accommodating the Demands of Pregnancy, 94 Colum. L. Rev. 2154, 2183-2189 (1994). Although arguing that equal opportunity requires preferential treatment departs from the clear mandate of Title VII's language, interpreting the PDA to require accommodation or preferential treatment to provide equal employment opportunity for pregnant women is consistent with Congress' intent when it passed the PDA.

Page 544.   Add the following new text to carryover
Note 26:

See Melissa B. Kessler, Note, Civil Rights—Childrearing Leave Policy and Employment Discrimination Under Title VII, 64 Temp. L.Q. 1047 (1991). In Maganuco v. Leyden Community High Sch. Dist. 212, 939 F.2d 440 (7th Cir. 1991), the court held that requiring a pregnant employee to choose between maternity leave or sick leave was not prohibited by the PDA because plaintiff was, in effect, claiming childrearing leave: "The impact of the leave policy that Maganuco contests then is dependent not on the biological fact that pregnancy and childbirth cause some period of disability, but on a Leyden schoolteacher's choice to forego returning to work in favor of spending time at home with her newborn child." Id. at 444. The court distinguished earlier cases:

> The establishment of a maternity leave policy more favorable to recent mothers than other leave policies are to other employees does not itself violate Title VII [citing *Harness*]. The failure to allow fathers to avail themselves of a more generous child-raising leave available to women employees might [citing *Schafer*].

Id. at 445. See also Fisher v. Vasser College, 66 F.3d 379 (2d Cir. 1995) (no violation for college to deny tenure based in part on plaintiff's long absence from academia to bear and raise children; choice of remaining home for an extended period following birth of child is not the inevitable consequence of pregnancy or a medical condition related to pregnancy as required by the PDA).

In Barnes v. Hewlett-Packard Co., 846 F. Supp. 442, 443-444 (D.C. Md. 1994), the court wrote: "There is . . . a point at which pregnancy and immediate post-partum requirements—clearly gender-based in nature—end and gender-neutral child care activities begin. . . . [A]ttending to the medical needs of one of [Barnes'] children—the reason she requested parental leave—could have been administered as well by her husband as by herself." If the court had ruled in Barnes's favor, would it have been perpetuating stereotypical views regarding the child care responsibilities of women, precisely the sort of stereotypical views that Title VII was designed to undermine?

Page 545.   Add new Notes 28a, 28b, and 28c:

28a. Even though pregnancy-related medical conditions end shortly after pregnancy, an employee who is discriminated against months later may nonetheless be able to assert pregnancy-based discrimination. In Ribando v. United Airlines, 1994 WL 91985 (N.D. Ill. 1994), plaintiff, after giving birth to a child with significant medical problems, was singled out for disciplinary action, denied health insurance coverage, and then discharged. The plaintiff presented evidence that United did not treat as harshly as it had treated her similarly situated employees who had not been pregnant or delivered a child. The court stated:

> the actions taken against Ribando relevant to her [Title VII claim] may have been due to Ribando's child bearing and therefore also tend to demonstrate that Ribando was discriminated against because of her gender and pregnancy-related condition.

28b. In Turic v. Holland Hospitality, Inc., 849 F. Supp. 544 (W.D. Mich. 1994), the court held that the phrase "related medical conditions" encompasses a woman's constitutional right to have an abortion. Id. at 549. The court based its conclusions on the EEOC guidelines and the PDA's legislative history. The plaintiff did not actually have an abortion but was discharged because she contemplated having one, thereby offending the hotel's "very Christian staff." The court stated:

> It is clear that defendant's actions, and the employee uproar, were in response to plaintiff's consideration of abortion. It would be perverse to reward an employer's rapid termination in response to such a disclosure with insulation from liability, simply because it failed to wait and see what the employee would decide. For purposes of Title VII analysis, there is no rational distinction between an employee's communication of the fact that she intends to have an abortion, she is considering having an abortion, or she has had an abortion. Logic dictates that discharge on the basis of any of these "statuses" violates the PDA.

28c. Is infertility a "related medical condition" covered by the PDA? In Pacourek v. Inland Steel Co., 858 F. Supp. 1393 (N.D. Ill. 1994), the plaintiff was diagnosed with esphofical reflux, a medical condition that prevented her from becoming pregnant naturally. She began experimental treatments in order to become pregnant. Subsequently, her supervisor told her that her medical condition was "a problem" and placed her on probation. Later she was told that she was considered a "high risk" and would inevitably be terminated. Pacourek's complaint under the PDA alleged that she was reproached for trying to become pregnant, that her ability to combine pregnancy and a career was questioned, and that a leave policy was disparately applied against her.

The defendant argued that inability to become pregnant naturally is not a covered condition under the PDA. The court held that the PDA covers discrimination against employees based on intended or potential pregnancy: "discrimination against persons who intend to or can potentially become pregnant is discrimination against women, which is the kind of truism the PDA wrote into law." Id. at 1401. The court concluded that the PDA's expansive language and legislative history indicate that infertility is a pregnancy-related medical condition. In addition, the court drew support from *Johnson Controls*, which condemned as illegal under the PDA classification of employees on the basis of potential for pregnancy, and from *Turic*, which interpreted "related medical conditions" to include a woman's constitutional right to have an abortion:

> If the coverage of the PDA is thought of in concentric circles, discrimination based on the fact of being pregnant may be thought of as the core wrong that the PDA was meant to address, or the inner-most concentric circle. The next concentric circle might contain the abortion decision. The court can find no reason why the same circle that contains termination of a pregnancy would not also include the initiation of a pregnancy.

Id. at 1403. See also Cleese v. Hewlett-Packard Co., 911 F. Supp. 1312 (D. Or. 1995); Erickson v. Board of Governors of State Colleges and Universities for Northeastern Ill. Univ., 911 F. Supp. 316 (N.D. Ill. 1995).

Unless an employer knows that an employee has had a hysterectomy or tubal ligation, has experienced menopause, or is infertile and not seeking fertility treatment, the employer knows that any female employee could become pregnant. Under the reasoning in *Pacourek*, does PDA coverage of women have any limits? Can any adverse employment decision relating to a female employee be attributed to the employer's awareness of pregnancy potential?

Page 546. Add the following new text after note 31:

TROUPE v. MAY DEPARTMENT STORES CO.
20 F.3d 734 (7th Cir. 1994)

[Kimberly Hern Troupe, a department store saleswoman, had been placed on probation for repeated tardiness ascribed to severe morning sickness. During her probation Troupe was late to work 11 more days. On the day before she planned to begin her maternity leave, Troupe was fired. She testified at trial that her supervisor told her that the company terminated her because she was not expected to return to work after she had her baby. Troupe filed suit under the PDA.

In an opinion written by Judge Posner, the Seventh Circuit found that Troupe was not a victim of pregnancy discrimination. Although the timing of Troupe's discharge suggested discrimination, her repeated tardiness and her supervisor's statement that she was being terminated because no one expected her to return to work after her maternity leave suggested alternative explanations. Posner framed the main issue on appeal as whether termination of a pregnant employee to avoid paying the costs of maternity leave is discrimination under the PDA. Id. at 737. "Standing alone," he asserted, "it is not."]

If the discharge of an unsatisfactory worker were a purely remedial measure rather than also, or instead, a deterrent one, the inference that Troupe wasn't really fired because of her tardiness would therefore be a powerful one. But that is a big "if." We must remember that after two warnings Troupe had been placed on probation for sixty days and that she had violated the implicit terms of probation by being as tardy during the probationary period as she had been before. If the company did not fire her, its warnings and threats would seem empty. Employees would be encouraged to flout work rules knowing that the only sanction would be a toothless warning or a meaningless period of probation. . . .

[Title VII does not bar a financially motivated dismissal, but requires a finding that the employer] failed to exhibit similar rapacity toward similarly situated employees. . . .We must imagine a hypothetical Mr. Troupe, who is as tardy as Ms. Troupe was, also because of health problems, and who is about to take a protracted sick leave growing out of those problems at an expense to Lord & Taylor equal to that of Ms. Troupe's maternity leave. If Lord & Taylor would have fired our hypothetical Mr. Troupe, this implies that it fired Ms. Troupe not because she was pregnant but because she caused the company more than she was worth to it. . . .

Employers can treat pregnant women as badly as they treat similarly affected but nonpregnant employees. . . . The Pregnancy Discrimination Act requires the employer to ignore an employee's pregnancy, but . . . not her absence from work, unless the employer overlooks the comparable absences of nonpregnant employees . . . in which event it would not be ignoring pregnancy after all. . . .

Troupe would be halfway home if she could find one nonpregnant employee had not been fired when about to begin a leave similar in length to hers.

[The court observed that its emphasis on comparative evidence could pose problems for a plaintiff in a situation lacking a comparison group, but reserved that issue for a case in which it is raised.]

NOTES

1. David C. Wyld, in Morning Sickness: Testing the Proper Bounds of Employee Protection and Employer Prerogative Under the Pregnancy Discrimi-

nation Act, 46 Lab. L.J. 95 (1995), pointed out that the court gave "unusually candid" assessments of both Lord & Taylor's actions toward the plaintiff and the plaintiff's work record, and that these assessments did not endorse either party in the case.

2. Insofar as *Troupe* accepts as nondiscriminatory the employer's concern that Troupe might not come back after leave, scholars have argued that "Kimberly Troupe appears to have fallen victim to sex stereotyping" because Lord & Taylor would probably not have concluded that a similarly situated employee, about to take disability leave, would not return to work after the leave. See Ann C. McGinley & Jeffrey W. Stempel, Condescending Contradiction: Richard Posner's Pragmatism and Pregnancy Discrimination, 46 Fla. L. Rev. 193, 221 (1994). By permitting the defendant to assume that Troupe would not return to work after her baby was born, Posner allowed use of exactly the type of stereotype about women, especially pregnant women, that the PDA was intended to overcome. Id.

3. *Troupe*, like most courts, adopts the interpretation of the PDA that prohibits only conduct that treats pregnant women differently than "similarly situated" nonpregnant people. In *Troupe*, however, the court further narrows the statute's protection by adopting restrictive rules about proving different treatment based on pregnancy. Does the court take into account the significance of the employer's disability and maternity leave policy? Arguably, the court could have found discrimination because of policy: by adopting a leave policy, the employer may have acknowledged that employees would receive that leave as long as they met the stated requirements. Depriving Troupe of her leave in order to save money would be inconsistent with the written terms of such a policy, leaving no explanation for her termination other than her pregnancy. This approach adopts the "equal treatment" interpretation of the PDA, but allows plaintiffs to prove different treatment based on stated policy rather than actual conduct. Under such an approach, the employer could assert a nondiscriminatory reason for its conduct by pointing to nonpregnant individuals who were also denied leave. The plaintiff, however, in her prima facie case could rely on the employer's stated policy. Would the analysis be different if the employer fired Troupe for her past tardiness, not her prospective leave? What is the proper analysis if (as appeared to be the case) the employer claimed both motivations?

4. White v. Frank, 8 F.3d 823 (4th Cir. 1993), addressed the issue left open in *Troupe* regarding the unavailability of comparative evidence. In *White*, the Fourth Circuit held that the USPS did not discriminate against White, a pregnant letter-carrier, when it denied her requests for light duty during her three pregnancies. Although affirming the district court's finding that the governing collective bargaining agreement, apparently barring light duty to rural carriers, would not do so in all circumstances, the record contained no evidence that any rural carrier anywhere actually received a light duty assign-

ment. The Fourth Circuit, therefore, held that White had failed to prove that similarly situated rural carriers would have been granted light duty. See also Elie v. K-Mart Corp., 64 FEP Cases (BNA) 957 (E.D. La. 1994).

5. In Byrd v. Lakeshore Hosp., 30 F.3d 1380 (11th Cir. 1994), the Eleventh Circuit took a different approach, holding that an employee alleging pregnancy discrimination need not show that the employer provided better treatment to nonpregnant employees. The plaintiff, a receptionist/secretary at a private hospital, missed ten days of work within two months due to pregnancy-related medical complications. In compliance with Lakeshore's employee sick leave policy, the plaintiff applied accrued sick leave to her absences, giving her supervisors sufficient notice on each occasion. Nevertheless, Lakeshore fired her for unsatisfactory performance and unwillingness to accept supervision. The court of appeals specifically rejected the defendant's claim that Byrd must show that other employees were either granted the guaranteed sick leave benefits or retained despite using them. Id. at 1383. According to the court,

> the only logical inference to be drawn in this case is that the Lakeshore policy customarily was followed. A contrary result would amount to a presumption . . . that Lakeshore Hospital commonly discharges employees for taking their allotted sick leave time. If such is the case, then the burden was on Lakeshore to prove this unusual scenario. The effect of our decision today is simple: it is a violation of the PDA for an employer to deny a pregnant employee the benefits commonly afforded temporarily disabled workers in similar positions, or to discharge a pregnant employee for using those benefits.

Id. at 1383-1384.

6. Despite their apparently opposite approaches, *Byrd* can be reconciled with *White*. In *Byrd*, the defendant's sick leave policy promised that employees would accumulate sick leave at a stated rate. The court found that defendant's policy implied that employees are entitled to take their sick leave. Consequently, the plaintiff was not required to prove that other employees had been granted sick leave. In contrast, the collective bargaining agreement governing White's employment apparently forbade the type of assignment she requested. Even though the employer acknowledged that in some circumstances rural carriers could receive light duty, the court could not determine what those circumstances might be because no rural carrier had ever received light duty. It was not possible, therefore, for the court to determine from the employer's policy alone whether similarly situated nonpregnant employees would have received light duty.

7. When comparative evidence is available and demonstrates that similarly situated disabled individuals were treated in the same way as pregnant women, courts have declined to find any violation of the PDA. See, e.g., Dodd v. Riverside Health System, Inc., 1996 WL 29246 (10th Cir. 1996) (pregnant employee discharged after taking more than six weeks' maternity

leave not discriminatorily discharged because nonpregnant employees subject to same policy); EEOC v. Elgin Teachers Assn., 27 F.3d 292 (7th Cir. 1994) (no violation of PDA because pregnant teachers were not denied options that other teachers possessed under leave policy).

Page 552.   Add new Notes 9-11:

9. Many work rules, even if facially neutral and applied equally to all employees, have a disparate impact on pregnant workers. Some pregnant women have asserted that such rules violate the PDA. Most courts have found disparate impact analysis applicable under the PDA. See, e.g., Maganuco v. Leyden Community High Sch. Dist. 212, 939 F.2d 440, 445 (7th Cir. 1991) (disparate impact claim available under PDA); Chambers v. Omaha Girls Club, Inc., 834 F.2d 697 (8th Cir. 1987) (disparate impact available but employer's rule prohibiting employment of unmarried staff who become pregnant or cause pregnancy is justified under the business necessity defense); Hayes v. Shelby Memorial Hosp., 726 F.2d 1543 (11th Cir. 1984) (fetal protection policy challenged under disparate impact theory); Abraham v. Graphic Arts Intl. Union, 660 F.2d 811 (D.C. Cir. 1981) (ten-day limit on temporary disabilities could violate Title VII because of its disparate impact on pregnant women). Some courts, however, have interpreted the PDA to prohibit disparate treatment only. See, e.g., Troupe v. May Dept. Stores Co., 20 F.3d 734 (7th Cir. 1994) (disparate impact not available under PDA); Connors v. University of Tenn. Press, 558 F. Supp. 38, 41 (E.D. Tenn. 1982) (disparate impact not available under PDA).

10. In Armstrong v. Flowers Hosp., Inc., 33 F.3d 1308 (11th Cir. 1994), the court held that a pregnant nurse was not entitled to be excused from treating an HIV-positive patient to protect her fetus because the employer required all nurses to treat all patients. Armstrong refused to care for an HIV-positive patient out of fear that she would put her fetus at risk. A written hospital policy provided that refusing to treat a patient was grounds for termination. After the hospital discharged Armstrong, she sued under the PDA, arguing that pregnant employees were adversely impacted by her employer's inflexible policy.

Armstrong asserted the policy required a woman to choose between her job and the health of her fetus, affecting pregnant employees more harshly than others. She claimed that her employer, therefore, must make alternative work available for pregnant employees. Flowers responded that Armstrong's claims of discrimination were more accurately seen as seeking preferential treatment by rescheduling assignments for pregnant employees. A pregnant employee would be entitled to refuse to work on a given patient if she believed the patient posed a special risk to herself and her fetus, while nonpregnant employees would have no such right.

In rejecting Armstrong's disparate impact claim, the court stated that the PDA's legislative history makes it clear that the Act does not require employers to extend benefits to pregnant women that they do not provide to other disabled employees. Arguably, however, the health care service's policy did not have a cognizable impact even if disparate impact was applied. Armstrong did not allege that women disproportionately lost their jobs as a result of the policy. Rather, she argued that the policy had a disparate psychological impact on pregnant women.

11. Any question about whether disparate impact analysis applies in pregnancy discrimination cases may have been resolved by The Civil Rights Act of 1991, which provides, for the first time, a statutory basis for the judicially created disparate impact theory of discrimination. In confirming statutory authority for disparate impact claims, Congress made no exceptions of cases alleging pregnancy discrimination. Pub. L. No. 102-166, §3(3), 105 Stat. 1071 (1991). The legislative history of the PDA also supports the application of disparate impact analysis to pregnancy discrimination cases. See Deborah A. Calloway, Accommodating Pregnancy in the Workplace, 25 Stetson L. Rev. 1, 36-39 (1995).

Page 552.   Add the following new Note before the case heading:

NOTE ON ACCOMMODATING PREGNANCY UNDER THE AMERICANS WITH DISABILITIES ACT AND THE PDA

The Americans with Disabilities Act (ADA) requires employers to provide reasonable accommodations to the known physical limitations of otherwise qualified employees with disabilities, unless such accommodation would impose an undue hardship on the employer. 42 U.S.C. §12112(b)(5)(A). In order to be qualified, an individual must be able to perform the essential functions of the job in question. Under the ADA, an "individual with a disability" is a person who has or is perceived to have "an impairment that substantially limits one or more of the major life activities" of the individual. 42 U.S.C. §12102(2)(A). See Chapter 8 for a complete discussion of the ADA. The EEOC's interpretive guidance concludes that pregnancy is not an impairment, and pregnant women, therefore, are not entitled to the ADA's protection. 29 C.F.R. pt. 1630 app. §§1630.2(h), (j). The EEOC's regulations, however, are not binding on courts, and courts generally will not defer to regulations if they interpret statutory language unreasonably or inconsistently with legislative intent. See Chapter 8. One commentator has argued that the EEOC's interpretation of the ADA's coverage conflicts with legislative intent. Colette G. Matzzie, Substantive Equality and Antidiscrimination: Accommodating Pregnancy Under the Americans with Disabilities Act, 82 Geo. L.J. 193 (1993). The argument is that the ADA's broad language, the absence of an explicit statutory exclusion for pregnancy, and Congress's broad remedial purpose in enacting the ADA all support including pregnancy within its coverage. Id. at 217-218.

Even if the ADA does not directly protect pregnant women, however, the ADA may affect employers' willingness to accommodate pregnancy. Pregnancy is a disabling condition. The ADA is likely to raise the expectations of pregnant employees, who will view their situations as comparable to those of individuals who are disabled by accidents or illness and will demand similar accommodations. Deborah Calloway, Accommodating Pregnancy in the Workplace, 25 Stetson L. Rev. 1, 29-30 (1995).

One commentator has argued that, even without direct ADA coverage, pregnant women may demand the same accommodations to which disabled employees are entitled. Thus, individuals covered by the ADA may, like pregnant women, require leave from work to see a doctor. Also like pregnant women, disabled employees may be unable to conform to rigid work rules or perform job functions such as climbing stairs and lifting heavy weights. If an employer, in compliance with the ADA's reasonable accommodation requirement, grants leave, provides flexible work rules, or assigns a disabled employee to light duty, the PDA may require that employer to provide the same accommodations to pregnant employees who have similar requirements. More broadly, if an employer adopts a general policy of accommodating the needs of disabled individuals, which all employers covered by the ADA must do, the PDA requires that employer to apply the same policy to women disabled by pregnancy. Id. at 30.

Page 554.   Add new Note 6a:

6a. Women have sometimes successfully challenged adverse decisions by employers based on unwed pregnancy. See, e.g., Cumpiano aka Cumpiano Sanchez v. Banco Santander Puerto Rico, 902 F.2d 148 (1st Cir. 1990); Jacobs v. Martin Sweets Co., 550 F.2d 364 (6th Cir. 1977); Avery v. Homewood City Bd. of Educ., 674 F.2d 337 (5th Cir. 1982). Employers, however, have taken several different approaches to justify discharging unwed pregnant females. In Harvey v. Young Womens Christian Assn., 533 F. Supp. 949 (S.D.N.C. 1982), the court found that discharging a woman for an unwed pregnancy was justified by the YWCA's philosophy. Because the YWCA is a religious institution, the real basis for this holding may be that the YWCA's decision fell within the exemption for religious employers.

The court in Boyd v. Harding Academy of Memphis, 887 F. Supp. 157 (W.D. Tenn. 1995), approached a similar case by finding that the employer's actions were based on a legitimate nondiscriminatory reason. The *Boyd* court ruled that Harding Academy, a religious school, did not violate Title VII when it discharged an unmarried pregnant teacher for violating the New Testament's proscription of premarital sex. The defendant testified that Boyd had not been terminated because of her pregnancy per se, but because her pregnancy indicated that she had engaged in sex outside of marriage. The Academy demonstrated that it had consistently terminated both male and female employees who engaged in sex outside of marriage, whether or not pregnancy resulted from the conduct. In addition, many married women had become pregnant while working at the Academy and had remained employed during and after their pregnancies. Similarly, in Kelly v. K.D. Construction of Fla., 866 F. Supp. 1406 (S.D. Fla. 1994), the court granted summary judgment to an employer who terminated an employee who was pregnant with a co-worker's child. Initially, before Kelly disclosed that a co-worker had fathered the child, her employer seemed pleased at the news of her pregnancy. When, however, the employer learned of Kelly's affair with a co-worker, he discharged both employees. The court accepted the defendant's claim that Kelly was dismissed, not because she was pregnant, but because she had an affair with another high-level company employee. The evidence showed that earlier, after Kelly had an affair with another high-level employee, her employer had warned her that he would not accept such behavior in the future.

2. Sexual Harassment

Page 563.   Add the following new text to Note 3:

Although past conduct may be relevant to the question of whether sexual advances were unwelcome, Rule 412 of the Federal Rules of Evidence regulates the admissibility of evidence of past sexual conduct. In trials relating to sexual misconduct, Rule 412 makes inadmissible

> evidence offered to prove that any alleged victim engaged in other sexual behavior . . . [or] . . . to prove any alleged victim's sexual predisposition . . . [unless] its probative value substantially outweighs the danger of harm to any victim and of unfair prejudice to any party. Evidence of an alleged victim's reputation is admissible only if it has been placed in controversy by the alleged victim.

Page 563.   Add the following new text to Note 5:

Similarly, in EEOC v. Domino's Pizza, 909 F. Supp. 1529 (M.D. Fla. 1995), the court awarded $237,257 to a male restaurant manager who was fired after turning down his supervisor's sexual advances. Theoretically, complaints by male employees should be subject to the same analysis as claims by female employees.

Page 564.   Add the following new text to carryover Note 6:

See Carr v. Allison Gas Turbine Div., 32 F.3d 1007 (7th Cir. 1994) (inquiry into plaintiff's personal and home-life problems would have been appropriate if she had been seeking damage for mental anguish caused by sexual harassment).

Page 565.   Add the following new text after "(a classifica-
tion courts have held is not protected under title
VII)." in the first full paragraph:

Cf. Pritchett v. Sizeler Real Estate Mgmt., 67 FEP Cases 1377 (E.D. La. 1995) (although Title VII does not protect a homosexual who is discriminated against based on sexual orientation, "to conclude that same gender harassment is not actionable under Title VII is to exempt homosexuals from the very laws that govern the workplace conduct of heterosexual").

Page 565.   Add the following new text after "such as
personal dislike, it is not actionable?" in the
first full paragraph:

See Vandeventer v. Wabash Natl. Corp., 867 F. Supp. 790 (N.D. Ind. 1994) (plaintiff not harassed "because he was a man"; rather he "was 'razzed' in a way designed to be the most annoying to him personally").

Page 565.   Add the following new text at the end of the
first full paragraph:

The question whether Title VII covers same-sex harassment has been the subject of numerous recent opinions. Most courts addressing this issue have ruled in favor of Title VII liability. See, e.g., Prescott v. Independent Life & Accident, 67 FEP Cases 876 (M.D. Ala. 1995) (Title VII's ban on "sex" discrimination covers homosexual as well as heterosexual harassment); EEOC v. Walden Book Co., 885 F. Supp. 1100 (M.D. Tenn. 1995) ("[i]t would simply be untenable to allow reverse discrimination cases but not same-sex sexual harassment cases under Title VII"; "When a homosexual supervisor is making offensive sexual advances to a subordinate of the same sex, and not doing so to employees of the opposite sex, it absolutely is a situation where, but for the subordinate's sex, he would not be subjected to that treatment"); Ecklund v. Fuisz Technology, 905 F. Supp. 335 (E.D. Va. 1995) (female former employee allegedly harassed by female co-worker may sue for sexual harassment because she was harassed solely because she is female); Sardinia v. Dellwood Foods, Inc., 69 FEP Cases 705 (S.D.N.Y. 1995) (male employee who claims that male supervisors grabbed his genitals or his buttocks and made sexual comments to him states claim of discrimination because of sex); Pritchett v. Sizeler Real Estate Mgmt., 67 FEP Cases 1377 (E.D. La. 1995) (sexual harassment of female subordinate by female supervisor is gender discrimination because "but for" her gender, she would not have been subjected to harassment); Raney v. District of Columbia, 892 F. Supp. 283 (D.C. 1995) (Title VII encompasses male employee's claim that he was sexually harassed by male supervisor); King v. M.R. Brown, Inc., 911 F. Supp. 161 (E.D. Penn. 1995) (same-sex sexual harassment is actionable under Title VII).

A number of courts, however, including two circuit courts, have ruled that same-sex harassment is not actionable under Title VII. See, e.g., Garcia v. Elf Atochem, 28 F.3d 446 (5th Cir. 1994) (Title VII does not cover same-sex sexual harassment); Ulane v. Eastern Airlines, 742 F.2d 1081 (7th Cir. 1984), cert. denied, 471 U.S. 1017 (1985) (same); Fredette v. BVP Management Assocs., 905 F. Supp. 1034 (M.D. Fla. 1995) (same-sex harassment not actionable under Title VII; harassment based not on fact that employee is a man, but on the fact that he refused manager's propositions and did not share his sexual orientation); Hopkins v. Baltimore Gas & Electric Co., 871 F. Supp. 822 (D. Md. 1994) (it would strain the language of Title VII "beyond its manifest intent" to hold that sexual harassment against someone of the same gender constitutes sex discrimination); Benekritis v. Johnson, 882 F. Supp. 521 (D.S.C. 1995) (same-sex harassment not the type of conduct Congress intended to prohibit when it enacted Title VII).

In the most recent court of appeals ruling on this issue, the Fourth Circuit held that a hostile environment employment discrimination claim does not lie where both the alleged harassers and the victim are heterosexuals of the same sex. The taunting and sexual remarks endured by the plaintiff in that case were "shameful" but not "because" of the offended worker's sex as required by the statute. The court speculated that the alleged harassing conduct was

"because of" the victim's known or believed prudery, or shyness, or other form of vulnerability to sexually-focussed speech or conduct. Perhaps "because of" the perpetrators' own sexual perversion, or obsession, or insecurity. Certainly, "because of" their vulgarity and insensitivity and meanness of spirit. But not specifically "because of" the victim's sex.

McWilliams v. Fairfax Cty. Bd. of Supervisors, 72 F.3d 1191 (4th Cir. 1996) What approach is most persuasive? Why?

Several courts that have found no liability in same-sex harassment cases have justified this result on the ground that Title VII's prohibition against sexual harassment is designed to prevent an atmosphere that denigrates women and interferes with female employment opportunities. These courts view sexual harassment liability primarily as a means of preventing the dominant male work culture from repressing women and as therefore inapplicable to male harassment of male employees in a male-dominated workplace. See, e.g., Mayo v. Kiwest Corp., 898 F. Supp. 335 (E.D. Va. 1995) (male supervisor's harassment of male subordinate does not prevent men from having the same employment opportunities as women); Vandeventer v. Wabash Natl. Corp., 867 F. Supp. 790 (N.D. Ind. 1994) (same-sex harassment not actionable under Title VII; statute is "aimed at gender-biased atmosphere; an atmosphere of oppression by a 'dominant' gender"); Goluszek v. Smith, 697 F. Supp. 1452 (N.D. Ill. 1988) (same-sex harassment not covered because actionable sexual harassment "is the exploitation of a powerful position to impose sexual demands or pressures on an unwilling but less powerful person"; harassment of male employee by male employee in male-dominated environment not cognizable).

One court that recognized a Title VII claim for same-sex harassment noted the illogic of exempting such behavior from coverage:

> To deny a claim of same gender sexual harassment allows a homosexual supervisor to sexually harass his or her subordinates either on a quid pro quo basis or by creating a hostile work environment, when a heterosexual supervisor may be sued under Title VII for similar conduct. Although it is clear that Title VII does not protect a homosexual who is discriminated against based on his or her sexual orientation, here it is not the homosexual who seeks to be protected.

Pritchett v. Sizeler Real Estate Mgmt., 67 FEP Cases 1377, 1379 (D. La. 1995).

Employers should be advised that, in jurisdictions recognizing same-sex harassment liability under Title VII, damages can be quite extensive. See, e.g., EEOC v. Walden Book Co., 885 F. Supp. 1100 (M.D. Tenn. 1995) (jury awarded $1.6 million in punitive damages and $75,000 in compensatory damages to male victim of same-sex harassment).

Page 566.   ***Add the following new text at the end of the carryover paragraph:***

Similarly, the Ninth Circuit, in Steiner v. Showboard Operating Co., 25 F.3d 1459 (9th Cir. 1994), found actionable sexual harassment despite the fact that a supervisor abused both male and female employees. The court found that the nature of his abuse of women was different and more sexually explicit than his abuse of men, some of which involved racial harassment. The court, however, noted that even if the supervisor used sexual epithets and sexual references in an equally degrading manner with men, that would not "cure" the harassment directed toward the women—it is possible that both male and female employees have viable claims against the same supervisor for sexual harassment. Id.

Page 566.   Add the following new text at the end of the first full paragraph:

Several courts have stated or held that, in order to have a cognizable sexual harassment claim, the perpetrator must single out employees of one gender. See, e.g., Raney v. District of Columbia, 892 F. Supp. 283 (D.C. 1995) (Title VII protections are invoked if bisexual supervisor singles out employees of one sex for harassment); EEOC v. Walden Book Co., 885 F. Supp. 1100 (M.D. Tenn. 1995) ("when a homosexual supervisor is making offensive sexual advances to a subordinate of same sex, *and not doing so to employees of the opposite sex*," victim of harassment states a claim under Title VII); Fox v. Sierra Dev. Co., 876 F. Supp. 1169 (D. Nev. 1995) (work environment saturated with homosexual reference is not discriminatory, because it is potentially abusive or hostile to men and women in equal measure); Ryczek v. Guest Services, Inc., 877 F. Supp. 754 (D.C. 1995) (sexual harassment by a supervisor who is bisexual is not a Title VII violation because the harassment would apply to both men and women).

Page 566.   Add the following new text after the final paragraph:

In Childress v. City of Richmond, 907 F. Supp. 934 (E.D. Va. 1995), male and female police officers complained about vulgar sex-biased comments made by their male supervisor about female officers. The court held that, although the female officers stated a claim of sexual harassment, the male officers did not have standing to challenge remarks that discriminated against female officers. See also Ramirez v. Bravo's Holding Co., 67 FEP Cases 733 (D. Kan. 1995) (male supervisor may not seek damages for emotional distress stemming from work environment that is sexually hostile to women he supervised). In addition, insofar as the male officers were offended, the court held that Title VII does not cover same-sex harassment unless it is either quid pro quo or involves a sexual component.

Page 568. Add the following new text at the end of the carryover paragraph:

The Seventh Circuit has ruled that a white district sales manager's use of the word "nigger" on just two occasions constituted racial harassment even though black employees in the same workplace sometimes used the word. Rodgers v. Western-Southern Life Ins. Co., 12 F.3d 668 (7th Cir. 1993).

Page 568. Add the following new text at the end of the second full paragraph:

The EEOC's proposed regulation proved controversial, particularly with respect to its definition of "reasonable" as encompassing the perspective of the victim. The proposed guidelines have been withdrawn. 59 Fed. Reg. 51396. The EEOC's regulations on gender harassment that is sexual in nature are treated separately and do not specify the perspective from which sexual harassment must be assessed.

Page 573. Add the following new text Note 1:

A number of courts have applied the *Harris* standard. In DeAngelis v. El Paso M.P.O. Assn., 51 F.3d 591 (5th Cir. 1995), the Fifth Circuit held that derogatory conduct does not constitute actionable harassment unless it is sufficiently egregious to alter conditions of employment and destroy equal employment opportunity. The court rejected a harassment claim based on four derogatory references to a female police sergeant printed in a police union newsletter at irregular intervals over a period of two and one-half years. In Davis v. Chevron U.S.A., Inc., 14 F.3d 1082 (5th Cir. 1994), the same court concluded that staring at a female applicant from the neck down does not constitute direct evidence of sexual harassment where the applicant was in poor physical condition and was applying for a physically demanding job. Similarly, the Seventh Circuit found insufficient evidence of sexual harassment where an employee alleged that her supervisor fondled and forcibly kissed her during an after-work meeting at a nightclub and, weeks later, made forcible advances in a park on the way back to work after lunch. The employee admonished the supervisor and, after the incident in the park, there were no further incidents. The behavior, while inappropriate, was not actionable because, even if the plaintiff felt harassed, a reasonable person would not have considered the relatively isolated incidents sufficiently severe to constitute harassment. See Saxton v. AT&T, 10 F.3d 526 (7th Cir. 1993).

Are these results consistent with the standard articulated in *Harris*?

Page 573. Add the following new text to Note 2:

In Faragher v. City of Boca Raton, 76 F.3d 1155 (11th Cir. 1996), the court concluded that one of the plaintiffs did not satisfy the "subjectively harassed" prong of the *Harris* test because she "tolerated such conduct not because she felt she had to but because it wasn't that important to her." The court ruled that it was insufficient that she found her employer's conduct to be offensive after the fact:

> Title VII is not violated when the victim of harassment does not perceive her work environment to be abusive at the time that she is employed. . . . An employee's conditions of employment are not affected by what happens after she resigns. After-the-fact realization of the offensiveness of conduct thus does not satisfy *Harris*; it is irrelevant to whether the employee's conditions of employment were altered.

Id. at. 1161 *16. The court also indicated that the district court should not have relied on any conduct of which the plaintiff was unaware in determining that the harassment was severe and pervasive.

Page 573. Add the following new text to Note 4:

The Seventh Circuit found insufficient evidence of harassment in Baskerville v. Culligan Intl. Co., 50 F.3d 428 (7th Cir. 1995), where a secretary cited nine incidents involving her supervisor over a six-month period, including his calling her a pretty girl, grunting in approval of a leather skirt, saying his office was hot after she came in, and saying he was lonely in his hotel room. The court noted that the supervisor never touched or assaulted the plaintiff, never asked her to have sex, never threatened her or exposed himself or showed her dirty pictures. "He never said anything to her that could not be repeated on prime-time television." Id. at 431.

Page 573. Add the following subsequent history after
*   Vance v. Southern Bell Tel. & Tel. in Note 5:*

, *cert. denied*, 115 S. Ct. 1546 (1995)

Page 573. Add the following new text at the end of Note 5:

On whether a single incident of severe harassment is actionable, the Second Circuit, in Tomka v. Seiler Corp., 66 F.3d 1295 (2d Cir. 1995), held that a plaintiff can make out a harassment claim based on a single incident that sufficiently alters the conditions of her employment. In *Tomka*, the plaintiff alleged that she was raped by three managers following a business dinner. Id. at 1300.

Page 574. Add the following new text to carryover Note 7:

As already noted, see page 123, this supplement (casebook page 568), the EEOC's proposed regulation proved controversial, particularly with respect to its definition of "reasonable" as encompassing the perspective of the victim. The proposed guidelines have been withdrawn. 59 Fed. Reg. 51396. The EEOC's regulations on gender harassment that is sexual in nature are treated separately and do not specify the perspective from which sexual harassment must be assessed.

Page 578. Add the following new text to Note 2:

The debate over the appropriate standard for assessing reasonableness in the context of discriminatory harassment cases has attracted considerable attention in the academic community. See, e.g., Nancy Ehrenreich, Pluralist Myths and Powerless Men: The Ideology of Reasonableness in Sexual Harassment Law, 99 Yale L.J. 1177, 1207-1208 (1990) (men tend to view some forms of sexual harassment as "harmless social interactions to which only overly-sensitive women would object"); Kathryn Abrams, Gender Discrimination and the Transformation of Workplace Norms, 42 Vand. L. Rev. 1183, 1203 (1989) (the characteristically male view depicts sexual harassment as comparatively harmless amusement); Robert Adler & Ellen Pierce, The Legal, Ethical, and Social Implications of the "Reasonable Woman" Standard in Sexual Harassment Cases, 61 Fordham L. Rev. 772 (1993); Comment, Sexual Harassment Claims of Abusive Work Environment Under Title VII, 97 Harv. L. Rev. 1449, 1459 (1984).

Page 579. Add the following new text to Note 5:

On remand, the district court concluded that Harris's case must be limited to the single harassing incident that occurred after she complained because, although the company president had made some inappropriate comments and gestures before she complained, he was unaware that she was offended until she informed him that his remarks and conduct were unwelcome. Harris v. Forklift Systems, Inc., 66 FEP Cases 1886 (M.D. Tenn. 1994).

Page 583.   Add the following new text to Note 2:

Neither *Burns* nor *Meritor* directly considered whether "welcoming" is a question of objective appearance or subjective interest. If it is an objective issue, neither court considers whether the victim's allegedly welcoming conduct should be viewed from the perspective of a reasonable person or, perhaps, a reasonable man. The definition of "unwelcome" used by both courts, requiring the conduct to be both uninvited and offensive, suggests that "welcomeness" is a subjective issue. In Henson v. City of Dundee, 682 F.2d 897 (11th Cir. 1982), the Eleventh Circuit expressly adopted a subjective standard, stating that the conduct "must be unwelcome in the sense that the employee regarded the conduct as undesirable or offensive." Id. at 905.

Does a women who has a private consensual sexual relationship with a married co-worker "welcome" sexual advances at work? See Stacks v. Southwestern Bell Yellow Pages, Inc., 27 F.3d 1316 (8th Cir. 1994) (no).

Page 583.   Add the following new text to Note 3:

In determining whether a victim's behavior precludes recovery because she welcomed sexually charged comments or behavior, most courts seem to weigh the victim's conduct against that of the alleged perpetrators. Thus, in Carr v. Allison Gas Turbine, 32 F.3d 1007 (7th Cir. 1994), the Seventh Circuit ruled that plaintiff's bawdy behavior and use of foul language could not constitute welcoming behavior justifying four years of extensive sexual harassment by many men that included derogatory comments of a sexual nature, foul names, sex-related pranks, sexual graffiti, and sexual pictures. In Balletti v. Sun-Sentinel Co., 909 F. Supp. 1539 (S.D. Fla. 1995), the court used a similar analysis to foreclose a harassment claim by a woman who acknowledged that she joined in the frequent gags in her workplace, engaged in vulgarities with her co-workers, and on one occasion grabbed a male co-worker's pants pockets and tried to pull down his pants, ripping them and exposing his buttocks. The court noted that this behavior was worse than anything she complained about and concluded: "These are not the actions of an employee who subjectively perceives her work environment to be abusive or of one who seeks to convey to her co-workers that their behaviors are unwelcome." Id. at 1548.

Page 583.   Add the following new text to Note 4:

In Weinsheimer v. Rockwell, 57 FEP Cases 1224 (11th Cir. 1991), the Eleventh Circuit held that an employee who once welcomed sexual or vulgar actions at work must show that at some point she made co-workers and her employer aware that such conduct would no longer be welcome.

Page 585.   Add new Note 10a:

10a. A final question with respect to welcoming behavior has not yet been litigated in the circuit courts but is quite likely to arise. The question relates to establishments such as the Hooters restaurant chain, which hires females as waitresses, dresses them in outfits designed to be provocative, and advertises not just its food, but its sexually attractive personnel. If a waitress in such an establishment complains of sexual harassment by customers, can the employer say that she welcomed harassment by taking the job or that putting up with some level of harassment is a bfoq? The same question arises with respect to dancers in clubs.

Page 585.   Add the following subsequent history after the
citation to De Cintio v. Westchester County
Medical Center in the second paragraph of the
Note on "Reverse Harassment":

, *cert. denied*, 484 U.S. 825 (1987)

Page 587.   Add the following new text at the end of the
carryover paragraph:

In Dirksen v. City of Springfield, 842 F. Supp. 1117 (C.D. Ill. 1994), the court found quid pro quo harassment where a supervisor explicitly told the plaintiff that promotion was conditioned on sexual relations with him and then, while the plaintiff was on leave, replaced her with a woman with whom he was having a sexual relationship and placed the plaintiff in a dead-end job.

Page 587.   Add the following new text at the end of the
first full paragraph:

In another sexual favoritism case, Thompson v. Olson, No. A2-94-23 (D.N.D. 1994), the court followed this reasoning, holding that workplace advantages granted to a female worker who was having a romantic relationship with her supervisor did not constitute sexual harassment of a male co-worker. The supervisor preferred the co-worker not because of her gender, but because of their romantic relationship. On the other hand, in Phillips v. Martin Marietta, 400 U.S. 532 (1971), an employer refused to hire women with pre-school-age children because of concerns about absenteeism. The Court held this to be sex discrimination. The fact that sex plus some other factor—young children—caused the discrimination did not mean that it was not sex discrimination. Harassing a particular woman could be characterized the same way—sex plus attractiveness.

Page 593. Add the following new citation after Kotcher *v. Rosa and Sullivan Applicance Ctr., Inc., in Note 8:*

; Lankford v. City of Hobart, 27 F.3d 477 (10th Cir. 1994) (city may be liable for harassing actions of police chief; chief may be agent because he exercises some control over hirings, firings, promotions, demotions, and other conditions of employment).

Page 594. Add the following new text to carryover Note 8:

The Second Circuit, in Karibian v. Columbia Univ., 14 F.3d 773 (2d Cir. 1994), ruled that, in a quid pro quo case, the employer is strictly liable because the quid pro quo harasser, by definition, wields the employer's authority to alter terms and conditions of employment either in fact or apparently. In addition, the court held that it is not necessary in a quid pro quo case for the employee to demonstrate actual economic loss; threatened loss is sufficient.

Page 595. Add the following new text to Note 13:

In Bouton v. BMW of North Am., Inc., 29 F.3d 103 (3d Cir. 1994), the Third Circuit held that the actions of even a high-level supervisor cannot be imputed to the employer if the employer maintains an effective grievance procedure: "[A]n effective grievance procedure—one that is known to the victim and that timely stops the harassment—shields the employer from Title VII liability for a hostile environment. . . . A policy known to potential victims . . . eradicates apparent authority the harasser might otherwise possess." Id. at 110. The District of Columbia Circuit took the same approach in a case in which a supervisor allegedly raped an employee, but the employer maintained a well-published and enforced sexual harassment policy and had no notice of the supervisor's harassing conduct until after the incident. Gary v. Long, 59 F.3d 1391 (D.C. Cir. 1995) (supervisor not an agent because he was acting outside of his scope of authority). In order to be effective to preclude liability, employees must be aware of the policy and feel free to report harassment without adverse consequences.

*Page 598.   Add the following new text after "Title VII" in
the carryover sentence:*

In Menchaca v. Rose Records, Inc., 67 FEP Cases 1334 (N.D. Ill. 1995), the
court held that an employer whose store manager observed a regular customer
harassing a cashier can be liable under Title VII.

*Page 598.   Add the following new citation at the end of the
third full paragraph in the Note on Adequate
Responses to Sexual Harassment:*

See also Reed v. Delta Air Lines, 19 F.3d 19 (6th Cir. 1994) (employer who
fired supervisor as soon as it learned of harassment not liable).

*Page 599.   Add the following new citation at the end of the
carryover paragraph:*

See Fuller v. City of Oakland, 47 F.3d 1522 (9th Cir. 1995) (employer who
failed to act because it believed harassment had ended was liable; inaction
ratifies prior harassment even if harasser chooses to cease misconduct).

*Page 600.   Add the following new citation after "879 F.2d
at 107" in the carryover sentence:*

See also Spicer v. Virginia, 44 F.3d 218 (4th Cir. 1995) (counseling and training sessions immediately after complaint were not an adequate response; sessions were haphazard, no employees were disciplined, and the harassment
continued).

*Page 600.   Add the following new text at the end of the
first full paragraph:*

The Eleventh Circuit held that an employer was not shielded from liability
for the harassment of several female employees even though the victims
failed to take advantage of the employer's procedures specifically designed to
deal with sexual harassment complaints. The employees' failure to use the
procedures was relevant to whether the employer was aware of the harass-

ment, but other evidence indicated that the employer had actual knowledge. Cross v. State of Alabama, 49 F.3d 1490 (11th Cir. 1995).

Page 601. *Add the following new text at the end of the carryover paragraph:*

In Saxton v. AT&T Co., 10 F.3d 526 (7th Cir. 1993), the Seventh Circuit ruled that prompt investigation and transfer of the offending supervisor constituted an adequate response. See Carmon v. Lubrizol Corp., 17 F.3d 791 (5th Cir. 1994); Nash v. Electrospace System, Inc., 9 F.3d 401 (5th Cir. 1993); Gary v. Long, 59 F.3d 1391 (D.C. Cir. 1995) (same).

Page 601. *Add the following new text at the end of the first full paragraph:*

Employers who have disciplined harassers have been sued, sometimes successfully, for violating the employment rights of the harassing employee. See, e.g., Chalmers v. Quaker Oats Co., 61 F.3d 1340 (7th Cir. 1995) (employer did not violate ERISA when it denied severance benefits to former vice president after discharging him for violating company policy against sexual harassment even though conduct may not have been sufficiently severe to violate Title VII; employer is free to take a more stringent stance against harassment); Scherer v. Rockwell Intl. Corp., 975 F.2d 356 (7th Cir. 1992) (employer must give executive with employment contract three years' notice of termination before discharging him unless he is guilty of misconduct, including sexual harassment; good faith belief that supervisor was guilty of sexual harassment would be insufficient to justify discharge without notice); Customized Transportation, Inc., 102 LA 1179 (1994) (discharge for racial harassment excessive in absence of effective progressive discipline). In Pierce v. Commonwealth Life Ins. Co., 40 F.3d 796 (6th Cir. 1994), a supervisor demoted for violating the employer's sexual harassment policy asserted that because the victim, who was a willing participant, was not disciplined, he was a victim of reverse discrimination. The court, however, ruled that his status as a supervisor was a legitimate nondiscriminatory reason justifying the different treatment. See also Castleberry v. Boeing Co., 880 F. Supp. 1435 (D. Kan. 1995) (two male managers and a female nonmanager bought and displayed a sex gadget for an employee; firing the managers while only suspending the nonmanager did not constitute reverse discrimination).

Page 608.   Add the following new text at the bottom of the page:

In the public sector, the Supreme Court has developed First Amendment doctrine outside of the harassment context to accommodate both government employees' free speech rights and government employers' interest in controlling the behavior of their own employees in the workplace. In this context, the Court has ruled that public employees may not be disciplined or discharged for engaging in speech on a matter of public concern unless the government can assert some interest in restricting that speech, such as disruption of the workplace, that outweighs the employees' interest in speaking. See Charles A. Sullivan, Deborah A. Calloway & Michael J. Zimmer, Cases and Materials on Employment Law 647-759 (1993). Most of the cases in which employees have asserted First Amendment defenses to disciplinary responses to sexual and racial harassment have arisen in the context of public employment. Both prongs of the analysis are illustrated by Tindle v. Caudell, 56 F.3d 966 (8th Cir. 1995), in which the Eighth Circuit found that an employee who was suspended for appearing in blackface at an office Halloween party was not protected by the First Amendment. The costume was not intended to express any message on a matter of public concern and the employee's interest in wearing the costume did not outweigh the department's interest in maintaining discipline and harmonious working relationships. Id. at 971. See also Jeffries v. Harleston, 52 F.3d 9 (2d Cir. 1995) (demotion of state college professor for anti-Semitic remarks does not violate the First Amendment because trustees who voted to demote the professor reasonably believed that the speech would disrupt college operations). Similarly, the Sixth Circuit held that a university coach's discharge for using the word "nigger" in addressing players did not violate the First Amendment because his speech did not involve a matter of public concern and the university had a countervailing interest in defining valid means of motivating players. In the course of its opinion, however, the court stated that the university's policy prohibiting behavior "that subjects an individual to an intimidating, hostile or offensive educational, employment or living environment" is overbroad, vague, and a content- and viewpoint-discrimination violation of the First Amendment. Dambrot v. Central Mich. Univ., 55 F.3d 1177 (6th Cir. 1995).

Employees in one public employee sexual harassment case prevailed on the basis of the First Amendment. In Johnson v. Los Angeles Cty. Fire Dept., 865 F. Supp. 1430 (C.D. Cal. 1994), a county fire department prohibited employees from reading Playboy magazine in private at the workplace. The court concluded that reading the magazine amounts to expression relating to matters of public concern because it contains articles concerning politics, sports, arts, and entertainment. The ban was content-oriented because it was based on the department's disagreement with the manner in which the magazine portrays women. The department's interest in eliminating sexual harassment was not weighty enough to support a content-based restriction.

Page 609. Add the following new citations at the end of the first paragraph:

See also McGanty v. Staudenraus, 901 P.2d 841 (Or. Sup. Ct. 1995) (employee who alleges sexual harassment and abuse by supervisor and that employer knew or should have known these acts would cause severe emotional distress states a claim for intentional infliction of emotional distress even though she did not allege that supervisor or employer had specific purpose of inflicting distress); Truman v. United States, 26 F.3d 592 (11th Cir. 1994) (sexual harassment claim for intentional infliction of emotional distress not barred by Federal Tort Claims Act's exceptions to waiver of sovereign immunity); Dennis v. Consolidated Rail Corp., 1994 U.S. Dist. LEXIS 12716 (E.D. Pa. 1994) (allegation that manager grabbed and squeezed an employee's buttocks during a department Christmas luncheon states a claim for negligent infliction of emotional distress cognizable under the Federal Employers' Liability Act).

Page 610. Add the following citation after McMormick v. A.T.& T. Technologies, Inc. in the carryover paragraph:

and Baker v. Farmers Elec. Co-op, Inc., 34 F.3d 274 (5th Cir. 1994) (claim preempted)

3. Grooming and Dress Codes

Page 620. Add new Note 16:

16. Litigants with complaints regarding grooming and dress codes should also explore the possibility of a claim under state or local antidiscrimination provisions. The District of Columbia Human Rights Act, for example, prohibits discrimination based on personal appearance. D.C. Code Ann. §1-2501-2514. In a recent case, a transsexual employee stated a claim for personal appearance discrimination under that provision. The employee allegedly was discharged "because she is a transsexual and retains some masculine traits." Underwood v. Archer Management Servs., Inc., 857 F. Supp. 96 (D.C. 1994).

4. *Sexual Orientation*

Page 627. *Add new Notes 11a and 11b:*

11a. In Romer v. Evans, 116 S. Ct. — (1996), the Court struck down an amendment to the Colorado state constitution. Justice Kennedy's majority opinion in *Romer* (joined by Justices Stevens, O'Connor, Souter, Ginsburg, and Breyer) holds unconstitutional Amendment 2 of the Colorado Constitution, which invalidates all local ordinances protecting persons from discrimination by reason of their sexual orientation.

The core of the majority's opinion is that equal protection does not allow classifications to be drawn for the sole purpose of disadvantaging a group. The Court found that "the amendment imposes a special disability upon those persons [homosexuals] alone." Since the sole purpose of Amendment 2 is a backlash against homosexual conduct and by extension, homosexuals, there was no rational relation of the Amendment to any legitimate state interest. "Amendment 2 classifies homosexuals not to further a proper legislative end but to make them unequal to everyone else."

The dissent in *Romer*, authored by Justice Scalia and joined by Chief Justice Rehnquist and Justice Thomas, would uphold the constitutionality of Colorado's Amendment 2 because it "prohibits special treatment of homosexuals, and nothing more." Because the majority did not overrule Bowers v. Hardwick, which upheld criminalizing certain homosexual conduct, the Court could not logically invalidate the lesser state action of prohibiting localities from making discrimination against homosexuals illegal. Justice Scalia believed the majority has entangled the Court in a "kulturekampf" over whether a state may democratically deny homosexuals preferential treatment. The dissent would allow the state to engage in what in essence it saw as a leveling of the playing field. Since homosexual conduct and by extension homosexuals do not receive any constitutional protection, antidiscrimination ordinances passed in favor of homosexuals "are subject to . . . lawful, democratic countermeasures."

Therefore, absent legislation that works a direct infringement on the rights of homosexuals in relation to the rights of the "majority" of Colorado citizens, the dissent would permit the democratic process of a state to run its course (in either direction) with regards to legislation that serves to grant or deny special rights to individual groups.

In contrast to the dissent's view that Amendment 2 leveled the playing field, the majority concluded that it would have the effect of "depriving gays and lesbians . . . the protection of general laws and policies that prohibit arbitrary discrimination in governmental and private settings." Based on that assumption, the Amendment did not level the playing field but tilted it in favor of the political majority out of animus against gays and lesbians and homosexuality.

11b. In Shahar v. Bowers, 70 F.3d 1218 (11th Cir. 1995), the Eleventh Circuit held that a female attorney's First Amendment right to intimate association may have been violated when the state attorney general withdrew a job offer that he had previously extended after learning that she had married a woman in a private Jewish religious ceremony conducted by a rabbi and followed by a weekend of celebration of Jewish marriage. The court emphasized that the basis for protection was not just the intimate relationship, but the intimate relationship "inextricably entwined with Shahar's exercise of her religious beliefs." Id. at 1225. The court remanded the case to the district court with instructions "to determine under a strict scrutiny standard" whether the state attorney general's interference with Shahar's rights violated the Constitution.

Page 630.   Add new Note 17a:

17a. In De Parrie v. Portland, 906 P.2d 844 (Or. Ct. App. 1996), the court considered whether Oregon's statute prohibiting discrimination on the basis of sexual orientation also prohibits preferential treatment for homosexuals. The plaintiffs complained that Portland expended funds to recruit homosexuals for city employment and offered employment solely on the basis of homosexual sexual orientation. The court concluded that the statute, which forbids local governments to "single out" or "grant rights, privileges or treatment" on the basis of sexual orientation, both forbids discrimination and outlaws preferential treatment.

In Tumeo v. University of Alaska, 1995 WL 238359 (Alaska Super.), plaintiff used a state statute prohibiting discrimination on the basis of marital status to secure the right to health coverage for the same-sex partner. The court ruled that, by favoring married couples over same-sex domestic partners, the terms of the university's insurance plan constituted "marital status" discrimination.

Page 632.   Add new Note 21 after the carryover paragraph:

21. *Wright* and *Dillon* are factually and legally distinguishable because while Wright was harassed because of his supervisor's attraction to males, Dillon was harassed because of his co-worker's dislike of homosexuals. Because courts have uniformly viewed homosexuality or sexual preference as beyond Title VII's proscription, different treatment on that basis is legitimate and nondiscriminatory. *Wright*, on the other hand, falls easily within standard Title VII disparate treatment or sexual harassment analysis. Wright was harassed because of his gender. Although the analysis in *Wright* is relatively straightforward, not all courts have been willing to find same-sex harassment

based on the victim's gender actionable under Title VII. See Chapter 7, Section C.2.

D. RELIGIOUS DISCRIMINATION

2. *The Special Duty to Accommodate Employees' Religious Practices*

Page 663.   Add the following to Note 6:

In Brown v. Polk Cty., Iowa, 61 F.3d 650 (8th Cir. 1995) (en banc), plaintiff was a born-again Christian who served as director of the county data-processing department. He was reprimanded after an internal investigation revealed that he had directed a secretary to type Bible study notes for him, that several employees had said prayers in his office before the beginning of some workdays, that several employees had said prayers in plaintiff's office during department meetings, and that, in addressing one meeting of employees, plaintiff had affirmed his Christianity and had referred to Biblical passages related to slothfulness and "work ethics." Shortly thereafter, he was reprimanded and then fired. In reversing judgment for the employer, the court first rejected the argument that plaintiff had no claim of religious discrimination because he never explicitly asked for accommodation for his religious activities. Because "the reprimand related directly to religious activities . . . defendants were well aware of the potential for conflict between their expectations and [plaintiff's] religious activities." Second, it was "undisputed that the defendants made no attempt to accommodate any of [plaintiff's] religious activities. In those circumstances, the defendants may prevail only if they can show that allowing those activities 'could not be accomplished without undue hardship.' United States v. Board of Education, 911 F.2d 882, 887 (3rd Cir. 1990)." Third, the defendants' arguments that accommodating plaintiff's religious practices caused an undue hardship failed because they presented no evidence to show that plaintiff's "personnel decisions actually were affected by his religious beliefs or that employee concerns in that respect were either reasonable or legitimate. . . . In our view, the defendant's examples of the burden that they would have to bear by tolerating trifling instances such as those complained of are insufficiently 'real' . . . and too 'hypothetical,' to satisfy the standard required to show undue hardship."

In contrast, in Wilson v. United States West Communications, 58 F.3d 1337 (8th Cir. 1995), the court held that an employer requiring a Roman Catholic employee to cover an anti-abortion button that had a graphic photograph of a fetus was a reasonable accommodation. The button was causing substantial disruption in the office, and a supervisor had been unsuccessful in requesting co-workers to ignore the pin. The employer's alternative allowed the employee to wear the pin in adherence to her religious beliefs, and it respected fellow workers' requests not to have to see it. Since the employer had offered an accommodation that was reasonable, the statutory inquiry was complete.

Page 665. Add the following after the carryover paragraph:

PROBLEM 7.2A

The National Basketball Association's rule book states, "Players, coaches and trainers are to stand and line up in a dignified posture along the sidelines or the foul line during the playing of the National Anthem." Mahmoud Abdul-Rauf, a player for the Denver Nuggets in the NBA who is a Muslim, refused to stand for the playing of the national anthem. He said that the United States flag is a "symbol of oppression, of tyranny. This country has a long history of that. I don't think you can argue the facts. You can't be for God and for oppression. It's clear in the Koran, Islam is the only way."

Sayyed M. Syeed, secretary general of the Islamic Society of North America, was quoted as saying that the decision whether to stand up for the anthem and the flag is a subjective one, and believers are responsible to their own consciences.

Though Abdul-Rauf had been not standing during the national anthem for some time, the issue came to a head after it was raised on radio talk shows. The league responded by suspending Abdul-Rauf without notice and without his pay of $31,707 for each game. The office of the Deputy Commissioner issued a statement, which read: "The N.B.A's rule on this point is very clear and all our rules apply equally to all players." Subsequently, Abdul-Rauf decided to stand during the playing of the national anthem but to pray for the victims of oppression. See The New York Times, Thursday, Mar. 14, 1996, at B13.

Did the NBA or the Denver Nuggets violate Abdul-Rauf's right to the reasonable accommodation of his religious beliefs?

3.   *The Constitutionality of Title VII's Treatment of Religion*

Page 673.   Add the following to Note 4:

Like Title VII, ADEA statutory coverage has sometimes been limited by constitutional considerations of freedom of religion. E.g., Scharon v. Saint

Luke's Episcopal Presbyterian Hosp., 929 F.2d 360 (8th Cir. 1991); Minker v. Baltimore Annual Conference of United Methodist Church, 894 F.2d 1354 (D.C. Cir. 1990). Cf. Weissman v. Congregation Shaare Emeth, 38 F.3d 1038 (8th Cir. 1994) (lay temple administrator could prosecute suit with little likelihood of religious entanglement); Geary v. Visitation of the Blessed Virgin Mary Parish Sch., 7 F.3d 324 (3d Cir. 1993) (lay teacher in a religious elementary school protected as long as plaintiff does not challenge the validity of a religious tenet, but merely argues that a supposed religious reason was a mere pretext for discrimination); Demarco v. Holy Cross High Sch., 4 F.3d 166 (2d Cir. 1993) (no excessive entanglement in determining whether age caused discharge of lay teacher in religious school, even where religion was the articulated basis for the discharge).

Page 673.   Add new Note 4a:

4a. In Brown v. Polk Cty., Iowa, 61 F.3d 650, 659 (8th Cir. 1995), the employer investigated plaintiff's religious activities conducted on the job and then reprimanded him:

> The reprimand directed Mr. Brown "immediately [to] cease any activities that could be considered to be religious proselytizing, witnessing, or counseling and . . . further [to] cease to utilize County resources in any way [that] could be perceived as to be supporting a religious activity or religious organization." The reprimand also directed Mr. Brown to "insure a work environment that is free of the types of activities described. Subsequently . . . the county administrator directed Mr. Brown to remove from his office all items with a religious connotation, including a Bible in his desk." The court found that these actions violated the free exercise rights of the plaintiff.
>
> We may concede for the sake of argument that Polk County has a legal right to ensure that its workplace is free from religious activity that harasses or intimidates. But any interference with religious activity that the exercise of the right entails must be reasonably related to the exercise of that right and must be narrowly tailored to its achievement. See, e.g., Thomas v. Review Board, 450 U.S. 707, 718 (1981). Here, there was not the least attempt to confine the prohibition to harassing or intimidating speech. Instead, Polk County baldly directed Mr. Brown to "cease any activities that *could be considered* to be religious proselytizing, witnessing, or counseling" (emphasis supplied). That order exhibited a hostility to religion that our Constitution simply prohibits. It would seem to require no argument that to forbid speech "that could be considered" religious is not narrowly tailored to the aim of prohibiting harassment, although it is certainly capable of doing that. If Mr. Brown asked someone to attend his church, for instance, we suppose that "could be considered" proselytizing, but its prohibition runs afoul of the free exercise clause. Similarly, a statement to the effect that one's religion was important in one's life "could be considered" witnessing, yet for the government to forbid it would be unconstitutional.

The defendants would have us hold that their "interest" in avoiding a claim against them that they have violated the establishment clause allows them to prohibit religious expression altogether in their workplaces. Such a position is too extravagant to maintain, for it gives a dominance to the establishment clause that it does not have and that would allow it to trump the free exercise clause. One might just as well justify erecting a cross and a creche on county property at Christmas as a means of avoiding a claim that employees had been denied their free exercise rights. The clauses cannot, in the nature of things, make conflicting demands on a government, and government is charged with making sure that its activities are confined to the ample and well-defined space that separates them.

Mr. Brown also complains about the directive to remove from his office all items with a religious connotation, including a Bible that was in his desk. It is here, perhaps, that the zealotry of the county administrator is most clearly revealed. Mr Brown had to remove a plaque containing the serenity prayer ("God, grant me the serenity to accept the things I cannot change, the courage to change the things I can, and the wisdom to know the difference"), another that said, "God be in my life and in my commitment," and a third containing the Lord's Prayer. Most intrusive of all was the order to take down a poster that proclaimed some non-religious inspirational commonplaces that were deemed inappropriate because their author, although he occupied no religious office had "Cardinal" in his name. Mr. Brown testified that he was told that these items had to go because they might be considered "offensive to employees."

Absent some showing of disruption of work or any interference with the efficient performance of governmental functions, the court found that the county's actions were not justified. "[E]ven if employees found Mr. Brown's displays 'offensive,' Polk County could not legally remove them if their 'offensiveness' was based on the content of their message. In that case, the county would be taking sides in a religious dispute, which, of course, it cannot do under either the establishment clause or the equal protection clause." Id.

Four of the eleven members of the en banc court dissented on the ground that plaintiff had not shown any substantial burden on his religious practices. "The record lacks any evidence that Brown's born-again Christianity required him to display religious items in his office or to engage in the religious activities restricted by the reprimand." Id. at 660.

Page 675. Add the following to the end of Note 9:

d. In Brown v. Polk Cty., Iowa, 61 F.3d 650 (8th Cir. 1995), the employer fired plaintiff, the director of the county's data-processing department, because he had directed a secretary to type his Bible study notes, several employees had prayed in his office before work, others had prayed in department meetings in his office, and, in addressing department meetings, plaintiff had affirmed that he was a born-again Christian and had referred to Bible passages related to slothfulness and "work ethics." In finding that the employer had failed to even attempt to accommodate plaintiff's religious beliefs, the court described the relationship between Title VII's religious accommodation duty and the free exercise clause of the First Amendment:

> With specific reference to the free exercise clause, we hold that in the governmental context, the first amendment protects at least as much religious activity as Title VII does. . . . Another way of framing that holding is to say that any religious activities of employees that can be accommodated without undue hardship to the governmental employer . . . are also protected by the first amendment. In other words, if a governmental employer has violated Title VII, it has also violated the guarantees of the first amendment.

Id. at 653.

E. NATIONAL ORIGIN AND ALIENAGE DISCRIMINATION

1. National Origin Discrimination

Page 685. Add the following to Note 7:

In Odima v. Westin Tucson Hotel, 53 F.3d 1484 (9th Cir. 1995), the court found the defendant's reason for not promoting the Nigerian-born plaintiff outside the laundry room was a pretext for discrimination based on race and national origin. The employer claimed that it had denied the plaintiff's requests for transfer because the plaintiff's accent would interfere with his communications with the public.

Page 685. Add the following to Note 9:

See David T. Wiley, Note, Whose Proof? Deference to EEOC Guidelines on Disparate Discrimination Analysis of "English-Only" Rules, 29 Ga. L. Rev. 539 (1995).

Page 687. Add new Note 12a:

12a. Government imposition of English-only rules raises First Amendment issues. See Yniguez v. Mofford, 42 F.3d 1217 (9th Cir. 1995) (striking down Arizona state constitutional amendment making English the state's official language on the ground that, as broadly drafted, it violated the First Amendment), *cert. granted sub nom.* Arizonans for Official English v. Arizona, 116 S. Ct. 1316 (1996).

Page 687.   Add the following to Note 13:

See Barbara Flagg, Fashioning a Title VII Remedy for Transparently White Subjective Decisionmaking, 104 Yale L.J. 2009 (1995).

Page 687.   Add new Note 13a:

13a. Juan F. Perea, Ethnicity and Prejudice: Reevaluating "National Origin" Discrimination Under Title VII, 35 Wm. & Mary L. Rev. 805, 807-808 (1994), stresses the limits of Title VII's present prohibition of national origin discrimination:

> Courts have been largely unsympathetic to claims of discrimination as experienced by persons whose ethnicity differs from that of the majority. Thus Mexican American employees must endure insults such as "wetback" and demeaning labor which "Americans . . . [do] not have to do." Employees may be fired or disciplined for speaking languages other than English in the workplace, even if employees are doing their jobs at the time or if their conversations do not interfere with job performance. Persons who speak with "foreign" accents may be denied employment, despite excellent qualifications and verbal skills, because of the discomfort and displeasure they cause interviewers. African American women may be denied the ability to express their ethnic identity by wearing their hair in cornrows.

He goes on to argue

> that the "national origin" term does not, and cannot, correctly encompass the protection of ethnic traits or ethnicity. Indeed, the concept of "national origin" discrimination is not helpful in describing accurately or recognizing the kind of discrimination that should be prohibited under Title VII. The continuing and exclusive reliance on "national origin" as the statutory source of protection in Title VII against discrimination because of ethnic traits is increasingly incompatible with more ethnic diversity in the workplace and the predictably increasing demand for equal treatment.

Id. at 809-810.

Professor Perea sees one basic problem with the application of the statute:

As long as traits such as language and accent are protected solely as proxies for protected "national origin," the protection of ethnic traits becomes solely a matter of the interpretive preferences of judges. These preferences manifest themselves in the threshold judicial decisions regarding whether a trait may function at all as a proxy for "national origin," and, if so, whether a trait is a close enough proxy to merit protection.

Id. at 845. Is the problem similar to the one we saw with respect to age discrimination in Hazen Paper Co. v. Biggin: discrimination on the basis of traits highly correlated with national origin (e.g., speaking Spanish) is not the same as discrimination on national origin grounds? Thus, it can be found discriminatory only when the articulated basis hides a real national origin bias?

H. AGE DISCRIMINATION

5. Early Retirement Incentive Plans

Page 732.   Add the following at the end of the first full paragraph:

Cf. Erica Worth, Note, In Defense of Targeted ERIPs: Understanding the Interaction of Life-Cycle Employment and Early Retirement Plans, 74 Tex. L. Rev. 411 (1995).

Page 733.   Add the following after the first full paragraph:

The courts have begun to address the questions generated by the OWBPA. Thus, they may also consider nonstatutory factors in deciding whether a waiver was truly voluntary. Griffin v. Kraft General Foods, 62 F.3d 368 (11th Cir. 1995). The consideration provided for waivers of ADEA rights need not be greater than the consideration paid younger workers who have no ADEA rights to waive. DiBiase v. SmithKline Beecham Corp., 48 F.3d 719 (3d Cir.), *cert. denied*, 116 S. Ct. 306 (1995); *Griffin*, supra. There also has been some dispute as to what information is required to satisfy the OWBPA. E.g., *Griffin*, supra (employers may be required to provide information about employees outside the facility directly affected).

*Page 733.   Add the following at the end of the last full
              paragraph:*

, *cert denied*, 115 S. Ct. 1403 (1995). See also Fleming v. United States Postal
Serv., 27 F.3d 259 (7th Cir. 1994). See generally N. Jansen Calamita, Note,
The Older Worker Benefit Protection Act of 1990: The End of Ratification
and Tender Back in ADEA Cases, 73 B.U. L. Rev. 639 (1993).

PART III

ALTERNATIVE APPROACHES TO DISCRIMINATION

Chapter 8

Disability Discrimination

A. INTRODUCTION

*Page 744.   Add the following at the end of the first full
paragraph in the carryover footnote:*

See generally Rebecca Hanner White, The EEOC, the Courts, and Employment Discriminaiton Policy: Recognizing the Agency's Leading Role in Statutory Interpretation, 1995 Utah L. Rev. 51.

B. PROVING MEMBERSHIP IN THE PROTECTED CLASS

1. The Meaning of "Disability"

Page 752.   Add the following new text at the end of Note 8:

In Doe v. Kohn, Nast & Graf, 862 F. Supp. 1310 (E.D. Penn. 1994), the court concluded that the HIV-infected plaintiff suffered from a physical impairment, citing symptoms including fever, skin rash, and disorder of the hemic and lymphatic systems. Further, the court held that procreation may be a major life activity because the activities listed in the regulations are not exclusive and because the ADA's legislative history suggests that HIV is a covered condition. Id at 1321. Finally, HIV substantially limits procreation because of the risk of transmitting the disease to a sex partner or to a child. Id.

The Fourth Circuit, however, took a different approach to ADA coverage for asymptomatic HIV-infected individuals in Ennis v. National Assn. of Business and Educational Radio, Inc., 53 F.3d 55 (4th Cir. 1995). In *Ennis* a former employee sued under the ADA, alleging discrimination on the basis of her relationship with her HIV-infected son. In considering whether the plaintiff's son had a disability within the meaning of the ADA, the court stated:

> We believe that [§3(2) defining "disability"] requires that a finding of disability be made on an individual-by-individual basis. The term "disability" is specifically defined, for each of subparts (A), (B), and (C), "with respect to [the] individual" and the individualized focus is reinforced by the requirement that the underlying impairment substantially limit a major life activity of the individual. . . . There is no evidence in the record before us that A.J. is impaired, to any degree, or that he currently endures any limitation, much less a substantial limitation, on any major life activity. . . . Were we to hold that A.J. was disabled under the ADA, therefore, we would have to conclude that HIV-positive status is per se a disability. The plain language of the statute, which contemplates case-by-case determinations of whether a given impairment substantially limits a major life activity . . . simply would not permit this conclusion.

Id. at 59. Which court has the stronger argument? Note that even if individuals with contagious diseases are "disabled," they still may not be entitled to protection because the contagious nature of their disease may mean that they are not qualified to work at many jobs.

Page 754.   Add the following new text to Note 13:

Courts have not consistently followed the EEOC's Interpretive Guidance on this issue. Compare EEOC v. Union Carbide Chem. & Plastics Co., 4 AD Cases 1409 (E.D. La. 1995) (ADA) (whether employee with bipolar disorder is disabled should be determined in his medicated or corrected condition) and Chandler v. City of Dallas, 2 F.3d 1385 (5th Cir. 1993) (Rehabilitation Act) (whether visual impairment is a disability must be considered in light of corrective glasses) with Canon v. Clark, 883 F. Supp. 718 (S.D. Fla. 1995) (diabetic plaintiff who is forced to rely on medical assistance to perform major life activities and to survive is disabled under the ADA) and Washington v.

HCA Health Servs. of Texas, Inc., 906 F. Supp. 386 (S.D. Tex. 1995) (employee with Adult Stills Disease, a degenerative disease affecting bones and joints, is disabled under the ADA because he would be bedridden if not medicated). In Coghlan v. H.J. Heinz Co., 851 F. Supp. 808 (N.D. Tex. 1994), the court ruled that a diabetic who, with medication, can perform all major life activities is not disabled under the ADA. The court found the EEOC's Interpretive Guidance to the contrary "directly at odds" with the statutory language. Do you agree? Why? Why not?

Page 756.   Add the following to the citation for Winston v. Maine Technical C. Sys. in carryover Note 20:

, *cert. denied*, 114 S. Ct. 1643 (1994)

Page 756.   Add new Notes 20a to 20d:

20a. In Vande Zande v. Wisconsin Dept. of Admin., 44 F.3d 538 (7th Cir. 1995), Vande Zande, who is paralyzed from the waist down, sought reasonable accommodations under the ADA relating to pressure ulcers caused by her paralysis. Her employer argued that because her ulcers were intermittent and episodic impairments, they did not fit the definition of a disability. The Seventh Circuit disagreed:

> [A]n intermittent impairment that is a characteristic manifestation of an admitted disability is, we believe, a part of the underlying disability. . . . Often the disabling aspect of a disability is, precisely, an intermittent manifestation of the disability, rather than the underlying impairment. The AIDS virus progressively destroys the infected person's immune system. The consequence is a series of opportunistic diseases which . . . often prevent the individual from working. If they are not part of the disability, then people with AIDS do not have a disability which seems to us a very odd interpretation of the law, and one expressly rejected by the regulations. We hold that Vande Zande's pressure ulcers are a part of her disability.

Id. at 543. *Vande Zande* raises an issue similar to that addressed by the Supreme Court in Hazen Paper Co. v. Biggins, 507 U.S. 604 (1993). In *Biggins*, the Court considered whether discharging an employee because he was about to vest in a pension plan amounted to discrimination on the basis of age. The Court ruled that it did not because, although eligibility for pension benefits correlates to a significant degree with age, "an employee's age is analytically distinct from his years of service." Id. at 611. In *Vande Zande* the Seventh Circuit held that a decision based on the symptoms of a disability, symptoms that may not be shared by all individuals suffering from the disability and that may be experienced by nondisabled individuals as well, are decisions based on the disability itself. Is there any reason to treat disability discrimination differently from age discrimination in this respect? Consider a case in which an alcoholic is arrested for drunk driving. Assume that the alcoholic's job does not include driving. If the employer fires the alcoholic for driving while drunk, has the employer acted on the basis of the individual's disability (alcoholism)? Why? See Section D.1, page 821 of the casebook.

20b. The First Circuit in Cook v. Rhode Island, 10 F.3d 17 (1st Cir. 1993), raised the question whether an individual is impaired under the Rehabilitation Act if her condition is one for which she is at least partially responsible. The defendant in *Cook* argued that "morbid obesity is a mutable condition and that, therefore, one who suffers from it is not [impaired] because she can simply lose weight and rid herself of any concomitant disability." Id. at 23. The court found that on the facts of the case, the metabolic dysfunction that caused plaintiff's condition was, in fact, immutable. The defendants also argued that the plaintiff's condition could not be an impairment because "morbid obesity is caused, or at least exacerbated, by voluntary conduct." Id. at 24. The court rejected this argument:

> The Rehabilitation Act contains no language suggesting that its protection is linked to how an individual became impaired, or whether an individual contributed to his or her impairment. On the contrary, the Act indisputably applies to numerous conditions that may be caused or exacerbated by voluntary conduct, such as alcoholism, AIDS, diabetes, cancer resulting from cigarette smoking, heart disease resulting from excesses of various types and the like. . . . Consequently, voluntariness, like mutability, is relevant only to determining whether a condition has a substantially limiting effect.

Id. Can excessive weight be distinguished from the other "voluntary" conditions listed by the court?

20c. Section 1630.2(j) of the EEOC's ADA Regulations, see the casebook, page 746, suggests that temporary disorders are not disabilities covered by the ADA. The Third Circuit, in McDonald v. Commonwealth, 62 F.3d 92 (3d Cir. 1995), recently considered whether inability to work for two months following abdominal surgery constitutes a disability within the meaning of the ADA. In a well-reasoned opinion relying on the legislative histories of both the Rehabilitation Act and the ADA, as well as administrative regulations under both statutes, the court concluded that the plaintiff's impairment "was not permanent, nor for such an extended time as to be of the type contemplated" by the Rehabilitation Act or the ADA. Id. at 96. See, e.g., Evans v. City of Dallas, 861 F.2d 846, 852-853 (5th Cir. 1988) (Rehabilitation Act contemplates impairment of a permanent nature); Hamm v. Runyon, 51 F.3d 721 (7th Cir. 1995) (ADA does not cover temporary impairments).

20d. Pregnancy shares many of the characteristics of a disability as defined by the ADA. Nonetheless, the EEOC ADA Guidance suggests that pregnancy is not a disability covered by the statute because pregnancy is not an impairment. 29 C.F.R. pt. 1630 app. §§1630.2(h), (i). One commentator has argued that pregnancy is covered by the ADA, Collette G. Matzzie, Substantive Equality and Antidiscrimination: Accommodating Pregnancy Under the Americans with Disabilities Act, 82 Geo. L.J. 193 (1993), and at least one court has reached the same conclusion but without significant discussion. See Chapsky v. Baxter Mueuller Div., 4 AD Cases 1047 (N.D. Ill. 1995).

Cases that have considered whether reproductive conditions other than normal pregnancy constitute disabilities have raised some interesting questions about the appropriate interpretation of the statutory and regulatory language. The regulations list reproduction among the body systems that, if disordered, meet the definition of "impairment" under the statute. An impairment is defined as "[a]ny physiological disorder . . . or condition" affecting one or more listed "body systems," including the "reproductive system." 29 C.F.R. §1630.2(h)(1). Reproduction, however, is not specified in §1630.2(i), which lists examples of major life activities that, when substantially limited by an impairment, constitute disabilities. The "major life activities" that are listed include "caring for oneself, performing manual tasks, walking, seeing, hearing, speaking, breathing, learning, and working."

In Pacourek v. Inland Steel Co., 858 F. Supp. 1393 (N.D. Ill. 1994), the court considered whether the inability to become pregnant naturally because of esphofical reflux is a disability under the ADA. It had no trouble concluding that infertility is an impairment because it is a physical disorder of the reproductive system. With respect to whether infertility substantially limits a major life activity, the court reasoned that, even though not specifically listed, reproduction must be a covered major life activity because "[o]therwise, it would have made no sense to include the reproductive system among the systems that can have an ADA physical impairment." Id. at 1404. Further, the court relied on McWright v. Alexander, 982 F.2d 222 (7th Cir. 1992), a case in which the Seventh Circuit stated that Rehabilitation Act "regulations define the protected class of handicapped individuals to include any person with a physiological disorder affecting the reproductive system." Pacourek, 858 F. Supp. at 1405 (citing McWright, 982 F.2d at 226-227).

Another district court reached the opposite conclusion in Zatarian v. WBSU-Television Inc., 881 F. Supp. 240 (E.D. La. 1995). While finding that the plaintiff's infertility was a physiological disorder of the reproductive system and therefore an impairment, the court went on to conclude that reproduction is not a major life activity under the Act:

[T]he structure of the ADA and its regulations indicate that the major life activity that is allegedly limited is separate and distinct from the impairment that limits it. Plaintiff's construction is faulty because it would allow her to bootstrap a finding of substantial limitation of a major life activity on to a finding of an impairment. . . . This analysis is circular and unpersuasive.

Furthermore, finding "reproduction" to be a "major life activity" would be inconsistent with the illustrative list of major life activities provided in the ADA regulations. Reproduction is not an activity engaged in with the same degree of frequency as the listed activities. . . . A person is required to walk, see, learn, speak, breath [breathe], and work throughout the day, day in and day out. However, a person is not called upon to reproduce throughout the day, every day.

Id. at 243. In Krauel v. Iowa Methodist Medical Center, 4 AD Cases 1736 (D. Mass. 1995), the court followed *Zatarian* but distinguished infertility from the enumerated major life activities not only because reproduction is engaged in less frequently but also because reproduction is a voluntary "lifestyle choice" rather than an activity such as walking, seeing, or hearing that all people do unless they are disabled. Id. at 1736-1738. Which court has the stronger argument with respect to ADA coverage for infertility? Why?

Page 760.   Add the following to the citation for Gupton
*   v. Virginia in Note 3:*

, *cert. denied*, 115 S. Ct. 59 (1994),

Page 761.   Add the following new text to Note 10:

The EEOC's recent "Guidance on the Definition of the Term 'Disability' Under ADA" states that an employer who discriminates on the basis of genetic information or genetic predisposition to disease is "regarding" an applicant or employee as disabled.

Page 762.   Add new Note 13:

13. Section 3(2) of the ADA defines disability to include having a record of an impairment that substantially limits a major life activity. In Doe v. Kohn Nast & Graf, 862 F. Supp. 1310 (E.D. Penn. 1994), the plaintiff, an attorney, was diagnosed with HIV in September 1992. In January 1993, the law firm informed him that it did not intend to renew his contract. The court rejected the plaintiff's attempt to establish that he was disabled based on having a

record of a substantially limiting impairment. The court, citing 29 C.F.R. §1630.2(k), reasoned that a "record" of impairment means a "history" of impairment. Doe did not have a record of impairment because the initial diagnosis in September 1992 led directly to the events that gave rise to the lawsuit: "[T]hat is not a long enough record to constitute a history of impairment. His disease was virtually brand new." Id. at 1322. Can you argue that this conclusion incorrectly interprets the statute?

2. The Meaning of "Qualified Individual with a Disability"

Page 768.   Add new Notes 3 and 4:

3. An individual with an infectious disease is not a qualified individual if he poses a significant risk of communicating his disease to others in the workplace. In School Board of Nassau Cty. v. Arline, 480 U.S. 273 (1987), the Supreme Court stated that the appropriate inquiry for determining whether an individual with a contagious disease is "qualified" should include

> [findings of] facts, based on reasonable medical judgments given the state of medical knowledge, about (a) the nature of the risk (how the disease is transmitted), (b) the duration of the risk (how long is the carrier infectious), (c) the severity of the risk (what is the potential harm to third parties), and (d) the probabilities the disease will be transmitted and will cause varying degrees of harm.

Id. at 288.

Employers have sought to deny employment in the medical profession to individuals who are HIV-infected or suffering from active AIDS. The Center for Contagious Diseases has concluded that "if appropriate medical procedures are followed, . . . the risk of transmission of infection from a doctor with AIDS to a patient in the course of a routine physical examination is remote." See Doe v. Attorney General of the United States, 62 F.3d 1424 (9th Cir. 1995). Consider the case of a surgical technologist who is infected with the AIDS virus. A surgical technologist works in the sterile field within which surgery is performed and often comes within inches of open wounds. The job requires placing hands in a body approximately once each day and handing sharp instruments to surgeons handle-end first. Is a surgical technologist who is infected with the AIDS virus a "qualified" disabled individual? Compare Bradley v. University of Texas M.D. Anderson Cancer Ctr., 3 F.3d 922 (5th Cir. 1993) and Doe v. University of Maryland Medical System Corp., 50 F.3d 1261 (4th Cir. 1995) with Doe v. Attorney General of the United States, supra.

4. Can an applicant for employment who applied for and has been approved to receive disability benefits subsequently claim to be a qualified in-

dividual entitled to protection under the Rehabilitation Act or the ADA? The courts have disagreed on whether an individual is estopped from claiming disability discrimination under these circumstances. In McNemer v. Disney Stores, 4 AD Cases 897 (E.D. Penn. 1995), an assistant store manager contracted AIDS. Although his discharge a month later was allegedly based on his acknowledged violation of a store policy, he sued for disability discrimination under the ADA. After his dismissal he applied for and was awarded state and federal disability benefits. The court found that McNemer had failed to meet his burden of establishing a prima facie case:

> McNemer has admitted that he is not qualified to perform the job of Assistant Manager; on his applications for Social Security Disability benefits and New Jersey disability benefits, McNemer and his physicians certified under penalty of perjury that he was "totally and permanently disabled." In addition, McNemer's physician represented that McNemer suffered from a "total and permanent disability" in order to exempt McNemer from repaying his student loans. Accordingly, McNemer is estopped from arguing now that he is "qualified" under the ADA.

Id. at 899. Other courts have reached the same conclusion. See, e.g., Garcia-Paz v. Swift Textiles, 973 F. Supp. 547, 554 (D. Kan. 1995); Lewis v. Zilog, Inc., 908 F. Supp. 931 (N.D. Ga. 1995) (ADA).

In contrast, other courts have declined to give preclusive effect to Social Security or other disability benefits payors' findings that an individual is entitled to disability benefits. In Smith v. Dovenmuehle, 859 F. Supp. 1138 (N.D. Ill. 1994), the plaintiff developed full-blown AIDS. Dovenmuehle fired Smith, allegedly because he incurred costs for the company by failing to complete a project on time. After he was fired, Smith sought disability benefits from the Social Security Administration:

> In his application, Smith stated that he was suffering from AIDS, peripheral neuropath, and HIV wasting syndrome, and that his condition made him stop working on October 7, 1992. Smith's doctor, Andrew Pavlatos submitted a medical evidence report to the Illinois Bureau of Disability Determination Services on or about December 21, 1992 stating that "due to impaired cognitive skills [Smith] can only do ADLS [activities of daily living]." The SSA awarded Smith monthly disability benefits from October 7, 1992.

Id. at 1139-1140. Smith asserted that by November 1992 he had recovered sufficiently that he could perform the essential functions of his former job. In fact, in March 1994, he was re-employed full-time by another firm. Smith filed suit against Dovenmuehle, alleging that he was terminated and denied benefits because he had AIDS, in violation of the ADA. In considering whether Smith's successful benefits claim judicially estopped him from claiming to be a qualified disabled individual, the court first defined the elements of judicial estoppel:

> The doctrine of judicial estoppel prevents a party who has successfully maintained a position in one proceeding from asserting the contrary in another proceeding. Judicial estoppel consists of three elements: the later position must be clearly inconsistent with the earlier position, the facts at issue must be the same in both cases, and the party to be estopped must have been successful in convincing the first court to adopt its position.

Id. at 1141. The court concluded that the SSA's determination that Smith was entitled to disability benefits was not preclusive because it did not amount to a decision that Smith was not "qualified" within the meaning of the ADA. Id. (citing Overton v. Reilly, 977 F.2d 1190, 1196 (7th Cir. 1992) (Rehabilitation Act). The court also reasoned that an individual's assertion that he is disabled and unable to work at the time he applies for disability benefits is not necessarily inconsistent with his assertion at another time that he is qualified to work because his condition may have improved or deteriorated over time. Id. at 1142. The court also noted that applying the doctrine of judicial estoppel in this context would frustrate the intent of the ADA:

> Defendant's position would place plaintiff in the untenable position of choosing between his right to seek disability benefits and his right to seek redress for an alleged violation of the ADA. Moreover, it would conflict with one of the stated purposes of the ADA which is to combat "the continuing existence of unfair and unnecessary discrimination and prejudice [which] denies people with disabilities the opportunity to compete on an equal basis and to pursue those opportunities for which our free society is justifiably famous, and costs the United States billions of dollars in unnecessary expenses resulting from dependency and nonproductivity." 42 U.S.C. §12101(a)(9).

Id. Finally, the court distinguished some precedents to the contrary on the ground that, in those cases, plaintiffs seeking back pay and reinstatement had asserted in the context of securing disability benefits that they were not now, nor had they ever been, able to work. Id. at 1142. In contrast, Smith asserted that his condition had improved since his initial claim for disability benefits, thus explaining the apparent inconsistency between asserting that he was disabled and then later seeking relief under the ADA. Id. Other courts applying the Rehabilitation Act have taken the same approach as *Smith*. See, e.g., Overton v. Reilly, 977 F.2d 1190, 1196 (7th Cir. 1992); Kupferschmidt v. Runyon, 827 F. Supp. 570 (E.D. Wis. 1993); Lawrence v. United States ICC, 629 F. Supp. 819 (E.D. Pa. 1985).

Which approach do you find to be more persuasive? Why?

Page 768.   Replace the second paragraph in the Note on
Essential Functions with the following new
text:

Numerous courts have held that regular and timely attendance at work is an essential job function and, therefore, a disabled individual who cannot meet that requirement is not "qualified" within the meaning of the ADA or the Rehabilitation Act. See, e.g., Tyndall v. National Education Centers, 31 F.3d 209 (4th Cir. 1994); Jackson v. Veterans Administration, 22 F.3d 277 (11th Cir. 1994); Carr v. Reno, 23 F.3d 525 (D.C. Cir. 1992) (Rehabilitation Act). Would an employer's concern over possible absenteeism constitute a legitimate basis to deny employment to a disabled individual? See Cook v. Rhode Island, 10 F.3d 17 (1st Cir. 1993) (no; the reasonable accommodation provision requires employers to bear some costs associated with hiring disabled employees).

Page 769.   Add the following to the citation for Guice-
Mills v. Derwinski in the carryover paragraph:

, *aff'd*, 967 F.2d 794 (1992)

Page 771.   Add the following new text at the end of first
full paragraph:

In Milton v. Scrivener, Inc., 53 F.3d 1118 (10th Cir. 1995), the Tenth Circuit considered whether a production standard imposed by a grocery warehouse on its "selectors" constituted an essential function of the job. Selectors were required to take orders for items in the warehouse and load the ordered items in correct amounts onto pallets. In order to increase efficiency and profitability, the warehouse established new production standards, which were applied to all selectors. Noting that the ADA does not prohibit employers from making changes designed to increase profits, the court concluded that speed is an essential function of the selector job. Id. at 1124.

Page 773.   Add the following to the citation for Guice-
Mills v. Derwinski in the carryover paragraph:

, *aff'd*, 967 F.2d 794 (1992)

*Page 773.   Add the following new text at the end of the
              carryover paragraph:*

Many disabled individuals could work productively if they could work at
home some or all of the time. The Seventh Circuit, in Vande Zande v. Wisconsin Dept. of Administration, 44 F.3d 538 (7th Cir. 1995), considered
whether working at home is a reasonable accommodation under the ADA.
The plaintiff, who was paralyzed from the waist down, suffered intermittent-
ly from pressure ulcers that required her to stay home for several weeks at a
time. Vande Zande did clerical, secretarial, and administrative-assistant work.
When Vande Zande's ulcers forced her to stay at home for eight weeks, she
asked her employer to provide her with a computer that would permit her to
work full-time at home. Her employer refused, causing her to lose 16.5 work
hours. In response to her allegation that her employer failed to reasonably accommodate her, the court stated:

> Most jobs in organizations public or private involve team work under supervi-
> sion rather than solitary unsupervised work, and team work under supervision
> generally cannot be performed at home without a substantial reduction in the
> quality of the employee's performance. This will no doubt change as commu-
> nications technology advances, but is the situation today. Generally, therefore,
> an employer is not required to accommodate a disability by allowing the dis-
> abled worker to work, by himself, without supervision, at home.

Id. at 544. While acknowledging that employers must consider working at
home as a reasonable accommodation for employees in some jobs, other
courts have agreed that working at home is not a reasonable accommodation
for most employees. See, e.g., Tyndall v. National Education Centers, 31 F.3d
209, 213 (4th Cir. 1994) (ADA) ("except in the unusual case where an employee can effectively perform all work-related duties at home, an employee
'who does not come to work cannot perform any of his job functions, essential or otherwise'") (quoting Wimbley v. Olger, 642 F. Supp. 481, 485 (W.D.
Tenn. 1986), aff'd, 831 F.2d 298 (6th Cir. 1987)); Carr v. Reno, 23 F.3d 525
(D.C. Cir. 1994) (Rehabilitation Act) (although agencies are required to consider work at home as a reasonable accommodation, plaintiff could not work
at home because coding clerk job involves tight deadlines).

In contrast, in Langon v. Department of Health & Human Services, 959
F.2d 1053 (D.C. Cir. 1992), a computer programmer with multiple sclerosis
asked to be allowed to work at home. HHS denied Langon's request, even
though the agency had a work-at-home policy, on the ground that her position
required exactness, meeting short deadlines, and frequent face-to-face con-
tacts, and therefore did not "lend itself to working at home." Id. at 1055. The
D.C. Circuit held that summary judgement was not appropriate on these facts

and instructed the district court to determine whether Langon's job could reasonably be performed at home. Id. at 1061. Similarly, in Spath v. Berry Plastics, 900 F. Supp. 893 (N.D. Ohio 1995), a regional sales manager suffered an ankle injury that prevented her from travelling. The court, in discussing whether she was a qualified disabled individual, noted that she had demonstrated that she could perform the essential functions of her job by planning and making sales calls by phone from her home. The court suggested that Berry could have accommodated her injury because other salespeople used their homes as their business location. In both *Langon* and *Spath*, the employers followed a policy of permitting work at home. This might be important if such a policy existed for nondisabled persons, but it should not be relevant if the "work at home" policies existed only as an accommodation to disabled employees. Courts have ruled that employers are free to extend benefits beyond those required to some disabled employees without being bound to extend those same benefits to others. See page 167, Note 18, this Supplement (casebook page 799). Do these cases disagree on the law or can they be distinguished on their facts?

Many employers provide light duty positions for employees with injuries or illnesses that prevent them from performing their regularly assigned jobs. The courts are divided on the question whether an employee who is qualified to perform only "light duty" positions is a qualified individual under the ADA and the Rehabilitation Act. In Valdez v. Albuquerque Public Schools, 875 F. Supp. 740 (D.N.M. 1994), the plaintiff, who was hired as a heavy equipment operator in 1974, was reassigned to an on-site supervisor position after he sustained incapacitating injuries to his right arm in 1979. In 1993, Valdez's employer APS obtained a "Functional Capacities Evaluation" of Valdez, which concluded that he was able to perform only work involving "light physical demand." Valdez's original job of heavy equipment operator was rated as requiring "heavy physical demand." Shortly after the capacities evaluation, Valdez was told that, because his disability rendered him unqualified as an equipment operator, he must either accept a transfer to an educational aide position paying $6,700 with no benefits, or be discharged from his current position, which paid $23,000 and included medical and other benefits. APS asserted that Valdez was hired to operate heavy equipment and that the supervisory position he held was a light duty position to which he was assigned to accommodate his disability. Therefore, because he could not perform the functions of his original position, APS argued it was entitled to discharge Valdez. The court, citing Rehabilitation Act precedent, concluded that the "employment position" referred to in the ADA definition of "qualified" is the "work in which he was engaged when the alleged discrimination occurred," not the classification to which the individual is officially assigned. Id. at 73 (quoting Taylor v. Garrett, 820 F. Supp. 933 (E.D. Pa. 1993)). Do you agree? Section 101(8) of the ADA provides: "The term 'qualified individual with a disability' means an individual with a disability who, with or without reasonable accommodation, can perform the essential functions of the employment position that such individual holds or desires."

Other courts have taken a somewhat different view of this issue. See Santos v. Port Authority of New York and New Jersey, 4 AD Cases 1245 (S.D.N.Y. 1995) (police officer working light duty after injuring his achilles tendon had no right to permanent light duty status because the ability to do more than clerical work is an essential function of the position of officer); Howell v. Michelin Tire Corp., 860 F. Supp. 1488 (M.D. Ala. 1994) (reassignment to temporary light duty job as an accommodation is required only for as long as the temporary position exists).

*Page 773.   Add the following new text at the end of the
                  first full paragraph:*

In Lyons v. Legal Aid Society, 68 F.3d 1512 (2d Cir. 1995), the Second Circuit relied on the legislative history of the ADA as well as the EEOC Interpretive Guidance to conclude that providing an employee with a parking space near the office can be a reasonable accommodation to perform the essential function of getting to work regularly and on time. See H.R. Rep. No. 485, 101st Cong., 2d Sess., pt. 2, at 61 (1990), *reprinted in* 1990 U.S.C.C.A.N. 303, 343; EEOC Interpretive Guidance at 407. The court noted, however, that whether providing a parking space is a reasonable accommodation might depend on a number of factors, including the employer's geographic location and financial resources. Id. at 1516.

*Page 774.   Add the following new text at the end of the
                  carryover paragraph:*

These provisions do not make it clear under what circumstances providing a reader, interpreter, page turner, or travel attendant would constitute "assisting the individual [with a disability] to perform the job" rather than "performing the job for the individual." In Hogue v. MQS Inspection, Inc., 3 AD Cases 1793 (D. Colo. 1993), a materials inspector supervisor injured his knee and ankle in two separate accidents on the job. Physical restrictions caused by these injuries made it impossible for Hogue to personally conduct all aspects of the field inspections that he might be assigned to supervise. Hogue proposed, as an accommodation, that MQS assign a helper to perform physical tasks beyond his capabilities. Without extensive discussion, the court denied MQS's motion for summary judgment, characterizing Hogue's request as seeking an aide to assist in performing the job rather than an aide to perform the job. Id. at 1798.

The Second Circuit, in Borkowski v. Valley Central Sch. Dist., 63 F.3d 131 (2d Cir. 1995), considered a library teacher's request for accommodation in the form of a teacher's aide to assist her in maintaining control of students. Borkowski's position put her in charge of two elementary school libraries and also required her to teach library skills to students. As a result of a motor vehicle accident, Borkowski developed difficulties with memory and concentration, especially in contexts involving multiple simultaneous stimuli. The court discussed whether classroom control is an essential function for a classroom teacher:

> A number of factors might be relevant . . . . One might be the age of the students. . . . [C]hildren of different ages may require different degrees of supervision. Another would be the availability of teacher's aides within the School District. . . . [W]ere other teachers within the school system provided with teacher's aides to assist in maintaining appropriate student behavior? If so, then classroom management might not be considered an essential function.

Id. at 141. The court went on to consider the legal implications of a variety of possible findings:

> [E]ither (a) classroom management was an essential function . . . and [the] proposed accommodation would eliminate that function; or (b) classroom management was an essential function . . . but providing Ms. Borkowski with an assistant would permit *her* to perform that function, though with assistance; or (c) classroom management was not an essential function . . . and it does not matter whether [the] proposed accommodation would result in her performing the function, albeit with assistance, or in the reassignment of that function to the teacher's aide.

Only the first finding would mean that Borkowski was not "qualified." Id.

C. PROVING DISABILITY DISCRIMINATION

1. *Individual Disparate Treatment*

Page 778.   Add the following new text to Note 1:

In Ennis v. National Assn. of Business and Educational Radio, Inc., 53 F.2d 55 (4th Cir. 1995), the Fourth Circuit ruled that, to establish disparate treatment under the ADA, the plaintiff must prove by the preponderance of the evidence that (1) she was in the protected class; (2) she was discharged; (3) at the time of the discharge, she was performing her job at a level that met her employer's legitimate expectations; and (4) her discharge occurred under circumstances that raise a reasonable inference of unlawful discrimination.

Id. at 57. The court characterized this formulation as easing a disabled employee's burden by dispensing with any requirement that she prove that she was replaced by a person outside the protected class, a difficult task given the large number of protected class individuals who are not easily identifiable (e.g., individuals with hidden disabilities and individuals who are associated in some way with a disabled individual). Does the Fourth Circuit's approach make proving discrimination easier or more difficult? Why? If, for example, a disabled employee is discharged for performing poorly but other employees with similar performance are retained, should there be a prima facie case?

Is it disability discrimination to treat a disabled person less favorably than a person with a lesser or more easily accommodated disability? See Hutchinson v. United Parcel Service, Inc., 883 F. Supp. 379 (N.D. Iowa 1995) (yes); Fink v. Kitzman, 881 F. Supp. 1347 (N.D. Iowa 1995) (yes).

Page 779. *Add the following new text to Note 3:*

Haysman v. Food Lion, Inc., 893 F. Supp. 1092 (S.D. Ga. 1995), ruled that harassment on the basis of an individual's disability is actionable discrimination under the ADA:

> The ADA prohibits discrimination in the "[t]erms, conditions or privileges of employment." . . . Referring to identical language in Title II, the Supreme Court stated: "harassment [that is] sufficiently severe or pervasive to 'alter the conditions of employment and create an abusive working environment,' is actionable under Title VII because it affects a term, condition or privilege of employment." Patterson v. McLean Credit Union, 491 U.S. 164, 180 (1989). Interpreting Title VII, the Supreme Court found that the "terms, conditions and privileges" language "evinces a congressional intent to strike at the entire spectrum of disparate treatment," and that Title VII affords employees the right to work in an environment free from discriminatory intimidation and insult. Meritor Savings Bank v. Vinson [reproduced at page 558 of the casebook]. It would seem illogical to hold that ADA language identical to that of Title VII was intended to afford disabled individuals less protection than those groups covered by Title VII. . . . Further, EEOC regulations to the ADA state that "it is unlawful to coerce, intimidate, threaten, *harass* or interfere with any individual in the exercise or enjoyment of . . . any right granted or protected by this part." 29 C.F.R. §1630.12 (emphasis added).

Id. at 1106. Employees who quit their jobs as a result of discriminatory harassment may be able to establish that they were constructively discharged. See page 178, Note 6, this supplement (casebook page 825). In addition, they may be able to establish intentional infliction of emotional distress entitling them to tort damages.

Page 779. Add the following new text to Note 4:

The Eighth Circuit, in Pedigo v. P.A.M. Transport, Inc., 4 AD Cases 1180 (8th Cir. 1995), followed the approach to mixed motives taken in the 1991 Civil Rights Act, overruling a jury verdict awarding compensatory damages to a truck driver discharged in violation of the ADA because the jury found that the employer would have made the same decision based on legitimate, nondiscriminatory reasons. The case was remanded to the district court to devise different remedies. Relying again on the 1991 Civil Rights Act, the court, however, rejected the employer's contention that the jury's findings barred all relief.

Page 780. Add the following new text to carryover Note 5:

See, e.g., Hedberg v. Indiana Bell Telephone Co., 47 F.3d 928 (7th Cir. 1995) (because the employer had no knowledge of the disability, it could not be liable under the ADA); Miller v. National Casualty Co., 4 AD Cases 1089 (8th Cir. 1995) (employer not required to accommodate manic-depressive employee who was discharged for excessive absence because employee did not apprise her employer of her condition and her condition was not obvious); Lyons v. Legal Aid Society, 4 AD Cases 1694, 1696 (2d Cir. 1995) (notice of disability listed as an element of a reasonable accommodation claim). Because the employer's knowledge regarding the employee's disability at the time of the adverse employment action is critical, medical evidence obtained after the discharge that establishes that an individual was disabled at the time of discharge is not relevant in an ADA action. See Heilweil v. Mount Sinai Hosp., 32 F.3d 718 (2d Cir. 1994) (medical evidence acquired after discharge suggesting that former employee was suffering from something more serious than asthma is irrelevant).

Page 781. Add the following new text to carryover Note 10:

In disability cases, employers often cite, as a legitimate nondiscriminatory reason, evidence of misconduct that is caused by an individual's disability.

In Borkowski v. Valley Central, 4 AD Cases 1265 (2d Cir. 1995), the Second Circuit ruled that denying a teacher tenure for inadequate performance amounted to denying tenure because of the teacher's disabilities: the school district knew of her disabilities and had an affirmative duty to make reasonable accommodation. The court stated that an employer's failure to consider accommodation amounts to discharge solely because of a disability if it leads to discharge for performance inadequacies resulting from the disability. See Teahan v. Metro-North Commuter RR, 951 F.2d 511 (2d Cir. 1991) (disciplining an employee because of excessive absenteeism resulting from her disability constitutes acting on the basis of her disability).

This same issue has arisen in a number of cases concerning individuals who have engaged in misconduct caused by or related to their alcoholism or drug addiction. In that context, courts have tended to rule that acting on the basis of misconduct, even if causally related to alcoholism or drug addiction, does not amount to acting on the basis of the plaintiff's disability. See, e.g., Maddox v. University of Tennessee, 62 F.3d 843 (6th Cir. 1995) (employee who becomes intoxicated and sexually assaults a co-worker is not protected under the ADA or the Rehabilitation Act merely because he is an alcoholic and claims his conduct was caused by his disability). In addition, numerous cases have found employers to be justified in discharging employees based on misconduct relating to their disability by ruling that disability-related conduct renders plaintiffs unqualified to perform the essential functions of their jobs. Which approach correctly construes the statute? Why? Does the statute suggest that alcoholism and drug addiction should be treated differently than other disabilities?

Page 784. *Add the following new text at the end of the Note on Burden of Proof in Disability Cases:*

In Borkowski v. Valley Central Sch. Dist., 63 F.3d 131 (2d Cir. 1995), a Rehabilitation Act case, the Second Circuit indicated that both the plaintiff and the defendant must meet their reasonable accommodation burdens by offering a cost/benefit analysis of proposed accommodations. The court went on to state that

> while the plaintiff could meet her burden of production by identifying an accommodation that facially achieves a rough proportionality between costs and benefits, an employer seeking to meet its burden of persuasion on reasonable accommodation and undue hardship must undertake a more refined analysis . . . considering the industry to which the employer belongs as well as the individual characteristics of the particular defendant-employer.

Id. at 139. According to the court, if the employer meets its burden with respect to reasonable accommodation, it will also have met its burden on the defense of undue hardship. Id.

In a recent case, Benson v. Northwest Airlines, Inc., 62 F.3d 1108 (8th Cir. 1995), the Eighth Circuit considered the allocation of the burden of proof under the ADA. Benson, a mechanic, suffered an attack of brachial plexopathy or Parsonage-Turner syndrome, "a rare neurological disorder which can cause pain, weakness or numbness in the arm and shoulder." Due to his condition, his doctor recommended that he not engage in work requiring either extensive use of his left arm or repetitive motion of his left shoulder. After his initial attack, Benson returned to work where he was transferred to the Recycling Unit "where employees with work-related injuries worked until able to return to their former positions or find alternative positions." Id. After being bumped from this position by a more senior employee, Benson ultimately was discharged because he was unable to find an open job within the company that he could perform with his impairment.

On appeal, the Eighth Circuit concluded that the lower court had improperly allocated the burden of proof. First, because Northwest argued that Benson could not perform the essential functions of the mechanic's job, the airline was required to

> put on some evidence of those essential functions. . . . Although Benson retains the ultimate burden of persuading the trier of fact that he can perform the essential functions of the job, with or without accommodation, much of the information which determines those essential functions lies uniquely with the employer.

Id. at 1113. In reaching this conclusion, the court noted that the ADA regulations direct courts to consider "the employer's judgment as to what functions of the job are essential." Id. (citing 42 U.S.C. §12111(8)). With respect to reasonable accommodation and burden of proof, the court followed the approach adopted in Gilbert under the Rehabilitation Act, holding that "once [the plaintiff] makes a facial showing that other reasonable accommodation is possible, the burden is on Northwest to present evidence that reasonable accommodation is not possible." Id. See Mason v. Frank, 32 F.3d 315, 318-319 (8th Cir. 1994) (Rehabilitation Act); Hall v. United States Postal Service, 857 F.2d 1073, 1080 (6th Cir. 1988). Borkowski also read a prior Seventh Circuit decision, Vande Zande v. Wisconsin Dept. of Admin., 44 F.3d 538 (7th Cir. 1995), to suggest that the burden of persuasion on reasonable accommodation rests with the plaintiff. Borkowski, 63 F.3d at 139 n.4.

Finally, in Barth v. Gelb, 2 F.3d 1180 (D.C. Cir. 1993), the D.C. Circuit discussed the allocation of the burden of proof in disability discrimination cases, concluding that there are three categories of disability cases requiring three different allocations of burden of proof. In the standard case in which the issue is whether the employer acted on the basis of the employee's disability, the traditional *Burdine* three-step analysis applies. The court described the burdens in the second category of cases, where the disability is admittedly relevant because "the fact that the plaintiff's handicap was taken into explicit account in the agency's employment or personnel decision is acknowledged." In such cases, the issue is whether the employee is nevertheless qualified to perform the job:

> In the second category, for example, a plaintiff must establish that (a) he is handicapped but, (b) with reasonable accommodation (which he must describe), he is (c) able to perform "the essential functions" of the position he holds or seeks. See 29 C.F.R. §1613.702(f); see also id. §1613.704(a), (b). As in the usual case, it would then be up to the employing agency to refute that evidence. The burden, however, remains with the plaintiff to prove his case by a preponderance of the evidence.

Id. at 1186. The court's third category involved cases in which the employer asserts an undue hardship defense. In these cases, the court allocated the burden of persuasion on undue hardship to the defendant. Burden of proof in undue hardship cases is discussed further at page 171, Note 8, this supplement (casebook page 811).

2. Systemic Disparate Treatment

Page 789. Add the following new text to Note 2:

Several ADA cases have considered the permissibility of blanket exclusions with mixed results. Although some of these opinions involve licensing decisions, in each case the license sought was a necessary prerequisite to obtaining employment, and the issues addressed are identical to those that would be addressed in an employment case. In Stillwell v. Kansas City Bd. of Police Commrs., 872 F. Supp. 682 (W.D. Miss. 1995), the court followed the approach taken in *Galloway* requiring individualized assessments of disabled individuals to determine if they could meet the requirements of a position. In *Stillwell*, the plaintiff, who was born without a left hand, worked as a private security guard, licensed and registered with the Kansas City Police Department, for nearly 20 years. In 1992, his application for recertification was denied based on a recent state regulation requiring private security guards to meet the physical requirements and qualifications of police officers. In support of their decision, the defendants asserted that two hands were necessary to successfully perform defensive tactics, including neck restraint, knife defense, and handcuffing. Stillwell challenged the Board's blanket rule that one-handed applicants cannot meet these standards. The court rejected the defendants' argument that licensing one-handed applicants would be a direct threat to health and safety. Citing the Supreme Court's decision in *Arline*, the court concluded that "[t]he determination that a person poses a direct threat to the health or safety of others may not be based on generalization or stereotypes about the effects of a particular disability; it must be based on an individual assessment. . . ." Id. at 1831 (quoting *Arline*, 480 U.S. at 287). Thus, the plaintiff could not be denied a license without an individualized assessment of his ability to meet the required physical standards. Other courts have followed the approach taken in *Galloway* and *Stillwell*, striking down blanket exclusions of insulin-dependant individuals from policing positions, see Bombrys v. City of Toledo, 849 F. Supp. 1210, 1216-1219 (N.D. Ohio 1993) (ADA), and from positions requiring driving. See Sarsycki v. United Parcel Service, 862 F. Supp. 336 (W.D. Okla. 1994). Of course, individualized assessment does not guarantee that a disabled individual will qualify for the job.

The District of Columbia and Fifth Circuits have taken a different approach in cases involving DOT regulations imposing restrictions on hearing-impaired truck drivers. In Buck v. Department of Transportation, 56 F.3d 1406 (D.C. Cir. 1995), the D.C. Circuit considered a Federal Highway Administration regulation "requiring that drivers of commercial motor vehicles in interstate commerce be able to hear." Id. Three deaf truck drivers who had previously operated commercial motor vehicles intra-state without any difficulty requested and were denied waivers of the hearing regulation. Challenging the denials under the Rehabilitation Act, the plaintiffs argued that "studies show that a deaf person can drive a truck safely and that the agency's hearing regulation violates . . . the Rehabilitation Act by excluding handicapped individuals on the basis of an absolute standard rather than allowing for the individualized assessment of their ability safely to operate a commercial motor vehicle." Id. at 1407. The D.C. Circuit disagreed, ruling that once the FHWA reasonably concluded that a certain hearing acuity is necessary in order to operate a truck safely, individual safe-driving assessments were not required. The court found unpersuasive the plaintiffs' evidence that the FHWA rule was not reasonably related to safe driving. The plaintiffs' evidence included their own anecdotal experience driving trucks intra-state and a study that, although relevant, concluded that hearing-impaired drivers have a risk of crashing that is from .7 to 2.0 times that of other drivers. Id. at 1409. Plaintiffs were entitled to individualized assessment of their hearing ability but not individualized assessments of their ability to drive a truck safely in spite of their hearing loss.

The U.S. Department of Transportation also has a blanket policy prohibiting persons with insulin-dependent diabetes from operating commercial motor vehicles weighing over 10,000 pounds. State policies patterned after DOT's guidelines were challenged in Wood v. Omaha Sch. Dist., 25 F.3d 667

(8th Cir. 1994). The Eighth Circuit concluded that the plaintiffs were not qualified to drive because "hyperglycemia creates an increased risk of sudden and unexpected loss of vision or blurred vision and that hypoglycemia produces a danger of a sudden loss of consciousness." Id. at 668. The Eighth Circuit, however, took an individualized approach, noting that the plaintiffs are "poorly-controlled diabetics and are thus in danger of problems from hypoglycemia or hyperglycemia." In Daugherty v. City of El Paso, 4 AD Cases 995 (5th Cir. 1995), a bus driver was discharged after he was diagnosed as an insulin-dependant diabetic. Daugherty asserted that the city should, as a reasonable accommodation of his disability, seek a waiver of the DOT regulations. The Fifth Circuit concluded that a waiver would not change Daugherty's status as a disabled individual who was not qualified to drive a bus. The court held that, as a matter of law, a driver with insulin-dependent diabetes is a direct threat to safety. Therefore, the city's blanket restriction prohibiting insulin-dependent diabetics from driving buses did not violate the ADA. Id. at 995.

Can these cases be reconciled with each other? Under what circumstances should the ADA and the Rehabilitation Act be interpreted to permit blanket exclusions?

3. Failing to Make Reasonable Accommodations

Page 789.   Add the following to the citation for Johnson v. Sullivan:

, *cert. denied*, 115 S. Ct. 52 (1994)

Page 796.   Add the following to the citation for Barth v. Gelb in Note 12:

, *aff'd*, 2 F.3d 1180 (D.C. Cir. 1993), *cert. denied*, 114 S. Ct. 1538 (1994)

Page 796.   Add the following new text to Note 12:

An employee who fails to participate in discussions about accommodation needs may forfeit protection against disability discrimination. In Derbis v. U.S. Shoe Corp., 67 F.3d 294 (4th Cir. 1995), the Fourth Circuit ruled that U.S. Shoe had no obligation to employ Derbis because, although she needed an accommodation to permit her to work with her injured hand, she failed to provide the employer with information necessary to determine what accommodations might be appropriate. See, e.g., Czopek v. General Electric Co., 4 AD Cases 1231 (N.D. Ill. 1995) (by discussing alternative job opportunities, employer met obligation to accommodate employee who failed to provide the additional medical information required to craft necessary accommodations). Employers, however, cannot escape liability by making unreasonable requests for medical information. See Langon v. Department of Health and Human Services, 959 F.2d 1053 (D.C. Cir. 1992).

Page 798.   Add the following to the citation for Walders v. Garrett in carryover Note 15:

, cert. denied, 505 U.S. 1229 (1992)

Page 798.   Add new Note 16a:

16a. In Vande Zande v. Wisconsin Dept. of Admin., 44 F.3d 538 (7th Cir. 1995), in an opinion authored by Judge Posner, the Seventh Circuit considered what it means for an accommodation to be "reasonable":

> It is plain enough what "accommodation" means. The employer must be willing to consider making changes in its ordinary work rules, facilities, terms, and conditions in order to enable a disabled individual to work. The difficult term is "reasonable." The plaintiff in our case, a paraplegic, argues in effect that the term just means apt or efficacious. An accommodation is reasonable, she believes, when it is tailored to the particular individual's disability. A ramp or lift is thus a reasonable accommodation for a person who like this plaintiff is confined to a wheelchair. Consideration of costs do not enter into the term as the plaintiff would have us construe it. Cost is, she argues, the domain of "undue hardship" . . . a safe harbor for an employer that can show that it would go broke or suffer other excruciating financial distress were it compelled to make a reasonable accommodation in the sense of one effective in enabling the disabled person to overcome the vocational effects of the disability.
>
> These are questionable interpretations both of "reasonable" and of "undue hardship." To "accommodate" a disability is to make some change that will enable the disabled person to work. An unrelated, inefficacious change would not be an accommodation of the disability at all. So "reasonable" may be intended to qualify (in a sense of weaken) "accommodation," in just the same way that if one requires a "reasonable effort" of someone this means less than the maximum possible effort, or in law that the duty of "reasonable care," the cornerstone of the law of negligence requires something less than the maximum possible care. It is understood in that law that in deciding what care is reasonable the court considers the cost of increased care. . . . Similar reasons could be

used to flesh out the meaning of the word "reasonable" in the term "reasonable accommodations." It would not follow that the costs and benefits of altering a workplace to enable a disabled person to work would always have to be qualified, or even that an accommodation would have to be deemed unreasonable if the cost exceeded the benefit however slightly. But, at the very least, the cost could not be disproportionate to the benefit. Even if an employer is so large or wealthy . . . that it may not be able to plead "undue hardship," it would not be required to expend enormous sums in order to bring about a trivial improvement in the life of a disabled employee.

Id. at 542-543. The Second Circuit in Borkowski v. Valley Central Sch. Dist., 63 F.3d 131 (2d Cir. 1995), applying the Rehabilitation Act, followed *Vande Zande*. Judge Calabresi held that an accommodation is reasonable only if its costs are not clearly disproportionate to the benefits it will produce. Id. at 138. See also Lyons v. Legal Aid Society, 68 F.3d 1512 (2d Cir. 1995) (reasonableness depends on balancing of costs and benefits to both the employer and the employee, but accommodation is not unreasonable merely because it requires employee to assume more than de minimis cost). Citing the legislative history of the ADA for support, the *Borkowski* court went on to further explain the cost/benefit analysis:

In evaluating the costs and benefits of a proposed accommodation, it must be noted that Section 504 does not require that the *employer* receive a benefit commensurate with the cost of the accommodation. . . . The concept of reasonable accommodation permits the employer to expect the same level of performance from individual with disabilities as it expects from the rest of its workforce. . . . But the requirement of reasonable accommodation anticipates that it may cost more to obtain that level of performance from an employee with a disability than it would to obtain the same level of performance from a non-disabled employee. . . . Congress fully expected that the duty of reasonable accommodation would require employers to assume more than a de minimis cost. . . . It follows that an accommodation is not unreasonable simply because it would be more efficient, in the narrow sense of less costly for a given level of performance, to hire a non-disabled employee than a disabled one.

Id. at n.1.

Page 799.   Add the following new text to Note 18:

Two courts have recently considered the distinction between personal and work-related needs. Nelson v. Ryan, 860 F. Supp. 76 (W.D.N.Y. 1994), concerned a blind rehabilitation instructor who used a guide dog to assist in travelling to blind clients' homes to provide private instruction in daily living skills. After Nelson's first guide dog died, Nelson requested paid administrative leave to train another dog. The court, relying on ADA legislative history, concluded that seeing-eye dogs, even if used at work, are generally considered to be personal items (citing S. Rep. Nos. 101-116, 101st Cong., Sess. 32-33 (1989)). The court noted that while an employer may be required to accommodate a blind person by permitting him to use a guide dog at work, employers are not required to provide guide dogs to blind employees because they are personal items. The court went on to hold that

> [a]s an employer is not required to supply a guide dog to a blind employee, there is no basis on which to require an employer to supply administrative paid leave to a blind employee for purposes of training his guide dog, even if that employee uses the guide dog for some work purposes.

Id. at 83. The court noted that the accommodation the employer provided, advance sick leave, was reasonable and that requiring more would open the door to claims for paid administrative leave for training to use other personal items such as a hearing aid or a prosthesis.

In Lyons v. Legal Aid Society, 68 F.3d 1512 (2d Cir. 1995), a disabled attorney sought financial assistance to park her car near her office because injuries made it difficult for her to walk, stand for extended periods of time, and climb or descend stairs. Legal Aid, in defending its refusal to pay for parking, argued that the requested accommodation was merely "a matter of personal convenience" and therefore not within Legal Aid's obligation to provide accommodation. The Second Circuit ruled that a parking place was a work-related need, not merely a personal need. Lyons could not do her job without parking near the office, reaching the office and the courts was an essential function of her job, and there was no evidence on the record that she planned to use the space for any other purpose. Id. at 1517.

If an employer provides accommodations beyond those required by the ADA, does anyone have standing to challenge this action? Is an employer who provides accommodations beyond those that are required bound to provide the same accommodations for others? See Vande Zande v. Wisconsin Dept. of Admin., 44 F.3d 538, 545 (7th Cir. 1995) ("if the employer . . . goes further than the law requires—by allowing the worker to work at home, it must not be punished for its generosity by being deemed to have conceded the reasonableness of so far-reaching an accommodation. That would hurt rather than help disabled workers"); Myers v. Hose, 50 F.3d 278 (4th Cir. 1995) ("the fact that certain accommodations may have been offered . . . to some employees as a matter of good faith does not mean that they must be extended to Myers as a matter of law").

Page 800.   Add the following new text to Note 20:

The Seventh Circuit in Vande Zande v. Wisconsin Dept. of Admin., 44 F.3d 538 (7th Cir. 1995), discussed the degree of equality of access to benefits required by the ADA. In *Vande Zande*, the plaintiff, who was confined to a wheelchair, complained that the kitchenette sinks provided for employee use in her office building were inaccessible because they were too high. A bathroom sink located near her office was accessible. She argued that forcing her to use the bathroom sink for activities such as washing out coffee cups was stigmatizing. While acknowledging that emotional barriers to equal employment of disabled individuals are relevant to determining the reasonableness of an accommodation, the court ruled that the employer need not spend "even modest amounts of money to bring about an absolute identity in working conditions." The court went on to rule that "[a]ccess to a particular sink, when access to an equivalent sink, conveniently located, is provided, is not a legal duty of an employer." Id. at 546.

Consider an asthmatic employee who is capable of performing all essential job functions, including attending meetings in a smoke-filled conference room, but with a significant level of discomfort. Is this employee entitled to an accommodation in the form of restricted or prohibited smoking in the conference room? According to the court in Harmer v. Virginia Electric & Power Co., 831 F. Supp. 1300 (E.D. Va. 1993), the answer is probably no:

> the purpose of reasonable accommodation is to allow a disabled employee to perform the essential functions of his job or to enable him to enjoy equal privileges of nondisabled employees, such as access to bathrooms and cafeterias. . . . Harmer is not entitled to absolute accommodation under the ADA because he can perform the essential functions of his position with the reasonable accommodations made by Virginia Power as evidenced by his job performance appraisals, which indicate that he consistently met his job requirements.

Id. at 1306. Cf. Heilweil v. Mt. Sinai Hosp., 32 F.3d 718 (2d Cir. 1994) (asthmatic employee affected by fumes in the blood bank where she worked not disabled because her asthma only interfered with this particular job).

The Ninth Circuit, in Felde v. City of San Jose, 66 F.3d 335 (9th Cir. 1995), considered what equal treatment means in the context of eligibility for retirement benefits. In *Felde*, the employer offered two retirement options, regular service retirement or disability retirement. Regular service retirement was available to all employees, including disabled employees, and included a payment for 100 percent of unused sick leave. Disability retirement, available only to disabled employees, had the advantage of providing some tax benefits, but the disadvantage of providing a sick leave payout capped at 80 percent of a maximum number of hours. Felde claimed that this cap was discriminatory. The Ninth Circuit disagreed because disabled employees had unlimited access to regular service retirement. What Felde wanted was a better deal than was available to other employees—all the advantages of disability retirement plus the advantages of general retirement.

Page 800.   Add the following new text to Note 22:

With respect to reassignment as an accommodation, Rehabilitation Act regulations now require that disabled employees be accommodated by offering reassignment to a vacant position

> in the same commuting area . . . and at the same grade or level, the essential functions of which the individual would be able to perform with reasonable accommodation. . . . In the absence of a position at the same grade or level, an offer of reassignment to a vacant position at the highest available grade or level below the employee's current grade or level shall be required.

29 C.F.R. §1614.203.

Page 800.   Add the following new text to Note 23:

Reasonable accommodation does not require bumping other employees, see Eckles v. Consolidated Rail Corp., 890 F. Supp. 1391 (S.D. Ind. 1995) (ADA), assigning disabled employees in violation of other employees' rights under a bona fide seniority plan, id. at 1150, or discharging other employees. See, e.g., Wooten v. Farmland Foods, 58 F.3d 382 (8th Cir. 1995).

Is an employer required to create a new position to accommodate a disabled employee? See Benson v. Northwest Airlines, 4 AD Cases 1234 (8th Cir. 1995) (not if doing so requires reallocating essential functions); Fedro v. Reno, 21 F.3d 1391 (7th Cir. 1994) (employer not required to create new position by combining two part-time positions). Is an employer required to promote an employee to a vacant position as a reasonable accommodation? See Milton v. Scrivener, Inc., 53 F.3d 118 (10th Cir. 1995) (no). Must an employer accommodate an employee by transferring the individual to a different job to avoid a stressful relationship with a supervisor or co-workers that exacerbates the employee's mental or other disability? Compare Lewis v. Zilog, Inc., 908 F. Supp. 931 (N.D. Ga. 1995) ("[f]orcing transfers of employees . . . would undermine an employer's ability to control its own labor force . . . [and] give disabled employee preferential treatment") with Weiler v. Household Finance Corp., 3 AD Cases 1337 (N.D. Ill. 1994) (alleged failure to transfer away from stressful position states a cause of action).

5.   Defending Against Disparate Treatment and Reasonable Accommodation Claims: Undue Hardship and Direct Threat

Page 810.   Add the following to the citation for Barth v. Gelb in Note 6:

, *cert. denied*, 114 S. Ct. 1538 (1994)

Page 811.   Add new Note 8:

Most disability discrimination cases do not reach the stage of considering undue hardship, instead concluding that the proposed accommodation is not reasonable. In three cases, however, the D.C. Circuit, Second Circuit, and Seventh Circuit have discussed at length the defendant's burden to establish that a proposed accommodation would constitute an undue hardship. In each case the discussion of undue hardship was unavoidably wrapped up in the discussion of the closely related concept of "reasonable accommodations."

In Barth v. Gelb, 2 F.3d 1180 (D.C. Cir. 1993), *cert. denied*, 114 S. Ct. 1538 (1994), the D.C. Circuit imposed on plaintiffs a burden of persuasion with respect to the issue of reasonable accommodation, a burden that includes two elements. The plaintiff must prove both that the proposed accommodation is effective and that the accommodation is reasonable in terms of the burden that it would impose on a typical employer. Under this approach, undue hardship includes consideration of whether the proposed accommodation is unreasonable in the context of the employer's particular enterprise.

The Second Circuit in Borkowski v. Valley Central Sch. Dist., 63 F.3d 131 (2d Cir. 1995), disagreed with this approach because it creates the possibility that a defendant for whom a proposed accommodation would be reasonable would not be obligated to provide it because it would be unreasonable for most employers in the same industry. The Second Circuit also expressed concern that placing the burden of proof with respect to reasonableness on the plaintiff is unworkable because the employer possesses most of the information relevant to that issue. The Second Circuit, therefore, while placing a burden on the plaintiff to show that an accommodation exists that would allow the plaintiff to perform essential functions, imposes on the defendant the burden of proving that the proposed accommodation is not reasonable. According to the Second Circuit, the plaintiff's burden on the reasonableness of the accommodation is one of production that can be met by "suggest[ing] the existence of a plausible accommodation, the costs of which, facially, do not clearly exceed its benefits." Id. at 138. The burden then shifts to the defendant to show that the proposed accommodation is unreasonable. Under this approach, unreasonableness and undue hardship merge:

> At this point the defendant's burden of persuading the factfinder that the plaintiff's proposed accommodation is unreasonable merges, in effect, with its burden of showing, as an affirmative defense, that the proposed accommodation would cause it to suffer an undue hardship, for in practice meeting the burden of non-persuasion on the reasonableness of the accommodation and demonstrating that the accommodation imposes an undue hardship amount to the same thing.

Id. The court went on to discuss the elements of "unreasonable" or "undue hardship," citing Rehabilitation Act regulations that designate the factors relevant to determining whether an accommodation imposes an undue hardship:

(1) The overall size of the recipient's operation, including the number of employees, number and type of facilities, and size of budget;
(2) The type of the recipient's operation, including the composition and structure of the recipient's workforce; and
(3) the nature and cost of the accommodation needed.

34 C.F.R. §104.12(b). The court also cited ADA regulations, which require consideration of substantially the same factors. 42 U.S.C.A. §12111(10). The issue, according to the Second Circuit, is one of degree: "[E]ven this list of factors says little about how great a hardship an employer must bear before the hardship becomes undue. Does Section 504 require, for example, that employers be driven to the brink of insolvency before a hardship becomes too great?" Id. The court held that this showing is not required, relying on legislative history of the ADA rejecting a provision that would have defined an undue hardship as one that threatened the continued existence of the employer. Id. "Where the employer is a government entity, Congress could not have intended the only limit on the employer's duty to make reasonable accommodation to be the full extent of the tax base on which the government entity could draw." Id. The court concluded that in order to meet its burden of proving both that the proposed accommodation is unreasonable and that the hardship it would impose is undue, the employer must "undertake a refined analysis" of the relative costs and benefits of the accommodation, considering both "the industry to which the employer belongs as well as the individual characteristics of the particular defendant-employer." Id. The court further noted that "mathematical precision" and "complex economic formulae" are

not required. Rather, "a common-sense balancing of the costs and benefits in light of the factors listed in the regulations is all that is expected." Id. at 1271.

In Vande Zande v.Wisconsin Dept. of Admin., 44 F.3d 538 (1995), the Seventh Circuit, while not discussing the allocation of burdens of proof with respect to reasonableness and undue hardship, has adopted the same cost-benefit analysis utilized by the Second Circuit. The Seventh Circuit agreed that limiting undue hardship to a "failing company" defense is probably incorrect under the ADA:

> [Undue hardship] is a defined term in the Americans with Disabilities Act, and the definition is "an action requiring significant difficulty or expense." . . . The financial condition of the employer is only one consideration in determining whether an accommodation otherwise reasonable would impose an undue hardship. . . . The legislative history equates "undue hardship" to "unduly costly." . . . These are terms of relation. We must ask, "undue" in relation to what? Presumably (given the statutory definition and the legislative history) in relation to the benefits of the accommodation to the disabled worker as well as to the employer's resources.

Id. at 543. Like the Second Circuit, the Seventh Circuit raised the issue of undue hardship for an employer with above-average costs resulting in a precarious financial condition, suggesting that undue hardship could be interpreted to permit such an employer to demonstrate that, although reasonable for a normal employer, the accommodation would be an undue hardship in light of this employer's financial instability.

Which approach is most persuasive? Why?

Page 814. *Add the following text to Note 3:*

Courts assessing the risk of hiring individuals who are infected with HIV have reached different results depending on the nature of the work involved. In Chalk v. U.S. District Court, 840 F.2d 701 (9th Cir. 1988), the court held that a teacher with AIDS who taught hearing-impaired students did not pose a "significant risk" in the workplace, and that his condition could be monitored to ensure that any secondary infections he contracted would also not pose a significant risk. On the other hand, in Scoles v. Mercy Health Corp., 887 F. Supp. 765 (E.D. Penn. 1994), a hospital that required an HIV-positive surgeon to inform patients of his HIV status was not liable for violating either the Rehabilitation Act or the ADA because the doctor posed a direct threat to his patients. *Scoles* took the same approach followed by courts that have considered whether HIV-infected individuals are "qualified" disabled individuals, concluding that while the probability of surgeon-to-patient transmission is low, the risk cannot be eliminated and even a very low risk is a direct threat to patients when it involves a fatal disease. Id. at 769.

In another case involving the risk of transmitting a contagious disease, a district court concluded that a firefighter who had the hepatitis B virus did not pose a direct threat to persons to whom he gave mouth-to-mouth resuscitation because there exists no scientific evidence that hepatitis B virus has been transmitted by saliva. See Roe v. District of Columbia, 842 F. Supp. 563 (D.C. 1993).

In Altman v. NYC Health and Hospitals Corp., 903 F. Supp. 503 (S.D.N.Y. 1995), the court applied the ADA direct threat provision when a hospital refused to reinstate, as chief of medicine, a doctor who entered an alcohol treatment program after treating patients while visibly drunk. The court held that the hospital was justified in refusing reinstatement because of the danger that the doctor might suffer an undetected relapse, a danger that the court deemed was not insubstantial where only three months had passed since he sought treatment. The chief of medicine position entailed final and essentially unreviewable treatment decisions whenever there was uncertainty or disagreement among physicians, interns, and residents. Even if the plaintiff effectively sought to remove himself from the decision-making process whenever he relapsed or suffered from withdrawal symptoms, his abrupt withdrawal from hospital operations could pose significant risks to patients. Id. at 509.

The hospital accommodated Dr. Altman's alcoholism by reinstating him as an attending physician. On the question whether Dr. Altman's alcoholism could be accommodated to permit him to return to his position as chief of medicine, the court considered and rejected as ineffective a number of proposed methods of monitoring his condition to ensure against relapse. Problems associated with monitoring by colleagues included his ability to consume large quantities of alcohol without apparent effect and the awkwardness of placing medical staff in the position of monitoring their supervisor. Professional monitoring was rejected as ineffective on the ground that some of the doctor's duties were performed at odd hours and without warning. Id. at 512.

D.   SPECIAL PROBLEMS OF DISABILITY DISCRIMINATION

1.   Drug and Alcohol Users

Page 821.   Add the following new text at the end of section 1:

Several circuits have concluded that discharging employees for misconduct relating to alcoholism and drug addiction does not constitute unlawful discrimination on the basis of their disabling condition. Despears v. Milwaukee, 63 F.3d 635 (7th Cir. 1995), concerned an alcoholic maintenance worker who lost his driver's license after his fourth conviction for drunk driving. His employer responded by demoting him to a lower-paying position. Although Despears' job responsibilities included occasional driving, driving was not an essential function of his job. The Seventh Circuit nevertheless declined to find unlawful discrimination under either federal statute, ruling that driving under the influence, while related to Despears' alcoholism, was not a symptom of his alcoholism because he could have chosen not to drive. The court held, therefore, that being demoted because he lost his license did not amount to being demoted because of his alcoholism. See also Maddox v. University of Tenn., 62 F.3d 843 (6th Cir. 1995) (ADA) (firing university football coach because he was arrested for drunk driving lawful; discharge for unacceptable misconduct is not a discharge because of a disability); Ferby v. United States Postal Service, 70 F.3d 1271 (9th Cir. 1995) (employee may be discharged for a violent outburst related to his alcoholism). Is an employer who discharges a dyslexic because he doesn't read fast enough or an individual with multiple sclerosis because she cannot walk fast enough acting on the basis of these employees' disabilities? If the answer is yes, can these cases be distinguished from the alcoholism cases? See page 147, Note 20a, this supplement (casebook page 756).

Another recurring issue relates to the meaning of "currently engaging" in drug use as distinguished from "rehabilitated successfully." The Ninth Circuit in Collings v. Longview Fibre Co., 63 F.3d 828 (9th Cir. 1995), ruled that an employer, who fired eight employees who admitted buying or using drugs at work within the past few weeks or months, did not discriminate on the basis of their drug addiction. The employees alleged that they were not "currently engaging in the illegal use of drugs" because they were drug-free at the time of the discharge. The court held that "currently engaging" is not limited to drug use on the day of, or within a matter of days or weeks before, the adverse employment action. It is enough that the drug use occurred recently enough for the employer to conclude that the employees were active drug users. See Baustian v. Louisiana, 4 AD Cases 1692 (E.D. La. 1995) (seven weeks between an employee's last use of drugs and his discharge was not long enough to avoid being considered a current drug user).

In Altman v. NYC Health and Hospitals Corp., 4 AD Cases 1665 (S.D.N.Y. 1995), discussed at page 174, this supplement (casebook page 814), the court declined to treat a doctor returning from an alcohol rehabilitation program as successfully rehabilitated, citing the danger of relapse and ruling that the hospital was entitled to take precautions against the possibility of relapse. The court did not attempt to characterize the hospital's actions as a response to the physician's current use of alcohol. Instead, the court ruled that the hospital was justified in acting on the basis of his alcoholism, whether or not he was currently alcohol-free, because the danger of undetectable relapse posed a direct threat to patient safety.

McDaniel v. Mississippi Baptist Medical Center, 877 F. Supp. 321 (S.D. Miss. 1995), posed similar problems. McDaniel was a hospital employee who had been treated in the past for drug addiction. While employed at the hospital, he relapsed and checked into a treatment program from which he was released three weeks later. When the hospital refused to reinstate him, he sued under the ADA, alleging that the employer's conduct was unlawful discrimination because he was enrolled in a treatment program and no longer engaging in drug use. The court ruled against McDaniel, holding that McDaniel was not protected because he was fired for drug use before he ever entered the treatment program. Id. at 326. In an alternative holding, the court ruled that, even if McDaniels was discharged after he entered treatment, he was not protected because a rehabilitated drug addict is protected from adverse employment actions only after a drug-free period of some considerable length. The individual must have been recovered long enough for the recovery to become stable. Id. at 328-329. The case is currently on appeal to the Fifth Circuit. See ADA's Protection of Drug Abuser Is Probed by Court, 150 LRR 504 (12/18/95).

The court in Corbett v. National Products, 4 AD Cases 987 (E.D. Penn. 1995), took a somewhat different approach in the context of an alcoholic employee who needed treatment. Although the court emphasized that "an employer would not have to permit several leaves of absence for an alcoholic worker for whom a successful treatment is unlikely," id. at 990, see Myers v. Hose, 50 F.3d 278 (4th Cir. 1995), the court ruled that, absent evidence that an employee's attempt at rehabilitation would be futile, his employer should have accommodated him by allowing him to take a 28-day unpaid leave of absence to receive treatment for his alcoholism. 4 AD Cases at 990-991. See Schmidt v. Safeway, Inc., 864 F. Supp. 991 (D. Or. 1994) (same).

2.   Medical Examinations and Inquiries

Page 822.   Add the following new text at the end of section 2:

In Grenier v. Cyanamid Plastics, 70 F.3d 667 (1st Cir. 1995), an employee on disability leave due to psychological problems, including paranoia, sought reinstatement as an electrician. The employer asked whether his mental state might interfere with his ability to get along with co-workers and asked for medical documentation as to his limitations and his need for accommodation. The First Circuit ruled that the ADA does not preclude an employer, during the pre-offer stage, from asking an individual with a known disability whether he can perform the job. In addition, requests for medical documentation to confirm the existence of a disability or to determine ability to perform are permissible. The court reasoned that the ban on pre-offer inquiries is designed to ensure that a hidden disability stays hidden. Because the employer already was familiar with the former employee's disability, the employer had a right to assess his recovery and his ability to perform. See Brumley v. Pena, 62 F.3d 27 (8th Cir. 1995) (requiring former employee disabled by severe depression to provide verification of recovery prior to restoration to duty did not violate the Rehabilitation Act).

The court in Doe v. Kohn, Nast & Graf, 866 F. Supp. 190 (E.D. Pa. 1994), ruled that the employer's search of a current employee's office for the purpose of discovering whether he had AIDS was a prohibited medical inquiry.

The distinction between a medical inquiry and a job-related inquiry directed at current employees is apparent in the Ninth Circuit's struggle to resolve a case brought by a physician's estate complaining that the FBI's decision not to refer patients to him constituted discrimination on the basis of his disability, AIDS. In its original opinion, the Ninth Circuit affirmed the district court's ruling against Doe on the theory that the FBI was entitled to stop sending patients because Doe failed to provide sufficient information in response to the FBI's requests about necessary accommodations. The court concluded that the FBI had a right to ask Doe if he had AIDS because he was not forthcoming with information about necessary precautions to protect patients. Doe v. Attorney General of the United States, 34 F.3d 781 (9th Cir. 1994) (opinion withdrawn 1/17/95). After withdrawing the original opinion, however, the court finally concluded that while the FBI's inquiries about necessary precautions were permissible, the responses provided were adequate and that the FBI violated the statute by asking whether Doe had AIDS and by terminating him because he refused to answer that question. Doe v. Attorney General of the United States, 62 F.3d 1424 (9th Cir. 1995).

4. Protected Relationship

Page 822. Add the following new text at the end of section 4:

The Fourth Circuit, in Tyndall v. National Education Centers, 31 F.3d 209 (4th Cir. 1994), held, consistent with the EEOC view, that a business school was not required by the ADA to restructure an employee's work schedule to enable her to care for her disabled son. The court found further that the school had not discharged the plaintiff because of her association with her disabled son and unfounded fears that this would lead to increased costs or absences. Rather, the school discharged her because of her excessive absenteeism. Id. at 211.

In order to make out a case of discrimination based on association with a disabled individual, the plaintiff must show that the individual with whom she has a relationship is disabled and that the employer was aware of the third party's disability. Ennis v. National Association of Business and Educational Radio, Inc., 53 F.3d 55 (4th Cir. 1995). Even if these minimum requirements are satisfied, the employee must be fired because of the relationship. In *Ennis*, the court concluded that plaintiff was discharged for inadequate performance, not because of her relationship with her disabled son. Id. at 62.

5.   Constructive Discharge

Page 825.   Add new Note 6:

Discriminatory harassment may provide the basis for a constructive discharge claim. See Haysman v. Food Lion, Inc., 893 F. Supp. 1092, 1100 (S.D. Ga. 1995) (employee allegedly harassed by supervisors on the basis of his disability may have stated a case of constructive discharge under the ADA); Kent v. Derwinski, 790 F. Supp. 1032, 1041 (E.D. Wash. 1991) (Rehabilitation Act) (retarded and emotionally handicapped laundry employee constructively discharged because she was taunted by co-workers because of her handicap, inappropriately disciplined by supervisor, and employer failed to respond adequately).

6.   Health Insurance

Page 829.   Add new Note 5:

One unique aspect of lawsuits relating to health insurance plans is that, by the time the health insurance is needed, the plaintiff may be too impaired to seek the protection of the ADA because he or she is no longer a qualified individual with a disability. For example, in Parker v. Metropolitan Life Ins. Co., 875 F. Supp. 1321 (W.D. Tenn. 1995), the plaintiff complained that her former employer's long-term disability plan provided longer medical benefits coverage for individuals with physical disabilities than for individuals with mental disabilities. The court ruled that the plaintiff was not covered by the ADA. She was qualified but not disabled when she signed up for the insurance plan and disabled but not qualified when she sued.

7. *National Labor Relations Act*

Page 830. *Add the following new text at the end of section 7:*

The courts are in disagreement about the impact of collective bargaining agreements and seniority rights on an employer's obligation to accommodate disabled employees under the ADA. In Milton v. Scrivener, Inc., 53 F.3d 1118 (10th Cir. 1995), employees who, because of their disabilities, could not meet the employer's increased production standards requested that they be accommodated by a lighter workload or allowing them to bid for less demanding jobs within the company. The Tenth Circuit ruled that both proposed accommodations were unreasonable and not required by the ADA. Giving the disabled employees a lighter workload was unreasonable in part because it was barred by the collective bargaining agreement. Allowing them to bid for other jobs was unreasonable because it was prohibited by the collective bargaining agreement because they lacked the necessary seniority. Id. at 1124. See also Wooten v. Farmland Foods, 58 F.3d 382, 386 (8th Cir. 1995) (ADA does not require an employer to terminate other employees in violation of a collective bargaining agreement in order to accommodate disabled employees).

A district court reached a different conclusion in Emrick v. Libbey Owens Ford Co., 875 F. Supp. 393 (E.D. Tex. 1995). Noting that "decisions under the Rehabilitation Act are only persuasive authority for ADA decisions," id. at 395, the court found that the legislative history of the ADA identifies conflict with a collective bargaining agreement as only one factor to be considered in determining whether a proposed accommodation is reasonable. In light of this history, the court held that because reassignment is specifically listed as a possible accommodation,

> the per se rule adopted under the Rehabilitation Act does not apply to cases under the ADA. Rather, . . . when reassignment of an otherwise qualified employee would conflict with an otherwise valid collective bargaining agreement or seniority system, this conflict shall be weighed by the fact finder in evaluating the reasonableness of such an accommodation under the ADA.

Id. at 396-397.

Two recent grievance arbitrations, however, ruled that the employers' attempts to accommodate in order to comply with the ADA breached their collective bargaining agreements. See Olin Corp., 103 LA 481; Clark Cty. Sheriff's Dept., 102 LA 193. But, in another case, the arbitrator ruled that reassigning two police officers to different shifts in order to accommodate a diabetic officer's need to work the day shift in compliance with the ADA did

not violate the union contract despite a past practice of assigning shifts by seniority. City of Dearborn Heights, 101 LA 809. One district court has held
that for employers who have collective bargaining contracts, that contract
may provide the only remedy for disabled employees claiming that they were
not reasonably accommodated. See Austin v. Owens-Brockway Glass Container, Inc., 844 F. Supp. 1103 (W.D. Va. 1994) (dismissing plaintiff's ADA
suit because Owens-Brockway's collective bargaining contract provided for
mandatory arbitration of all disputes under the contract). Is this consistent
with the law developed under Title VII? See page 979 of the casebook.

In light of these cases, how would you advise an employer to respond if a
disabled employee requests an accommodation, such as a transfer to a vacant
position, that interferes with other employees' seniority rights under a collective bargaining agreement? Note that, even under the Rehabilitation Act, an
employer may accommodate a disabled employee by reassigning him to a vacant position without violating the rights of other employees if the contract
anticipates that such accommodation is a valid concern to be considered in
filling vacancies. See Buckingham v. United States, 998 F.2d 735, 740 (9th
Cir. 1993) (Rehabilitation Act).

8.   Family and Medical Leave Act

Pages 831-833.   Replace the Department of Labor, Preamble to Interim Regulations with the following new text:

EEOC's FMLA regulations define "serious health condition":

> "[S]erious health condition" entitling an employee to FMLA leave means an
> illness, injury, impairment, or physical or mental condition that involves—
>   (1) Inpatient care (i.e., an overnight stay) in a hospital, hospice, or residen-
> tial medical care facility, including any period of incapacity . . . or any subse-
> quent treatment in connection with such inpatient care; or
>   (2) Continuing treatment by a health care provider.

29 C.F.R. §825.114(a) (1993).

The regulations define "inpatient care" for purposes of this section to mean
inability to work or perform other regular daily activities. Id. The definition
of "continuing treatment by a health care provider" in the regulations provides for five different types of continuing treatment: (1) a period of incapacity of more than three consecutive calendar days; (2) a period of incapacity
due to pregnancy or prenatal care; (3) a period of incapacity due to a chronic
serious health condition (e.g., asthma, diabetes, epilepsy); (4) a period of incapacity that is permanent or long-term due to a condition for which treat-

180

ment may not be effective (e.g., Alzheimer's, stroke, terminal illness); and (5) a period of absence to receive multiple treatments for necessary restorative surgery or for conditions such as cancer, arthritis, or kidney disease that, without treatment, would result in absences of more than three days. In order to qualify for FMLA leave, each of these situations must involve specified levels of active treatment or supervision by health care professionals. 29 C.F.R. §825.114(a)(2)(i)-(v) (1993).

The regulations provide specific examples of conditions and treatments that are and are not eligible for FMLA leave. Routine physical, dental, or eye examinations are not covered. Cosmetic treatments that are not medically required do not constitute "serious health conditions," unless inpatient hospital care is required or complications arise. A variety of common short-term illnesses, such as colds and flu, do not qualify for FMLA leave, absent complications. On the other hand, restorative dental surgery following an accident or surgery to remove cancerous growths and treatments for allergies or stress or substance abuse are included if the other conditions of the regulation are met. Absence resulting from drug use without treatment clearly does not qualify for leave. 29 C.F.R. §825.114(b)-(d). Treating substance abuse as a "serious health condition" should not prevent an employer from taking employment action against an employee whose abuse interferes with job performance as long as the employer complies with the ADA and does not take action against the employee because the employee has exercised his or her right to take FMLA leave for treatment of that condition.

According to EEOC regulations, being "unable to perform the functions of the position of the employee" means "where the health care provider finds that the employee is unable to work at all or is unable to perform any one of the essential functions of the employee's position within the meaning of the Americans with Disabilities Act. . . ." 29 C.F.R. §825.115.

The FMLA regulations expressly provide that the FMLA does not modify the ADA in any way and that employers are obligated to comply with both statutes. 29 C.F.R. §825.702.

In the first case litigated by the Department of Labor under the FMLA, the question was whether an employee gave adequate notice that she was taking leave under the FMLA. Reich v. Midwest Plastic Eng., Inc., No. 1:94-CV-525 (W.D. Mich. 1995), concerned a pregnant employee who was fired for excessive absenteeism after contracting chicken pox. The statute requires 30 days' notice for foreseeable leave. Although the statute does not indicate when notice must be provided when the need for leave is unforeseeable, the regulations provide that "an employee should give notice to the employer of the need for FMLA leave as soon as practicable." 29 C.F.R. §825.303(a). Notice may be verbal but it must be "sufficient to make the employer aware that the employee needs FMLA-qualifying leave." 29 C.F.R. §825.302(c). Reich missed four days of work when her children contracted chicken pox and eight days of work when she contracted chicken pox herself. During her absence, she saw her doctor twice and was hospitalized for one night. The court held that Reich's employer did not violate her rights under the FMLA because, although she spoke with the employer on three occasions about her illness, she never made it clear that she was taking leave because of a serious health condition that qualified her for unpaid leave under the statute. *Reich.*

Manual v. Westlake Polymers Corp., 66 F.3d 758 (5th Cir. 1995), also concerned whether the employee must notify the employer of the need to take FMLA leave. Like *Reich, Manual* involved an unforeseeable leave. Manual was discharged for chronic absenteeism after missing a month of work due to complications relating to an ingrown toenail. In *Manual,* the Fifth Circuit, relying on EEOC's final regulations, see 29 C.F.R. §825.303(b), ruled that Manual was not required to expressly invoke the FMLA in order to seek the protection of the statute. Notice is adequate, the court ruled, if "the information imparted to the employer is sufficient to reasonably apprise it of the employee's request to take time off for a serious health condition." Id. at 764.

The definition of a "serious health condition" was at issue in Seidle v. Provident Mut. Life Ins. Co., 871 F. Supp. 238 (E.D. Pa. 1994). Seidle was absent from work for four days to tend to her son's ear infection. The court ruled that the plaintiff's absence met neither prong of the two-part definition of serious health condition. First, the illness must require an absence from work or school of more than three calendar days. The child in this case was absent from day care for four days, but his ear infection required only a three-day absence. Second, to qualify, the sick individual must see a health care provider at least twice or once followed by a regimen of health care. In this case, the child saw a doctor only once, did not take medication under a doctor's continuing supervision, and did not return for a follow-up visit. This case was decided prior to the EEOC's final regulations under the FMLA that specify an ear infection as an example of an illness that, absent complications, typically will not qualify as a serious health condition. 29 C.F.R. §825.114(c) (1993).

F.   THE REHABILITATION ACT OF 1973

2.   *Federal and Federally Assisted Programs*

Page 837.   Add the following to the citation for Kling
*   v. County of Los Angeles in the first full*
*   paragraph:*

, *rev'd,* 769 F.2d 532 (9th Cir.), *cert. granted and judgment rev'd,* 474 U.S. 936 (1985)

Chapter 9

Equal Pay for Equal Work

B. NARROWING THE GAP BETWEEN MEN'S AND WOMEN'S EARNINGS: EQUAL PAY FOR EQUAL WORK

3. Making the Equal Pay Act Prima Facie Case

Page 864. Add new Note 2a:

2a. It is not necessary that the predecessor male being used as a comparator have been employed during the statutory period allowed for suit. It is sufficient that the plaintiff can make out that she was paid less than a male comparator during the relevant time period. Brinkley-Obu v. Hughes Training, Inc., 36 F.3d 336 (4th Cir. 1994).

Page 864. Add the following to Note 3:

As professional jobs have become the focus of EPA attacks, some courts have found differences in skill to be almost definitional when the two jobs are distinct. For example, Strag v. Board of Trustees, Craven Community College, 55 F.3d 943 (4th Cir. 1995), seemed to find that the mere fact that the plaintiff taught in a different department than her chosen male comparator precluded a finding of equal work. More persuasive, however, is the court's focus on the actual differences between the two jobs, including the male's greater responsibility for lab supervision. See also Soble v. University of Md., 778 F.2d 164 (4th Cir. 1985).

Page 865.   Add the following to carryover Note 4:

See also Stanley v. University of S. Cal., 13 F.3d 1313 (9th Cir. 1994) (differences between responsibilities of coaches of men's and women's basketball teams, including greater public relations and promotional duties for men's coach whose team generated much higher revenues than women's team). See generally Joseph P. Williams, Lower Pay for Women's Coaches: Refuting Some Common Justifications, 21 J.C.&U.L. 643 (1995); Lisa A. Bireline Sarver, Athletics: Coaching Contracts Take On the Equal Pay Act: Can (and Should) Female Coaches Tie the Score?, 28 Creighton L. Rev. 885 (1995).

4.   Breaking an Equal Pay Act Prima Facie Case

*Page 880.   Add the following to the first paragraph of the
             "Economic Benefit" Note:*

Compare Byrd v. Ronayne, 61 F.3d 1026 (1st Cir. 1995) (greater revenues generated for law firm provided an affirmative defense for higher pay for one attorney as compared to plaintiff).

*Page 892.   Add the following after the Morgado citation in
             the second full paragraph:*

; Irby v. Bittick, 44 F.3d 949 (11th Cir. 1995)

5.   Using Title VII to Attack Gender-Based Wage Discrimination

Page 904.   Add new Note 3a:

3a. The courts have struggled with what will suffice to establish a case of gender discrimination in wages under Title VII. Generally, courts simply apply normal Title VII analysis. See Meeks v. Computer Assocs. Intl., 15 F.3d 1013 (11th Cir. 1994); Mulhall v. Advance Security, Inc., 19 F.3d 586 (11th Cir. 1994); Tidwell v. Fort Howard Corp., 989 F.2d 406 (10th Cir. 1993). Other courts have taken a stricter view of Title VII pay cases, seeming to require "direct" evidence or "clear" evidence of discrimination before allowing suit where the work performed in the jobs being compared is sufficiently different. EEOC v. Sears Roebuck & Co., 839 F.2d 302 (7th Cir. 1988); Plemer v. Parsons-Gilbane, 713 F.2d 1127 (5th Cir. 1983). But see Loyd v. Phillips Brothers, Inc., 25 F.3d 518, 525 n.6 (7th Cir. 1994). See also Automobile Workers v. Michigan, 886 F.2d 766, 769 (6th Cir. 1989).

PART IV

PROCEDURES AND REMEDIES

Chapter 10

Procedures for Enforcing Antidiscrimination Laws

B. PRIVATE ENFORCEMENT: THE ADMINISTRATIVE PHASE

3. Filing a Timely Charge: Deferral States

Page 979.   Add the following to the first full paragraph:

Meredith v. Beech Aircraft Corp., 18 F.3d 890 (10th Cir. 1994) (plaintiff B in the second suit could rely on a finding in the first suit that defendant's promotion decision was based on sex, but the defendant could not rely on a finding in the first suit that plaintiff A was the best qualified applicant. Plaintiff B, while allowed to use estoppel offensively, was not bound by the first suit because she was not a party, or in privity with a party, to that suit, and thus had no opportunity to litigate the best qualified issue).

*Page 981.   Add the following at the end of the first full
             paragraph:*

One circuit has even held that *Gilmer* in effect overruled *Gardner-Denver*, in
that arbitration clauses, even when contained in collective bargaining agreements, bar suit by individual employees. Austin v. Owens-Broadway Glass
Container, Inc., 78 F.3d 875 (4th Cir. 1996).

*Page 981.   Add the following after the second full
             paragraph:*

Of course, even if arbitration agreements are enforceable, the courts must
still determine whether a particular clause reaches the dispute in question.
Courts have struggled with whether general language in an arbitration agreement includes employment discrimination claims. Some courts seem hostile
to the notion. One held that the employee must have "knowingly" agreed to
arbitrate such claims, and this requirement is not satisfied unless the agreement refers to employment discrimination claims. Prudential Ins. Co. v. Lai,
42 F.3d 1299 (9th Cir. 1994). See also Kresock v. Bankers Trust Co., 21 F.3d
176 (7th Cir. 1994) (valid amendment to agreement not retroactive without
consent). Another decision carefully parsed the general language and concluded that employment discrimination disputes are not covered. Farrand v.
Lutheran Bhd., 993 F.2d 1253 (7th Cir. 1993). See also Tays v. Covenant Life
Ins. Co., 964 F.2d 501 (5th Cir. 1992). However, other courts have held that
general language includes discrimination claims. Kidd v. Equitable Life As-
surance Socy., 32 F.3d 516 (11th Cir. 1994); Bender v. A.G. Edwards & Sons,
Inc., 971 F.2d 698 (11th Cir. 1992).

   Recently, the Supreme Court held that state laws requiring special treatment of arbitration clauses are preempted by the Federal Arbitration Act.
Doctors Assocs., Inc. v. Casarotto, 64 U.S.L.W. 4370 (May 21, 1996). While
state law principles applicable to contracts generally are in effect incorporated into the FAA on its own terms, that statute precludes states from singling
out agreements to arbitrate for special treatment.

*Page 982.   Add the following at the end of the carryover
             paragraph:*

See generally Douglas E. Abrams, Arbitrability in Recent Federal Civil
Rights Legislation: The Need for Amendment, 26 Conn. L. Rev. 521 (1994)

(arguing that the texts of the ADA and the 1991 Civil Rights Act, "the only sources assured of judicial effectuation," favor enforcing arbitration agreements, even if the legislative histories "acknowledge qualifications on the binding effect arbitral awards would otherwise hold under the FAA").

Page 982.   Add the following at the end of the second full paragraph:

Contra Williams v. Cigna Financial Advisors, Inc., 56 F.3d 656 (5th Cir. 1995) (OWBPA is inapplicable to arbitration agreements). But see Douglas E. Abrams, Arbitrability in Recent Federal Civil Rights Legislation: The Need for Amendment, 26 Conn. L. Rev. 521, 556 n.187 (1994) (arguing that "Congress did not intend the OWBPA's waiver provision to affect the FAA mandate's operation with respect to either post-dispute or predispute arbitration agreements").

Page 983.   Add the following after the last paragraph:

State law actions can also be preempted by the Labor Management Relations Act, §301, 29 U.S.C.A. §185 (1978), or the Railway Labor Act, 45 U.S.C.A. §§151-188 (1986), when the action between an employee and an employer or union would require interpretation of a collective bargaining agreement. Hawaiian Airlines, Inc. v. Norris, 114 S. Ct. 2239 (1994); Hirras v. National R.R. Passenger Corp., 44 F.3d 278 (5th Cir. 1995); Ramirez v. Fox Television Station, Inc., 998 F.2d 743 (9th Cir. 1993); Jackson v. Kimel, 992 F.2d 1318 (4th Cir. 1993). However, there are several exceptions to this rule. Preemption does not occur when the state law regulates activity of "a merely peripheral concern" to the Act or where the regulated conduct touches interests that are deeply rooted in local responsibility and concerns or affects public interests that transcend the employment relationship. San Diego Unions v. Garmon, 359 U.S. 236 (1959); Cook v. Lindsay Olive Growers, 911 F.2d 233 (9th Cir. 1990). Also, state claims that involve "nonnegotiable state law rights" or state law that proscribes conduct or establishes rights independent of the collective bargaining agreement are not preempted. Livadas v. Bradshaw, 114 S. Ct. 2068 (1994); Hawaiian Airlines, Inc. v. Norris, 114 S. Ct. 2239 (1994); Martin Marietta v. Maryland Commn. on Human Rel., 38 F.3d 1392 (4th Cir. 1994). As a result, claims under state fair employment statutes would not normally be preempted. Ramirez v. Fox Television Station, Inc., 998 F.2d 743 (9th Cir. 1993). But see Davis v. Johnson Controls, Inc., 21 F.3d 866 (8th Cir. 1994).

D.   PRIVATE ENFORCEMENT:
RELATIONSHIP OF THE EEOC
CHARGE TO PRIVATE SUIT

1.   Proper Plaintiffs

Page 991.   Add the following to the citation for Fair
*   Employment Council of Greater Washington,*
*   Inc. v. BMC Marketing Corp. in the carryover*
*   paragraph:*

, *rev'd in part and aff'd in part*, 28 F.3d 1268 (D.C. Cir. 1994) (testers had no
standing to sue, although organization that employed them could have standing because of injury to its interests).

Page 991.   Add the following at the end of the carryover
*   paragraph:*

Leroy D. Clark, Employment Discrimination Testing: Theories of Standing
and a Reply to Professor Yelnosky, 28 U. Mich. J.L. Ref. 1 (1994); Jonathan
Levy, Comment, In Response to *Fair Employment Council of Greater Washington Inc. v. BMC Marketing Corp.*: Employment Testers Do Have a Leg to
Stand On, 80 Minn. L. Rev. 123 (1995).

Page 992.   Add the following at the end of the carryover
*   paragraph:*

See also Fair Employment Council of Greater Washington, Inc. v. BMC Marketing Corp., 28 F.3d 1268 (D.C. Cir 1994) (Council suffered injury in fact in
its own right even though it was pursuing the interests of third parties in being free of discrimination because of its broad goal of promoting equal employment opportunity).

H. TITLE VII SUIT AGAINST GOVERNMENTAL EMPLOYERS

2. Federal Eployment

Page 1027.   Add footnote ‡ callout at end of first paragraph:

. . . were also included.‡

‡Following the Republican election success in 1994, the Congressional Accountability Act of 1995, Pub. L. No. 104-1 (Jan. 23, 1995), part of the Contract with America, improved the protection accorded House and Senate employees from discrimination on the basis of race, sex, age, and handicap.

I. SETTLING DISCRIMINATION SUITS

Page 1031.   Add footnote ‡ callout after "pose few special problems" in the sixth line of the first full paragraph:

. . . pose few special problems,‡

‡There has been some question of whether settlements of federal discrimination suits could be enforced in federal court without an independent basis for federal jurisdiction. Although circuit court cases adopted a broader rule, at least for EEOC enforcement, the Supreme Court in Kokkonen v. Guardian Life Ins. Co. of Am., 114 S. Ct. 1673 (1994), held that, after a district court has dismissed the case, it has to have ancillary jurisdiction to enforce any underlying settlement agreement unless the district court specifically retained jurisdiction for that purpose or incorporated the agreement in the order for dismissal. Thus, for a federal court to enforce a settlement agreement where jurisdiction has not been retained for that purpose, Sheng v. Starkey Laboratories, Inc., 53 F.3d 192 (8th Cir. 1995) (reservation of jurisdiction for the parties to reopen the action is not sufficient to assert jurisdiction to enforce a settlement agreement), there must be an independent basis for federal jurisdiction. See Morris v. City of Hobart, 39 F.3d 1105 (10th Cir. 1994) (the mere fact that an agreement settles a federal claim does not mean that suit to enforce the agreement arises under federal law for federal question jurisdiction, but such jurisdiction will lie if resolution of the dispute requires decision of a substantial federal question).

Page 1033.   Add the following at the end of the first full paragraph:

See Patterson v. Newspaper & Mail Deliverers' Union, 13 F.3d 33 (2d Cir. 1993) (applying *Rufo* standard to a consent decree against private parties).

*Page 1034.   Add the following after the second full
             paragraph:*

Rufo's relaxed standards do not necessarily mean that consent decrees will be modified to be less rigorous. In Vanguards of Cleveland v. City of Cleveland, 23 F.3d 1013, 1019 (6th Cir. 1994), the court approved an extension of a decree because

> the lower than expected pass rates by minorities on the 1984 and 1985 promotional examinations and the resulting slower than expected promotion rate for minorities, a significant change in factual circumstances, caused the consent decree to become "unworkable" as well as "detrimental to the public interest" as a vehicle for curing the previously discriminatory promotion practices in the City's Division of Fire.

Chapter 11

Judicial Relief

B. RELIEF FOR INDIVIDUAL DISCRIMINATION

5. *Liquidated Damages*

Page 1086.   Add the following to Note 3:

See also Commissioner v. Schleier, 115 S. Ct. 2159, 2161 (1995) ("liquidated damages . . . serve no compensatory function").

7.   Lack of Causation as a Remedial Limitation

Pages 1098-1104.   Replace Wallace v. Dunn Construction
Co. and the accompanying Notes with
the following case and Notes:

MCKENNON v. NASHVILLE BANNER
PUBLISHING CO.
115 S. Ct. 879 (1995)

Justice KENNEDY delivered the opinion of the Court.

The question before us is whether an employee discharged in violation of the Age Discrimination in Employment Act of 1967 is barred from all relief when, after her discharge, the employer discovers evidence of wrongdoing that, in any event, would have led to the employee's termination on lawful and legitimate grounds.

I

For some 30 years, petitioner Christine McKennon worked for respondent Nashville Banner Publishing Company. She was discharged, the Banner claimed, as part of a work force reduction plan necessitated by cost considerations. McKennon, who was 62 years old when she lost her job, thought another reason explained her dismissal: her age. She filed suit in the United States District Court for the Middle District of Tennessee, alleging that her discharge violated the Age Discrimination in Employment Act of 1967 (ADEA). The ADEA makes it unlawful for any employer: "to discharge any individual or otherwise discriminate against any individual with respect to his compensation, terms, conditions, or privileges of employment, because of such individual's age." McKennon sought a variety of legal and equitable remedies available under the ADEA, including backpay.

In preparation of the case, the Banner took McKennon's deposition. She testified that, during her final year of employment, she had copied several confidential documents bearing upon the company's financial condition. She had access to these records as secretary to the Banner's comptroller. McKennon took the copies home and showed them to her husband. Her motivation, she averred, was an apprehension she was about to be fired because of her age. When she became concerned about her job, she removed and copied the documents for "insurance" and "protection." A few days after these deposition disclosures, the Banner sent McKennon a letter declaring that removal and copying of the records was in violation of her job responsibilities and advising her (again) that she was terminated. The Banner's letter also recited that had it known of McKennon's misconduct it would have discharged her at once for that reason.

For purposes of summary judgment, the Banner conceded its discrimination against McKennon. The District Court granted summary judgment for the Banner, holding that McKennon's misconduct was grounds for her termination and that neither backpay nor any other remedy was available to her under the ADEA. The United States Court of Appeals for the Sixth Circuit affirmed on the same rationale. We granted certiorari to resolve conflicting views among the Courts of Appeals on the question whether all relief must be denied when an employee has been discharged in violation of the ADEA and the employer later discovers some wrongful conduct that would have led to discharge if it had been discovered earlier. We now reverse.

II

We shall assume, as summary judgment procedures require us to assume, that the sole reason for McKennon's initial discharge was her age, a discharge violative of the ADEA. Our further premise is that the misconduct revealed by the deposition was so grave that McKennon's immediate discharge would have followed its disclosure in any event. The District Court and the Court of Appeals found no basis for contesting that proposition, and for purposes of our review we need not question it here. We do question the legal conclusion reached by those courts that after-acquired evidence of wrongdoing which would have resulted in discharge bars employees from any relief under the ADEA. That ruling is incorrect.

The Court of Appeals considered McKennon's misconduct, in effect, to be supervening grounds for termination. That may be so, but it does not follow, as the Court of Appeals said in citing one of its own earlier cases, that the misconduct renders it " 'irrelevant whether or not [McKennon] was discriminated against.' " We conclude that a violation of the ADEA cannot be so altogether disregarded.

The ADEA, enacted in 1967 as part of an ongoing congressional effort to eradicate discrimination in the workplace, reflects a societal condemnation of invidious bias in employment decisions. The ADEA is but part of a wider statutory scheme to protect employees in the workplace nationwide. See Title VII of the Civil Rights Act of 1964; the Americans with Disabilities Act of 1990; the National Labor Relations Act; the Equal Pay Act of 1963. The ADEA incorporates some features of both Title VII and the Fair Labor Standards Act, which has led us to describe it as "something of a hybrid." The substantive, antidiscrimination provisions of the ADEA are modeled upon the prohibitions of Title VII. Its remedial provisions incorporate by reference the provisions of the Fair Labor Standards Act of 1938. When confronted with a violation of the ADEA, a district court is authorized to afford relief by means of reinstatement, backpay, injunctive relief, declaratory judgment, and attorney's fees. In the case of a willful violation of the Act, the ADEA authorizes an award of liquidated damages equal to the backpay award. The Act also gives federal courts the discretion to "grant such legal or equitable relief as may be appropriate to effectuate the purposes of [the Act]."

The ADEA and Title VII share common substantive features and also a common purpose: "the elimination of discrimination in the workplace." Congress designed the remedial measures in these statutes to serve as a "spur or catalyst" to cause employers "to self-examine and to self-evaluate their employment practices and to endeavor to eliminate, so far as possible, the last vestiges" of discrimination. Deterrence is one object of these statutes. Compensation for injuries caused by the prohibited discrimination is another. The ADEA, in keeping with these purposes, contains a vital element found in both Title VII and the Fair Labor Standards Act: it grants an injured employee a right of action to obtain the authorized relief. The private litigant who seeks redress for his or her injuries vindicates both the deterrence and the compensation objectives of the ADEA. It would not accord with this scheme if after-acquired evidence of wrongdoing that would have resulted in termination operates, in every instance, to bar all relief for an earlier violation of the Act.

The objectives of the ADEA are furthered when even a single employee establishes that an employer has discriminated against him or her. The disclosure through litigation of incidents or practices which violate national policies respecting nondiscrimination in the work force is itself important, for the occurrence of violations may disclose patterns of noncompliance resulting from a misappreciation of the Act's operation or entrenched resistance to its commands, either of which can be of industry-wide significance. The efficacy of its enforcement mechanisms becomes one measure of the success of the Act.

The Court of Appeals in this case relied upon two of its earlier decisions, Johnson v. Honeywell Information Systems, Inc., 955 F.2d 409 (6th Cir. 1992); Milligan-Jensen v. Michigan Technological Univ., 975 F.2d 302 (6th Cir. 1992), and the opinion of the Court of Appeals for the Tenth Circuit in Summers v. State Farm Mutual Automobile Ins. Co., 864 F.2d 700 (1988). Consulting those authorities, it declared that it had "firmly endorsed the principle that after-acquired evidence is a complete bar to any recovery by the former employee where the employer can show it would have fired the employee on the basis of the evidence." Summers, in turn, relied upon our decision in Mt. Healthy City Bd. of Ed. v. Doyle, 429 U.S. 274 (1977), but that decision is inapplicable here.

In Mt. Healthy we addressed a mixed-motives case, in which two motives were said to be operative in the employer's decision to fire an employee. One was lawful, the other (an alleged constitutional violation) unlawful. We held that if the lawful reason alone would have sufficed to justify the firing, the employee could not prevail in a suit against the employer. The case was controlled by the difficulty, and what we thought was the lack of necessity, of disentangling the proper motive from the improper one where both played a part in the termination and the former motive would suffice to sustain the employer's action.

That is not the problem confronted here. As we have said, the case comes to us on the express assumption that an unlawful motive was the sole basis for the firing. McKennon's misconduct was not discovered until after she had been fired. The employer could not have been motivated by knowledge it did not have and it cannot now claim that the employee was fired for the nondiscriminatory reason. Mixed motive cases are inapposite here, except to the important extent they underscore the necessity of determining the employer's motives in ordering the discharge, an essential element in determining whether the employer violated the federal antidiscrimination law. As we have observed, "proving that the same decision would have been justified . . . is not the same as proving that the same decision would have been made."

Our inquiry is not at an end, however, for even though the employer has violated the Act, we must consider how the after-acquired evidence of the employee's wrongdoing bears on the specific remedy to be ordered. Equity's maxim that a suitor who engaged in his own reprehensible conduct in the course of the transaction at issue must be denied equitable relief because of unclean hands, a rule which in conventional formulation operated in limine to bar the suitor from invoking the aid of the equity court has not been applied where Congress authorizes broad equitable relief to serve important national policies. We have rejected the unclean hands defense "where a private suit serves important public purposes." That does not mean, however, the employee's own misconduct is irrelevant to all the remedies otherwise available under the statute. The statute controlling this case provides that "the court shall have jurisdiction to grant such legal or equitable relief as may be appropriate to effectuate the purposes of this chapter, including without limitation judgments compelling employment, reinstatement or promotion, or enforcing the liability for [amounts owing to a person as a result of a violation of this chapter]." In giving effect to the ADEA, we must recognize the duality between the legitimate interests of the employer and the important claims of the employee who invokes the national employment policy mandated by the Act. The employee's wrongdoing must be taken into account, we conclude, lest the employer's legitimate concerns be ignored. The ADEA, like Title VII, is not a general regulation of the workplace but a law which prohibits discrimination. The statute does not constrain employers from exercising significant other prerogatives and discretion in the course of the hiring, promoting, and discharging of their employees. In determining appropriate remedial action, the employee's wrongdoing becomes relevant not to punish the employee, or out of concern "for the relative moral worth of the parties," but to take due account of the lawful prerogatives of the employer in the usual course of its business and the corresponding equities that it has arising from the employee's wrongdoing.

The proper boundaries of remedial relief in the general class of cases where, after termination, it is discovered that the employee has engaged in wrongdoing must be addressed by the judicial system in the ordinary course of further decisions, for the factual permutations and the equitable considerations they raise will vary from case to case. We do conclude that here, and as a general rule in cases of this type, neither reinstatement nor front pay is an appropriate remedy. It would be both inequitable and pointless to order the reinstatement of someone the employer would have terminated, and will terminate, in any event and upon lawful grounds.

The proper measure of backpay presents a more difficult problem. Resolution of this question must give proper recognition to the fact that an ADEA violation has occurred which must be deterred and compensated without undue infringement upon the employer's rights and prerogatives. The object of compensation is to restore the employee to the position he or she would have been in absent the discrimination, but that principle is difficult to apply with precision where there is after-acquired evidence of wrongdoing that would have led to termination on legitimate grounds had the employer known about it. Once an employer learns about employee wrongdoing that would lead to a legitimate discharge, we cannot require the employer to ignore the information, even if it is acquired during the course of discovery in a suit against the employer and even if the information might have gone undiscovered absent the suit. The beginning point in the trial court's formulation of a remedy should be calculation of backpay from the date of the unlawful discharge to the date the new information was discovered. In determining the appropriate order for relief, the court can consider taking into further account extraordinary equitable circumstances that affect the legitimate interests of either party. An absolute rule barring any recovery of backpay, however, would undermine the ADEA's objective of forcing employers to consider and examine their motivations, and of penalizing them for employment decisions that spring from age discrimination.

Where an employer seeks to rely upon after-acquired evidence of wrongdoing, it must first establish that the wrongdoing was of such severity that the employee in fact would have been terminated on those grounds alone if the employer had known of it at the time of the discharge. The concern that employers might as a routine matter undertake extensive discovery into an employee's background or performance on the job to resist claims under the Act is not an insubstantial one, but we think the authority of the courts to award attorney's fees, mandated under the statute, and in appropriate cases to invoke the provisions of Rule 11 of the Federal Rules of Civil Procedure will deter most abuses.

The judgment is reversed. . . .

NOTES

1. *McKennon* was an ADEA action. In a private ADEA action, the unpaid wages (or backpay) award is a *legal* remedy that gives rise to the right to a jury trial. See page 1088 of the casebook. Yet, the Court's opinion seems to treat the award as an equitable remedy. For example, the Court said:

> The beginning point in the trial court's formulation of a remedy should be calculation of backpay from the date of the unlawful discharge to the date the new information was discovered. In determining the appropriate order for relief, the court can consider taking into further account . . . equitable circumstances.

After *McKennon*, how should a jury in an after-acquired evidence case be instructed on the availability of backpay and the appropriate amount?

2. The Court carefully distinguished between the factual situation before it and a mixed-motives case. If McKennon had been discharged because of both her age and her misconduct, but she would have been discharged even if her age had not been considered, would she have been eligible for backpay? See section (a) at page1096 of the casebook. Is §706(g)(2)(B) in Title VII limited to mixed-motives cases?

3. Suppose that McKennon's misconduct had been obtaining the position by submitting a fraudulent resume or job application. Should the "would have been terminated" standard or a "would not have been hired" standard be used to calculate backpay? Shatluck v. Kinetic Concepts, 49 F.3d 1106 (5th Cir. 1995) (using first standard).

4. The appellate courts have had no difficulty in concluding that *McKennon* is also applicable to backpay awards in Title VII actions. Wallace v. Dunn Constr. Co., 62 F.3d 374 (11th Cir. 1995); Wehr v. Ryan's Family Steak Houses, Inc., 49 F.3d 1150 (6th Cir. 1995).